A to Z
BABY NAMES

igloo

igloo

Published in 2012

by Igloo Books Ltd

Cottage Farm

Sywell

NN6 0BJ

www.igloo-books.com

CTP001 0712

10 9 8 7 6 5 4 3 2

ISBN 978-0-85780-505-8

Cover and content images © Copyright Thinkstock/Getty Images

Printed and manufactured in China

Introduction

Choosing a name for your baby is one of the most important decisions you will make for your child. You'll want to choose something that will last a lifetime, suit their personality and go with whatever paths their life take. So where to start? There are thousands of names listed in this book and it may seem daunting. Perhaps you need to narrow it down?

Introduction

This introductory section will help you decide what kind of name will suit your baby by thinking over certain questions:

- *Do you want a name with religious origins and a meaning particular to your beliefs?*

- *Do you want a name with cultural ties to your community?*

- *Do you want to name your child after a place or moment special to you?*

- *Do you want a name with a particular meaning, such as brave, strong, or healer?*

- *Do you want a name with mystical or mythological origins?*

- *Do you want a name that runs in the family or has ties to older generations?*

- *Or do you want something completely unique and unusual?*

Once you've thought about these questions, you will probably have a better idea of what kind of name you want for your child.

Now you will need to consider other factors, such as any siblings, cousins, etc. that the child will grow up with and how their names will sound together; calling your two sons Sam and Sammy could get confusing! You might also want to consider a middle name and, of course, how the baby's chosen name will fit with its surname; names like Jacob Jacobs could be problematic.

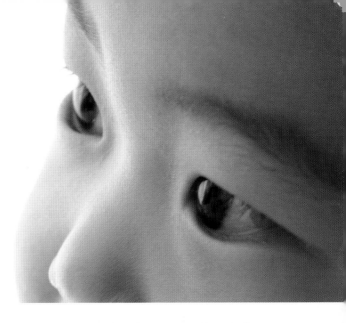

The following pages will cover the different types of names you can choose, including religious names from Christian, Jewish, Muslim, Sikh and Hindu backgrounds, as well as names from various cultures and historic traditions, such as Native American, African, Celtic, Persian, Sanskrit, Scandinavian, Aboriginal, Pan-Asian and Polynesian names.

There is also advice on rhythm, syllables, vowels, sustainability, popularity and meanings to help guide you. Follow the sound advice on how to make good decisions, as well as some helpful notes on what not to do, which covers pitfalls and oversights that once made will stay with a child for life!

We all know that names influence first impressions and often beget popular, or not so popular, nicknames. You will need to bear this in mind when choosing a name, as your child will have to live with it for the rest of their life (or at least until they can legally change it).

There will no doubt be helpful, or not so helpful, suggestions from family and friends who will all have an opinion. You may or may not want this kind of help and even if you think you don't want to hear what anybody else has to say, it's always worth keeping an open mind; you never know, someone might just stumble upon the perfect name. Remember if you don't want the name your Grandma is pressuring you to choose, you don't have to use it. As soon as she sees your beautiful baby, she will forget she ever disapproved of the modern, new age name you chose.

Choosing a name doesn't have to be tormenting. Why not see it as a fun and creative process? Picking the right name requires thought and preparation; you shouldn't just pluck one out of the air at the registry office. And even if you've always known what you were going to call your baby since you were a child, it's worth rethinking because tastes, and surnames, change.

Before you start trawling the pages and writing long lists of possibilities, perhaps stop and think about what it is you want for your baby's name. And most important of all, remember that even though you may be influenced by society, friends and family, the decision is ultimately yours. So, choose a name that you, and your child, will be proud of.

Some friendly advice

Often, the hardest part about choosing a name is where to begin. There are so many and even if you've narrowed it down to a particular type of name, be it religious, natural, meaningful or genealogical, there are still lots to choose from. Don't panic. First, why not sit down with pen and paper and write down all the names that come into your head. Have a think about people you admire, people whose names you've always thought were nice, people who have touched or inspired you, perhaps characters from books or films. Now add in family names you like, or that are important to you.

By now you should have a list of names that are at least worth considering. This will be your base and you can add to this list whenever you think of a good name. Why not use this book to look up the meanings and origins of the names you've listed. Perhaps a particular meaning will sway your decision for or against, for example: Cameron means crooked nose and Deidre means sorrowful. But just because a name has a negative meaning, it doesn't mean you can't choose it – it won't seal the fate of your unborn child. On the other hand you may find an unexpected deep meaning in some of your listed names, for example: Zoe and Eve both mean life and Kenneth means handsome. Some names may surprise you with their meanings, for example: Iris means Rainbow.

Once you've got a shortlist, say the names out loud with your partner, or close friends and family. How do you feel when you say the name? Often you will get a gut feeling when you say the right name out loud. Think about how the name fits with any siblings and if you do have other children or close relatives of a similar age, how do they sound together? If you're choosing a middle name, or names, say these together and in different orders to see which works best for you.

Now think about what nicknames might be derived from your chosen names; imagine the name being used in conversation, being shouted across the street, or being announced, as if at a degree ceremony or awards evening. Think about how the name will sound through various stages of your child's life from a baby through to childhood, teenage years, adulthood and as they get older.

It's so important to say names out loud. It may seem obvious, but make sure you pick a name that you and your family members can pronounce. It's worth bearing in mind any speech impediments or trouble with certain letters that could cause embarrassment for other family members and the child.

Saying the name aloud will help you think about rhythm, the amount of syllables, vowels and consonants. Does it roll off the tongue? And together with any middle names or surnames, does it create a balance of syllables when said altogether? For example, a name made up of names containing only one syllable each could sound flat: Ben John Smith. If your surname only has one syllable, perhaps think about adding variation to the first and, or, middle names: Benjamin John Smith, or Daniel Llyod Smith. On the other hand, a name can sound too long and rambling, such as Zachariah Alexander Johansson.

Bear in mind any rhyming which might occur; if your surname is Wray, naming your daughter Faye may sound pretty, but could lead to teasing in the playground. Subtle rhymes, however, work really well. Using names that have consonant or vowels similar to the surname or middle name can create melodic, flowing names such as Naomi Jayne.

Putting vowels too close together can lead to pronunciation problems, because of the way the sounds form in the mouth. If your surname, or chosen middle name, starts with a vowel, avoid ending your chosen name with the same vowel: Anna Adams, or Leonardo O'Connor. Conversely, it is often nice to put a vowel before a consonant – this make a name flow really well, for example: Erica May, or Milo Rowan.

Finally think about how the name fits within your family. Would you like a tradition of names that share a connection? Perhaps you want all of your children to have a name that starts with the same letter, or a name passed down through generations. If you are choosing names that start with the same letter, watch out for potential tongue-twisters and confusing situations and bear in mind that your child is an individual, not a duplicate of its sibling. Naming traditions can be really rewarding and provide great family bonds, but remember to make the name you choose unique to your child.

What not to do

Here is some top advice on common mistakes and pitfalls that should be avoided. Although the decision is ultimately yours, you do not want your child to suffer ridicule. You want give your child the best start possible. For example, choosing a name like Adolf might bring up negative connotations, whilst choosing a zany or unpronounceable name might simply leave your child counting down the days until he/she can change it legally.

Avoid Negative Associations

Some names just evoke bad feelings and that's something you have no control over. We've already mentioned Adolf, but some names have evolved and have meanings all of their own, such as: Gay/Gaylord, Willie, Woody, Dick, Fanny, Randy, or even Mary Jane. If you're naive to the many alternative and negative meanings associated with some names, it may be best to do a bit of internet research before you decide to call your child John Thomas. Often names have personal negative associations, for example you may love a girls' name you picked out when you were six, but for your partner, it could bring back memories of an ex-girlfriend, or a horrible teacher. Also bear in mind what bad feelings a name might have for friends and family. As a rule, try to avoid names that bring thoughts of harm or violence, such as diseases, disasters and murders. And make sure that if you have the surname of a famous serial killer, silly character or infamous celebrity – choose a different first name: for example if your surname is Bundy, try not to name your son Ted (or even Edward).

Don't Make it Sickly Sweet

It's great to give a baby a cute name, but remember the baby will grow up and it probably won't want to be stuck with a name like Blinky, Sweetie or Princess. These names may sound cute when your baby is under 12 months, but could be the butt of many jokes in future years. If you're overcome by your baby's cuteness and just can't resist immortalising it, be sensible and take a non-hormonal person with you to the registry office, just in case you need some sense talking into you. And keep the cutesy names reserved for pets only.

Think about the initials

Before you commit your baby's name to a legal document, just take a moment to consider the initials. Do they spell anything silly or offensive? Bear in mind initials appear more often than you think, especially during education. Here's some to watch out for:

BJ	**SOB**
WTF	**OMG**
DIE	**PIG**
LOL	**UFO**

Self-fulfilling prophecies

We've discussed how almost every name has a meaning, and you can find these out in the rest of the book. However, some names themselves have a meaning that is more obvious. Make sure that when you pick a name like Prudence, Chastity or Gay what the social impact on the child will be, and whether they will feel the need to rebel against their names.

Ironic Names

You may think you're a comedy genius for coming up clever puns using your child's name as material, but it is simply cruel. Peoples' names are spoken several times everyday and what might be funny once is certain to get old and embarrassing. You too will also have to say, or even shout, the name in public. Giving your child a silly name may impact their self-esteem and even their fondness of you. So, if your surname is Butts don't name your son Seymour, or if your surname is Rotch, don't name your child Mike. It may seem funny at the time, but your child will never forgive you for a name like Frank N. Stein, Grace Land or Pepe Roni.

Pet Names

Believe it or not, some people give their children names that should only be given to animals. Just like many of the pitfalls above, a child with a name reserved for pets will not go through life easily or without ridicule. Some names are just no-nos for humans, like Spotto, Bonzo or Tickles. Likewise if you had a childhood pet you adored, no matter how great, it's probably best not to name you child after the pet – it doesn't matter how amazing your beloved pet was, your child will not appreciate being named after a dog.

Original Spellings

Sometimes it's nice to be different, but be careful if you are thinking about picking a wacky spelling of a common name. Your child will likely spend their whole life correcting people and receiving documents with the incorrect spelling.

Place Names

It may be nice to name your child after a place or an event, think about Brooklyn Beckham, however, be clear why you are using that name. If you really want to name your child after the place or time they were conceived, such as Paris or Storm, consider how you are going to tell them when they are older. Do you want your child forever associating its name with your sexual behaviour? If you must do this, perhaps you could think of an alternative story to tell your child.

Middle Names

Many parents choose a middle name for their child and if this is the case for you, then you will need to put the same amount of thought into this name as you did into your baby's first name. As with choosing a first name, it's easy to narrow down your middle name options by asking yourself a similar set of questions as before?

- *Do you want the name to have a religious origin or meaning?*

- *Do you want to pass on a family tradition?*

- *Do you want to honour a relative or friend?*

- *Do you want more than one middle name?*

- *Do you want something zany or wacky?*

Middle names are often steeped in tradition. Often sons and daughters were given a middle name that was the same as their parent's first name. This isn't as common anymore, but perhaps this tradition appeals to you?

A middle name is often an opportunity to honour relatives or to preserve a mother's maiden name. It gives you the opportunity to continue a naming tradition that may be outdated, but nevertheless important to you, whilst sparing your child the embarrassment of having it as a first name.

In many states in America children are often addressed by both middle and first names at the same time, think of names like Betty Sue, Billy Bob and Mary Lou that have become naming traditions in their own right. Does this appeal to you?

When choosing a middle name, keep in mind how the child's full name will flow together; a name like Sarah Suzie Shackleford may turn into a bit of a tongue twister and could sound like a TV character. Remember the advice on vowels and consonants – this will help to pick names that flow together, like Emma Jane, or Thomas Alexander.

Bear in mind, middle names are often shortened to one initial, such and John F Kennedy, or Richard E Grant, so make sure the name will work in this scenario, too. In fact, some cultures only choose an initial not a whole name, which you may want to consider.

Remember, you don't have to stick to one name, perhaps you like two middle names – there's nothing to stop you choosing more than one. In British high society it is common for members of the aristocracy to have up to four middle names! On the other hand, you may decide you don't want a middle name for your child. Not everyone has one and you shouldn't feel pressured by society into giving your child a middle name. Not having a middle name can be unique in itself.

Considering siblings

If you already have children, or are expecting twins (or more!) you have the job of choosing more than one name. If you already have a child then you will want to pick a name that works well with the existing name – calling one Abraham and the other Mohammed may send mixed messages. So here are some ideas and pointers on how to narrow down your search for the perfect name, or names.

Perhaps you want your children's names to be linked, either in meaning, sound or origin. Thinking about this first is a great way to filter out inappropriate names and hone in on potential winners.

The most common way to name sibling is to use the same initial letter, although this could lead to problems if siblings share the same initials. Perhaps your first-born is called Mark, if you want to continue this tradition then turn straight to the M section in the book.

Perhaps you chose a name from the mother's side of the family for the first-born, now try finding a name from the father's side – this could add cohesion and balance to the family unit. But remember, you have to love the name and your child will have to be comfortable with it, so don't go naming your son Aloysius out of misguided family loyalty until you've thought about the consequences.

If your first-born's name has a particular meaning, like Jamal (meaning handsome), you may want to continue this tradition and name your second-born a different name with a similar meaning, such as Hassan for a boy or Nadia for a girl.

Perhaps your first-born has a name with religious meaning, such as Seth or Ethan, you could continue this tradition for your second-born. But remember not all religious names have good meanings; so don't forget to research the meaning if you plan to pick out names from holy texts.

You may want to involve an older sibling in the choice; this is a great way of involving other siblings and family members in your new baby's life and could help to alleviate any worries by getting older siblings excited about the baby's arrival. But remember, kids can be cruel: never promise an older sibling total control over the baby naming process.

The History of Names

The naming tradition dates back to the dawn of humanity and has been evolving ever since. The earliest known naming traditions are from the first human settlers, be they Sanskrit names from the Indus Valley, Celtic names from settlers in middle Europe, or Norse names from Scandinavian warriors. Many of these ancient names still exist today and can be found in this book. One of the oldest naming traditions still around today is the Norse tradition in Iceland. Even today Icelanders use the ancient patronymic naming system: this is where a child's surname will reflect the first name of the father plus the word son or dottir (daughter). For example the famous Viking, Lief Eriksson was the son of Erik Jonsson, his child would have then taken the surname Liefsson (for a boy) or Liefsdottir (for a girl). Where there is no father, the child will take the mother's first name to form its surname. So in Icelandic society, even today, most people are only referred to by their first name – amazing!

Throughout the ages, changes in culture and religious influence have had a big effect on naming traditions. From Greek, Roman and Norse gods to religious figures; there are also names inspired by authors, myths, nature and joyous events. Religious names were of utmost importance right up to the 1800s, with many children being given names of religious figures, perhaps mixed with Norse and Saxon names. Many wanted to give their children names they could live up to, such as Faith, Purity and Honor – remember the perils of choosing such names. As emigration increased and wars and battles raged, so naming became influenced by these events. Irish and Celtic names were taken to America by immigrants, meanwhile African Americans began to free themselves of slavery and take control of their own naming traditions once again.

During the 20th century, people began to experiment with names; shortened forms of names were taken as full names, such as Betty instead of Elizabeth and Nelle instead of Helen. People wanted their child to be different and chose names to set them apart from the crowd – this became heightened during the 1950s baby boom following the end of the Second World War.

By the 1960s, cultures from all over the world began to mix. People started to take interest in other cultures and started to adopt names that sounded beautiful, or had a meaning personal to them. At this time people also began to experiment with creating brand new names, using nature and art for inspiration. The unisex name came into its own at this time, with people embracing the ideals of free love and non-gender stereotyping – choosing as neutral a name as possible gave their child the opportunity to make their own mark on the world without having to live up to the connotations of an overtly butch or feminine name.

Towards the end of the 20th century the meaning and origin of names became important once again, as did family history and honouring past generations. As cultures lived together throughout the world, children started to inherit genealogy from more than one culture. This gave families a unique opportunity to celebrate diversity and choose names that they may not have considered before.

The celebrity culture and entertainment industries boomed at the end of the 20th century and continue to grow and captivate our imagination today. As with all other trends throughout history, the celebrity and entertainment culture has spawned all sorts of baby naming fashions. With celebrities giving their children wild and wacky names like:

- *Kal-El (Nicholas Cage's child after Superman's given alien name)*

- *Apple (Child of Gwyneth Paltrow and Chris Martin)*

- *Audio Science (Child of Shannyn Sossamon, actress)*

- *Moxie Crimefighter (Child of Penn Jilette, magician)*

- *Jermajesty (Child of Jermaine Jackson)*

And there's plenty more where they came from. As well as taking inspiration from what celebrities do, like naming your child after a place: Brooklyn Beckham, Memphis Eve (child of Bono). Sometimes we even choose to name our child after the celebrities themselves, popular names include: Keanu, Beckham, Bono and Beyonce.

Today you have thousands of names to choose from thanks to thousands of years of cultures and traditions coming together. Never before have we been so free to choose and had such information at our fingertips. Pretty much anything goes today so don't be afraid to experiment. Retro names like Otis, Walter and Edith are now considered cool; names inspired by nature can be beautiful and names that celebrate your culture and beliefs can hold deep meanings for you and your child.

The following pages will cover the various cultures and religions, including advice on mythological, created and unusual names.

African Names

African names are often steeped in history; following tradition that dates back to when the first humans walked the planet. In African culture, it is believed that a child's name will influence the path his or her life takes. With many names originating from the environment, they tend to be beautiful; hence their increasing popularity in British and American cultures. The African continent is huge and names and traditions vary from region to region. When choosing an African name, you may want to investigate its origins and whether it is derived from a native language, such as Zulu, Swahili, Kongo, Hausa or Yoruba; alternatively, whether European settlers influenced the name. These influences can be diverse ranging from French, Dutch, English, Arabic, and Portuguese. This extra information may impact your decision.

Popular African names are:

Girls: Afiya, Fatima, Salma

Boys: Abdul, Jumoke, Senwe

African American Names

When Africans were first brought to America as slaves, they were stripped of their native names and forced to take on new ones. The slave owners did not want them to take on American names, as they desired them to remain separate from the dominant white culture, therefore slaves were often given mythological names such as Hercules or Achilles. Some African names survived through a small percentage of owners who allowed slaves to be called by their original names. As slave families grew and the African slaves adopted Christianity, they began to take names from the bible. Owners maintained the distinction between black and white by enforcing the use of shortened versions or nick names, thus maintaining the assumed social hierarchy. Once slavery was abolished, African Americans began to phase out the names associated with their former lives and returned to their African roots, combining these with American culture to create new names. African Americans are known for their original and inventive names that incorporate style, culture and ancient tradition.

Popular African American names are:

Girls: April, Ebony, Kamala

Boys: Dale, Leroy, Tariq

Jewish names

In Jewish culture, naming a baby is a significant part of a child's life. The meaning of a child's name is very important. In fact, many Jews believe that a child's name will directly affect a child's path in life and the afterlife. If you want to give your child a Jewish name, it may be wise to investigate the name's meaning and how the Jewish community will perceive a person with that name. Jewish naming ceremonies are important events and celebrated with vigour. At these ceremonies, not only the birth of the child is celebrated but origins of the child's name are retold and the achievements of the child's namesakes are extolled.

Whilst Jewish names are gaining in popularity today, in the past Jewish parents actually chose to give their children less Jewish and more Anglo-American names. After the Second World War, many Jews had suffered terrible persecution during the holocaust and so wanted to help their child fit into mainstream society with English or American versions of traditional names.

Today Jewish communities live free of persecution and celebrate their heritage, returning to more unusual names used in Israel such as Ophir, Itzak and Livya, as well as names featured in the Torah.

Popular Jewish names are:

Girls: Deborah, Rebecca, Sarah

Boys: Jacob, Ethan, David

Christian Names

Christianity has spread throughout the world and has held as a dominant world religion for the last 2,000 years. Many Christians share names with Jewish communities, but Christian names are inspired by the New Testament and by the Judo-Christian names featured in the Old Testament, such as Eve, Adam, Seth, David and Rachel. Whilst the origins of Christian names come from Jewish cultures, they were soon influenced by Roman and Greek cultures and later, as Christianity grew, Celtic, Germanic, Slavic and even Scandinavian naming traditions. Christian names, like other religious names have meanings and accolades associated with their namesakes.

Popular Christian names are:

Girls: Mary, Ruth, Sarah

Boys: Matthew, Luke, Paul

Muslim Names

With roots in the Middle East, Africa, Europe, UK and America, Islam is one of the biggest religions in the world. The prophet Mohammed is a highly revered figure in the Muslim faith and his name is often taken as a boy's first or middle name. Often, when a boy becomes a man, he adopts Mohammed as his chosen name. As this practice is very common, many muslim men tend to use their middle, or surname as the name the are known by. For example, a man called Mohammed Haroon may chose to go by the name Haroon because many of his peers are also called Mohammed. Many Islamic names use Arabic words to make up names: popular combinations often involve the words abdul (meaning servant) allah (meaning God) and kahreem (meaning generous).

Muslim naming ceremonies, called Aqeeqahs, are held on the seventh day after a baby's birth. Traditionally, the ceremony involves the sacrifice of a goat or a sheep – two for a boy and one for a girl. Since the Torah and Qu'ran originate from the same holy texts, it is no surprise that Muslims and Jews share similar beliefs about a baby's name. They believe that a child's name is extremely important, it is understood to influence a child's path in life.

Popular Muslim names include:

Girls: Amina, Khadija, Salma

Boys: Mohammed, Abdul, Omar

Other cultures such as Turkish and Persian cultures have been influenced by Islam. However, these cultures have also been influenced by great rulers and revolutions from the Greek and Roman empires through to the Ottomans, Persians, Egyptians and Mongols.

In Turkey, only names derived from the official language are allowed, so ethnic groups are not recognised and Armenian, Greek, Jewish and Kurdish names, for example, are forbidden. Arabic middle names are allowed, but are often made more Turkish, a common example is the name Mehmet, which is the Turkish for Mohammed.

Popular Turkish names include:

Girls: Sibel, Azra, Selma

Boys: Ahmed, Ali, Hasan

Native American Names

Native American names are becoming increasingly popular in America, the UK and Australia. The English language version of native American names are most commonly adopted amongst non-descendants and the most popular of these include names like River, Bear and Forest.

Original Native American naming traditions vary from tribe to tribe, here are some examples of how naming babies work:

In the Navajo tribe, names are extremely important and powerful. They are deemed so precious that they are only spoken during the naming ceremony itself, which often means tribe members are referred to by their position, i.e. father, daughter, aunt, son, etc.

In the Miwok tribe, given names often describe water and the way in which the water was flowing when the baby was born. This name gives the child a deep connection with mother earth, as their name aligns them with the exact moment that the child enters the world.

In the Salish tribe, the name given to the baby only lasts until adolescence. At this time the child passes through a rite of passage and is given a new name by tribal leaders. The name given often represents the natural qualities of the child, for example, Standing Badger. When the child becomes an adult, he or she may change their name if they are given a specific task or mission, then their name will reflect the expectations that this person must live up to.

Sioux tribes have complicated naming systems where a person can have several names over the course of a lifetime. First, the child is given a name according to its gender and social position. Later, the child will be given a name that reflects it's character and, in adulthood, another name will be adopted dependant on kinship and social order. For example, a child would not be given the name Chief at birth, but rather must earn that title in later life.

It is hard to say which Native American names are most popular as they are ever changing, but here are some of the most famous names:

Red Cloud, Maria Tallchief, Crazy Horse, Squanto, Sacajawea, Pontiac, Geronimo, Sitting Bull, Black Hawk, Sequoiah and Pocahontas

Sanskrit Names

Many historians believe Sanskrit to be the origin of nearly all languages. It was most likely one of the only surviving languages of the ice age. Remaining true to its original form, it is one of the oldest languages on earth. Many words we know today have a Sanskrit origin, even words we believe to be of Hebrew, Arabic, or of other diverse, cultural descent. Sanskrit is most likely the origin for most Indian names.

Some popular names of Sanskrit origins are:

Girls: Divi, Priti, Usha

Boys: Abhay, Jeevan, Ravi

Indian Names

There are thousands of Indian baby names which will vary from region to region. The names are often influenced by the Hindu and Sikh religions, horoscopes, mythology, names of gods and goddesses, lucky names, Sanskrit names and Mother Nature. For many Indians, their birth name is different to their official name; a birth name is destined to start with the initial letter of a person's horoscope at the time of birth.

Naming traditions vary geographically, for example in Gujarat, a male child will take his father's name as his middle name and the family name as his surname, however when a woman marries, she will take her husband's first name as her middle name. To differentiate between genders, suffixes are added to the given names.

In many Indian traditions, the first-born son will take the name of his paternal grandfather and the second-born son will take the name of his maternal grandfather with the first-born daughter taking the name of her paternal grandmother and the second-born daughter taking the name of her maternal grandmother. Only after these names have been used can younger siblings be given different names, although these will usually relate to other family members, or important gods.

If you choose the give your child a name of Indian or Sanskrit origin, it is always useful to look up the origin and meaning of the name, especially if you do not belong to an Indian family, or are breaking from tradition.

Some of the most popular Indian baby names are:

Girls: Aditi, Sonia, Greeta

Boys: Jay, Sanjay, Dinesh

Celtic Names

Since the Celts invaded Britain and Ireland, their art, culture and traditions have been embraced and cherished. Their influence is most obvious in the Scottish Highlands, Wales, Ireland and the Isle of Man. Celtic names have endured most notably in Wales and Ireland, with distinct differences despite Anglo invasion and colonisation. Following the Irish Diaspora and an increase in emmigration, Celtic names have grown in popularity – most notably in America.

Popular Celtic names include:

Girls: Siobhan, Fiona, Aileen

Boys: Aiden, Kian, Alistair

Polynesian Names

Polynesian communities lived alone and unaware of the rest of the world for hundreds of years, and as such, their names and naming traditions remain entirely unique. In Hawai'i, your name, or Inoa, is considered your most precious possession. Hawaiians, Polynesians and Maoris traditionally believe that a god chooses the name of your child and it is revealed to you in signs, visions or dreams. It is also believed that if you ignore the signs and choose a name you prefer, your child will suffer throughout its life.

Aboriginal Names

Before Australia was discovered by the rest of the world, there were over 250 different Aboriginal languages with many people being able to speak and remember up to five different Aboriginal languages. Relying on an oral tradition, Aboriginal individuals became masters at remembering stories and words. Many Aboriginal names relate to nature and the earth.

American Names

American names are renowned for being creative and original. Whilst early Americans drew on virtues they found appealing in people, such as Prudence, Temperance and Honor, modern Americans have taken inspiration from everywhere including TV programmes, celebrities and food. Many American names are quite unique and have remained localised to the United States. Other popular American names are derived from Native American names, words and tribes, such as Dakota, Geronimo, Cherokee and Cheyenne. If you like these names you do need to be aware of their cultural context and meanings before naming your child, especially if you are not descended from Native Americans. Some names are precious and hold special meaning to Native Americans and it is best to carry out research to avoid causing offence.

Some popular American names are:

Girls: Brooke, Darlene, Honey

Boys: Brandon, Denzil, Rocky

Other world Names

In this book you will find names from all over the world including Russian, Slavic, French, Italian, Spanish, Latin, Greek, Chinese, Japanese, Australian, Dutch and Inuit. Globalisation has prompted the opening of varied cultures to a world market and therefore names from other countries and regions have spread across religious and cultural divides becoming quite commonplace. Great examples of these are names of Latin origin that are commonly found in French, Italian and Spanish speaking countries: Names like Gloria, Maria, Carlos, Jean, Eva and Amelia have become common throughout Europe, UK and America. Names of Russian and Slavic influence have also become popular, such as Natalie, Andréi, Nadia and Alexi.

Whilst Chinese and Japanese names have almost always been kept with the culture and direct descendants, even these are becoming popular with the wider world.

If you are looking for an exciting name for your child and are thinking about a name from a different ethic background, there is nothing stopping you. It is advised that you look up the meaning and cultural significance of each name you consider to ensure that the name is appropriate and will not cause offense to members of its original culture.

Mythological Names

Many people choose names from mythological tales, be they Greek, Roman, Norse or Celtic. Mythological heroes, by their very nature of myth, display traits that we admire, such as bravery, heroism and selflessness, however it is worth noting the ying yang nature of most mythological tales, although demonstrating feats of great human accomplishment myths often explore the darker and more sinister side to human nature. Mythological names can be unique and beautiful, but ensure that you research the stories the name comes from, what it means and what connotations the name evokes. For example, Odysseus may have been a hero king who won the Trojan War, however, he was also known to be cunning and cruel.

Some famous mythological names are:

Girls: Athena, Hebe, Iris

Boys: Ambrose, Hector, Homer

Created Names

People have been thinking up names for centuries, so there's nothing to stop you creating your own name, too. Many Arabic names are made up of two words put together, such as Abdulkahreem (meaning generous servant), or Abdulallah (menaing God's servant). More recently, Americans have relished creating their own names with varying degrees of success. Many modern names are inspired by nature, such as Willow, Cloud, Clementine or Wren. But this isn't a new phenomenon; think back to age-old classics like Holly, Ivy, Ash or Dale. Many created names are a fusion of two existing names, by taking two traditional names and fusing them together, you can create something unique and original. If you plan on creating your own name, think carefully about what meaning the new name will take on from its various origins and also whether it will stand the test of time. Is it a name people will take seriously when your child is fully grown?

Some popular created names are:

Girls: Brynlee, Donita, Elara, Izona, Jacelyn, Katesha, Mirella, Ranika, Shailyn, Tenaya, Zaryn

Boys: Arric, Branton, Deveron, Estin, Jareth, Kylun, Rizi, Saulth, Talano, Trendon, Wylden, Xanthius, Zevlin

Having a girl?

If you are having a girl, the first question you want to ask is how feminine do you want her name to be? Traditional feminine names tend to have more syllables than boys' names and often have a flair about them, maybe ending in –ella, -illy, -a, -ie, or –elle. Traditional girly names hold a sense of elegance and prettiness. Choosing a name for your daughter carries many responsibilities: Whilst a very feminine name may sound pretty, are you setting her up to be pigeon-holed and not taken seriously, or will she be more attractive with an attractive sounding name? If you choose a name that is derived from a male name are you taking away from her femininity, or are you giving her an advantage should she choose to enter a male-dominated work arena? These are questions only you can answer and they are most definitely subjective. Also, when choosing a name for your daughter, you must bear in mind any siblings:

If you have another daughter with a very feminine name, choosing a more masculine or unisex name for your second daughter may cause jealousy and perception issues as they grow older. Similarly if you have a son with a unisex or less masculine name, choosing a unisex or masculine name for your daughter may make your son feel inadequate.

Having a boy?

Boys traditionally have less name options than girls, so if you're having a boy, the decision is immediately easier. Boys' names are generally masculine with only one or two syllables. There are several tried and tested names that appear on most popular lists around the world. If you're looking for a good, strong traditional name for your son, then look no further than William, John, James or Ben. However, just because they are popular it doesn't mean you can't find something different and just as fitting. In the past less thought has gone into choosing boys' names, but times are changing and new trends are emerging. If you still want a historic, traditional name, but don't want your son to be another John or William, why not dig a bit deeper and investigate other common names like Daniel, Christopher, Jack or Luke. Religious texts are full of mens' names and all of these names carry meaning and honor, so why not think about less common names from various religious texts, such as Bartholomew, Moses, Jamal, Levi or Amos – perhaps not Judas or Herod though.

Again, you must bear in mind siblings, if you have one son with a very masculine name, choosing a more feminine or unisex name for your second son may cause feelings of inadequacy and jealousy and vice versa.

Unisex Names

Unisex names are more common in some cultures than other, however, unisex names are popular because they do not impose gender stereotypes onto a child, rather they enable the child to find its own way rather than having to subconsciously live up to its name. Many unisex names began life as boys' names and were taken on by women either through marital traditions or perhaps because they sounded more feminine and appealed to parents expecting girls. (Polynesian and Hawaiian names are the exception here). Some unisex names have made the jump from a boys' name all the way over to a girls' name (Lindsay, Whitney and Florence), but don't let this worry you. Evolutionary changes like these take hundreds of years; so choosing a unisex name now will not leave your son or daughter saddled with an inappropriate name in ten years' time.

Some of the most popular **unisex** names are:

Adrian, Alex, Bailey, Cameron, Casey, Chris, Drew, Finley, Jesse, Jody, Kai, Jordan, Kelly, Morgan, Paris, Parker, Quinn, Sacha, Sidney and Tracey

Are you ready?

Now you've read all of the advice, you've thought about what kind of name you're looking for and you've got a pen and notepad – are you ready to choose a name?

Naming your child is a huge responsibility. One of the most rewarding things you will do in life will be to give your child an identity. The name, or names, you pick will be one of the greatest gifts you give your child, so take your time and listen to your gut instincts.

Whilst all of the names listed ahead are steeped in tradition, culture and meaning, your child will take their chosen name and grow into it, they will embody that name and give it new meaning that you will cherish for the rest of your lives.

Boys' Names

Aaron
Origin/meaning: Hebrew 'high mountain' or Egyptian (no known meaning).
Aaron was the brother of Moses and first High Priest of Israel. Used as a first name after the 16th-century Reformation.
Variations: Aron (Eng), Aharon (Heb), Haroun (Ar).

Abbas
Origin/meaning: Arabic 'stern'.
Abbas, 566–652, was an uncle of Mohammed and became one of the Prophet's most ardent supporters. He was the founder of the Abbasides, Khalifs of Baghdad, 750–946.
Variation: Abasi (Swahili).

Abdul
Origin/meaning: Arabic 'servant of God'.
This is one of the commonest Muslim names, and is found in slightly varying forms in many countries.
Variations and abbreviations: Abdu (worshipper of God) (Swahili), Abdala (Swahili), Abdullah.

Abel
Origin/meaning: Hebrew 'breath' or 'son'.
Abel was the second son of Adam and Eve, killed by his brother Cain.
Variations and abbreviations: Abe, Abell, Able, Nab.

Abelard
Origin/meaning: Old German 'noble resolution' from 'adal' – 'noble', 'hard' – 'resolute'.
The French and best-known version of the name.
Variations and abbreviations: Adalard (Eng), Adalhard (Old Ger), Alard.

Abhay (pron. Ahbpóy)
Origin/meaning: Sanskrit/Gujerati, 'fearless'.

Abraham

Origin/meaning: Hebrew 'father of a multitude' from the Hebrew word 'abba' – 'father'. The name of the Patriarch of Israel whose name was changed by God from Abram to Abraham (Genesis ch.17). This was one of the names brought into use in the 13th century in England. Now more popular in the US than Britain because of President Abraham Lincoln.

Variations and abbreviations: Abe, Abey, Abie, Abrahamo (It), Abrahán (Sp), Abram, Abramo, Avram, Avrom, Bram, Ibrahim (Ar), Ham.

Absolom

Origin/meaning: Hebrew 'father of peace'.
The name of King David's son by Maacah (Samuel I + II). Popular in the 12th and 13th centuries.

Variations and abbreviations: Absolon (Fr), Axel (Ger/Scand).

Achilles

Origin/meaning: Greek. May mean 'tight-lipped' or be connected with the River Achellos. Still common in Greece and where there are large Greek communities.

Variation: Achille (Fr).

Adam

Origin/meaning: Hebrew 'red (earth)'.
In the Book of Genesis Adam, the first man, was fashioned from the earth and is presumed to have taken his name from its color. Adam became popular in Britain in the 13th century especially in the North. Many last names derive from it, e.g. Adams, Adamson, Atkins, MacAdam.

Variations and abbreviations: Ad, Adamh (Ir), Adamnan, Adamo (It), Adan (Sp), Adda (Wel), Addan, Adao (Port), Ade, Edom (Scot).

Ade

Origin/meaning: Yoruba 'royal'.

Adolph

Origin/meaning: Old German 'noble wolf'. The English version of Adolphus.

Variations: Adolf (Ger), Adolphe (Fr).

Adrian

Origin/meaning: Latin 'from Adria' (the port which gave its name to the Adriatic Sea). One of the best-known holders of this name is the Roman Emperor Hadrianus, who built Hadrian's Wall in the North of England to keep out the Scots.

Variations and abbreviations: Adriaen, Adrien (Fr), Arrien, Arne.

Ahmed

Origin/meaning: Arabic 'praiseworthy'.

This popular name is found in all Muslim countries in the same form. It was the name of three Turkish Sultans in the 17th and early 18th centuries.

Aidan

Origin/meaning: Old Irish 'little fire' or 'little fiery one'.

The name of an influential 7th-century Irish saint who converted the North of England to Christianity.

Variations: Adan, Eden.

Akbar

Origin/meaning: Sanskrit 'the great'.

This was the epithet applied to the great Mogul Emperor Jelal-ed-din-Mohammed, 1542–1605. In a few years he extended his Empire to the whole of India north of the Vindhya Mountains. He was a wise and humane ruler who practiced religious tolerance.

Akiiki (pron. Akee-éekee)

Origin/meaning: Muneyankole 'friend'.

Alan

Origin/meaning: 'handsome'.

A name originally introduced into England at the time of the Norman Conquest from Brittany, the Celtic area of France. It was originally found in its French form, Alain.

Variations and abbreviations: Ailean (Scot), Ailin (Ir), Al, Alain (Fr), Aland, Alano (It/Sp), Alein, Allan, Allayne, Allen, Alleyn.

Alastair

Origin/meaning: Ancient Greek 'defender of men'.

A Scottish form of Alexander q.v.

Variations and abbreviations: Al, Alasdair, Alistair, Alister, Allister.

Alban

Origin/meaning: Latin 'white', 'fair'.

This name has appeared consistently since at least ad 287 when St Alban was martyred at the Roman town of Verulamium, later named St Albans in his honor.

Variations: Albany, Alben, Albin (Ger), Albion, Alva (Sp), Aubin (Fr).

Albert

Origin/meaning: Old German 'noble bright' from 'adal' – 'noble', 'berhta' – 'bright'.
Its real popularity in the present form is almost entirely due to Queen Victoria's marriage in 1840 to the German Prince Albert.

Variations and abbreviations: Adalbert, Ailbert (Scan), Al, Alberto (It/Sp), Albrecht (Ger), Aubert (Fr), Bert, Bertie, Halbert.

Aldous

Origin/meaning: Old German 'old'.
One of the many 13th-century additions to the number of English first names. Usually found both as a first name or a last name on the East Coast of England.

Variations and abbreviations: Aldis, Aldo, Aldus.

Aldred

Origin/meaning: Old English 'old counsel'.
An Anglo-Saxon name still found occasionally after the Norman Conquest.

Alec

Origin/meaning: Ancient Greek 'defender of men'.
One of the many variations of Alexander q.v.

Variations and abbreviations: Alek, Aleck, Alic, Alick.

Alexander

Origin/meaning: Ancient Greek 'defender of men'.
The name of the famous Greek conqueror Alexander of Macedon, 356–323 bc, it has been popular ever since, particularly popular in Scotland where it often takes the form Alastair.

Variations and abbreviations: Al, Alasdair (Scot), Alastair (Scot), Alaster, Alec, Alejandry (Sp), Alek, Aleksandr (Russ), Alessandro (It), Alex, Alexan, Alexandre (Fr), Alexio (Port), Alexis, Alic, Alick, Alisander, Alistair (Scot), Alister, Allister, Sacha, Sander, Sandro (It), Sandy, Sasha, Saunder.

Alexis

Origin/meaning: Ancient Greek 'helper' or 'defender'.
Popular in Russia and Greece, Alexis has recently become more popular in English-speaking countries. Also a short form of Alexander q.v. Sometimes found as a short form of the girl's name Alexandra q.v.

Alfie

Origin/meaning: Old English 'elf-wise counselor' hence 'good counselor'.
A short form of Alfred, Alfie is now a very popular first name in its own right, due to the lead character from the 1966 Michael Caine film 'Alfie' that was remade with Jude Law in 2004.

Alfred

Origin/meaning: Old English 'elf counselor', 'good counselor'.

This was the name of one of the Saxon Kings of England, Alfred the Great, 849–901.

Variations and abbreviations: Al, Alf, Alfie, Alfredo (It/Sp), Alfy, Alured, Avery, Fred, Freddie, Freddy.

Algernon

Origin/meaning: Norman French 'bearded', 'with whiskers'.

This name began as a nickname some 900 years ago at a time when most men were clean-shaven.

Abbreviations: Algie, Algy.

Ali

Origin/meaning: Arabic 'exalted'.

Ali, d.661, was the cousin of the Prophet Mohammed, and the first convert to Mohammedanism. He married the Prophet's youngest daughter, Fatima q.v. He was fearless in his devotion to the Prophet and became Khalif, but was later assassinated.

Aloysius (pron. Allowíshus)

Origin/meaning: Old German 'glorious battle'.

It developed as the Latin, written form of the old Provençal name Aloys, meaning son of Loys (Louis). A 16th-century St Aloysius, one of the early Jesuits, popularized the name in Catholic Europe.

Variations and abbreviations: Alois (Ger), Aloisio (It), Aloisius, Aloys. See also Louis.

Alphonso

Origin/meaning: Old German 'adal-funs' – 'noble and ready'.

Now a comparatively rare name except in Spain where it was introduced in the 8th century.

Variations and abbreviations: Affonso (Port), Alfons (Ger), Alfonso (Sp/It/Scand), Alonzo, Alphonse (Fr), Alphonsus (Lat/Ir), Fons, Fonsie, Fonz, Fonzie.

Alvin

Origin/meaning: Old German 'noble friend'.

A form of the Old English name Aylwin q.v. which is more usually found in America.

Variations: Aloin (Fr), Aluin, Alvan, Alwin (Ger).

Amadeus

Origin/meaning: Latin 'beloved of God'.

Uncommon in English-speaking countries.

Variations and abbreviations: Amadeo (Sp/It), Amadis, Amado, Amando, Amédé (Fr).

Ambrose

Origin/meaning: Greek 'divine', 'immortal'.
The Greek gods fed on Ambrosia which ensured thèir immortality. St Ambrose,
a 4th-century saint, made the name popular.

Variations and abbreviations: Ambie, Ambrogio (It), Ambros (Ir/Ger), Ambrosi, Ambrosio
(Sp), Ambrosius (Ger/Scand), Amby, Emrys (Wel).

Amos

Origin/meaning: Hebrew 'burden' or 'bearer of burdens'.
A minor prophet of the Old Testament.

André

Origin/meaning: Greek 'manly'.
A French form of Andrew q.v.

Andrew

Origin/meaning: Greek 'manly'.
St Andrew, one of Jesus's Apostles, was an immensely popular saint who was patron saint of
Scotland and Russia. In England the name came into use after the Conquest.
Variations and abbreviations: Anders (Scand), Andie, André (Fr), Andrea (It), Andreas
(Ger/Dut), Andres (Sp), Andy, Drew.

Aneurin (pron. An-eye-rin)

Origin/meaning: Latin 'honorable'.
A common name in Wales. There was a 7th-century Welsh bard of that name whose poem
'Y Gododdin' describes a famous Welsh attack on the English at Catterick.

Variations and abbreviations: Aneirin, Neirin, Nye.

Angus

Origin/meaning: Old Gaelic 'one choice'.
A common name in Scotland. It is found in early legends and was the name for
a 9th-century saint. It has an Irish Gaelic equivalent – Aonghus, pronounced the same way.

Variations and abbreviations: Aonghus (Ir), Aeneas, Gus.

Anselm

Origin/meaning: Old German 'helmet of God'.
A Lombard name brought to England after the Norman Conquest. The name of
a 12th-century saint, who was Archbishop of Canterbury.

Variations and abbreviations: Anseaume (Fr), Anselmo (Ir), Elmo.

Antony

Origin/meaning: Latin – Antonius. The name of one of the great families of Rome. Meaning uncertain but is sometimes given as 'beyond price'.

The best known early holder of this name was Mark Antony, the famous Roman soldier and lover of Cleopatra. Two saints – St Antony the Great, 4th century, and St Antony of Padua, 13th century – helped to establish the popularity of the name.

Variations and abbreviations: Anthony, Antoine (Fr), Anton (Ger/Scand), Antoni, Antonio (It/Sp/Port), Antonius, Tony.

Archibald

Origin/meaning: Old German 'genuinely bold'.

This name has become unfashionable except in parts of Scotland.

Variations and abbreviations: Archaimbaud (Fr), Archambault (Fr), Archibaldo (Sp), Archibold, Archie, Archy.

Archie

Origin/meaning: Old German 'genuinely brave'.

This short version of Archibald has now become a far more popular first name than the original form.

Variation and abbreviation: Archy.

Arnold

Origin/meaning: Old German 'eagle-power'.

Brought to England by the Normans at the time of the Conquest, Arnold was very popular for several centuries, often in the French form Arnaud. Many last names derived from it, e.g. Arnott, Arnett, Arnell.

Variations and abbreviations: Arnoldo (Sp), Arnaud (Fr), Arni, Arnie, Arnoldo (It), Arny.

Arran

Origin/meaning: As in the Isle of Arran. Occasionally used as a male name.

Arthur

Origin/meaning: Old Welsh 'bear' or Old Irish 'stone' or Latin 'Artorius' (one of the patrician Roman families).

Early versions of the name were 'Arter' and 'Artar'. The 'h' appears around the 16th century.

Variations and abbreviations: Art, Artair (Scot), Arte, Arttois (Fr), Artie, Artur (Ir), Arturo (Sp/It), Artus (Fr), Arty.

Asher

Origin/meaning: Hebrew 'happy'.

Asher was one of the sons of Jacob by Zilpah, the maid of his wife Leah. He was the founder of one of the tribes of Israel. Asher is found both first and last names among Jewish people.

Ashley

Origin/meaning: Old English 'ash tree wood' or 'clearing'.

A widespread English last name which became popular during the 19th century when many last names were adopted as first names.

Variations and abbreviations: Ash, Ashlin.

Ashok (pron. Assówk)

Origin/meaning: Sanskrit 'tree'.

Ashok, 269–233 bc, was one of the most famous Indian Emperors. His symbol is incorporated into the modern Indian flag. During his reign Buddhism became widespread. He encouraged builders to use stone so their buildings would last.

Variations: Ashoka, Asoka.

Ashton

Origin/meaning: Old English 'ash tree settlement'.

This last name is now used as a first name, most commonly in the US.

Variation and abbreviation: Ash.

Athol

Origin/meaning: Old Scots 'new Ireland'.

The name of an area of Scotland found both as a last name and first name.

Variation: Atholl.

Auberon (pron. Oberon)

Origin/meaning: Old German 'little elf-ruler'.

Diminutive English form of the German Alberich, from its French version Auberi. It was not unusual in Medieval England. Shakespeare used the alternative spelling Oberon as the appropriate name for the King of the Fairies in 'A Midsummer Night's Dream'.

Variations and abbreviations: Oberon, Bron.

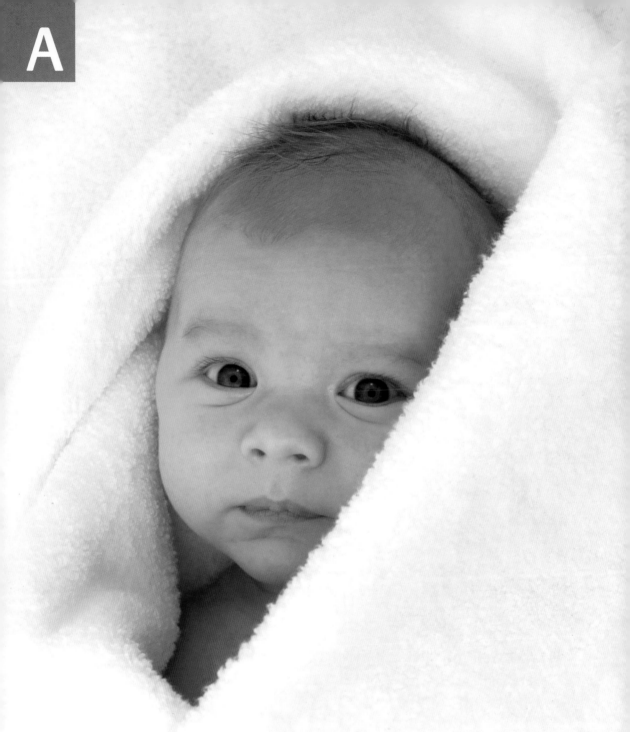

Aubrey

Origin/meaning: Old German 'elf-ruler'.
The English form of the German Alberich comes from its French version Auberi, as does Auberon q.v. Common in Medieval England.

Variations: Alberich (Ger), Alberik, Albery, Avery.

August

Origin/meaning: Latin 'venerable', 'majestic'.
A version of the old Roman name Augustus that is now found as a name in its own right.

Augustus

Origin/meaning: Latin 'venerable', 'majestic'. A title given to Roman emperors.
Brought to England by the Hanoverians in the 18th century, it was popular for about a century and was the second name of Queen Victoria's husband Albert.

Variations and abbreviations: Agosto (It), Aguistin (Ir), Agustin, Augie, August (Ger), Auguste (Fr), Augustin, Augustine, Augusto (Sp), Austen, Austin, Augy, Gus.

Avinash (pron. Aveenass)

Origin/meaning: Sanskrit 'indestructible'.
This is a Hindu name.

Axel

Origin/meaning: Hebrew 'father of peace'.
The Scandinavian and German form of Absolom q.v.

Azikiwe (pron. Azeekiwi)

Origin/meaning: Ibo 'vigorous'.
This is a name found in Nigeria.

Abbreviation: Zik.

Aziz

Origin/meaning: Arabic 'precious'.
This name is popular among Muslims.

Variation: Azizi (Swahili).

Babar

Origin/meaning: Sanskrit 'tiger'.

This Muslim name was first used as an epithet to Zahir-ud-Din-Mohammed, 1493–1530, the first of the Muslim Mogul Emperors of India. The character in French children's literature, Babar the elephant, is named after him.

Variation: Babur.

Badhur

Origin/meaning: Arabic 'born at the full moon'.

A popular Muslim name.

Variations: Badar, Badr, Badru (Swahili).

Bailey

Origin/meaning: various origins, English 'bailiff' or 'town dweller'.

This old last name is now found as a first name especially in the US and is also used for girls.

Barry

Origin/meaning: Old Irish 'spear'.

An exclusively Irish name until the 19th century when Irish emigrants spread it further afield.

Variation: Barrie.

Bartholomew

Origin/meaning: Hebrew 'son of Tolmai', 'son of a farmer'.

This is the patronymic (father's name) of the Apostle Nathanael, and the name by which he is best known. St Bartholomew was immensely popular in Medieval England.

Variations and abbreviations: Bart, Bartelmy, Barthel (Ger), Barthelemy (Fr), Bartholomé (Fr), Bartolome (Sp), Bartholomeus (Scand/Dut), Bartholomeo (It), Bat.

Baruch

Origin/meaning: Hebrew 'blessed'.

The name of the companion of the prophet Jeremiah. Popular in the 17th century like many other Biblical names.

Basil

Origin/meaning: Greek 'kingly'.

A popular name in the Eastern Christian Church because of St Basil the Great, 330–379. The name was probably brought to Western Europe by the Crusaders.

Variations and abbreviations: Baz, Basile (Fr), Basilio (It/Port/Sp), Basilius (Dut/Ger/Scand), Vasilis, Vassily (Slav/Russ).

Benedict

Origin/meaning: Latin 'blessed'.

A common name in England after the Norman Conquest. An old form is Benedick, used by Shakespeare in 'Much Ado About Nothing'. Its original popularity was largely due to the honor in which St Benedict, 480–547, the founder of the Benedictine Order, was held.

Variations and abbreviations: Ben, Bendix, Bendt (Dan), Benedetto (It), Benedicht (Swiss), Benedick, Benedicto (Sp), Benedikt (Ger/Scand), Benet, Bengt (Swed), Bennet, Bennett, Benito (It/Sp), Bennie, Benny, Benoit (Fr).

Benicio

Origin/meaning: Spanish 'benevolent person'.

The popularity of this Spanish name in the English-speaking world is mainly due to the Hollywood actor Benicio Del Toro.

Benet

Origin/meaning: Latin 'blessed'.

An English short form of Benedict q.v., more widespread in the Middle Ages than the original.

Variations and abbreviations: Ben, Benett, Bennet, Bennett.

Benjamin

Origin/meaning: Hebrew 'son of my right hand'.

In the Book of Genesis, ch.35, Rachel, Jacob's second wife, died giving birth to a son whom she called Ben-oni 'son of my sorrow'. He was then renamed by his father Benjamin 'son of the south' or 'son of my right hand'. The name Benjamin has come to be synonymous with a much loved youngest son.

Variations and abbreviations: Ben, Beniamino (It), Benji, Benjie, Bennie, Benny.

Bernard

Origin/meaning: Old German 'bear-hard', Old English 'noble and strong'.

A name popular in England for several centuries after the Norman Conquest. Often used to honor St Bernard of Clairvaux, 1091–1153, founder of the Cistercian Order of Monks.

Variations and abbreviations: Barnard, Barnet, Barney, Bearnard (Ir/Scot), Berend (Ger/Dan), Bern, Bernardo (It/Sp), Bernd (Ger), Berne, Bernhard (Ger), Bernt (Swed), Bernie, Berny, Burnard, Burnhard.

Bertram

Origin/meaning: Old German 'brilliant raven'.
One of many names brought to England at the time of the Norman Conquest. The raven was the device of Odin, Norse god of war.

Variations and abbreviations: Bart, Bartram, Beltrame (It), Beltrán (Sp), Bert, Bertie, Bertran, Bertrand (Fr), Bertrando (It), Berty.

Bevis

Origin/meaning: Old French, meaning uncertain. May be 'boy' or 'young calf'.
A name brought over by the Normans in 1066. Never widely popular.

Bharat (pron. B'rat)

Origin/meaning: Sanskrit 'the sustainer'.
This is one of the names of the Hindu god of fire Agni. He became a famous king and gave to the country the name (pron. Bhaar't), which many Indians still use today instead of India.

Bill

Origin/meaning: Old German 'will helmet' i.e. 'helmet of resolution'.
A popular short form of William q.v. sometimes given as an independent name.

Björn

Origin/meaning: Old German 'bear'.
The Scandinavian form of Bern, one of the short forms of Bernard q.v. Now widely known in English-speaking countries because of the former Swedish tennis champion Björn Borg.

Variation: Beorn (Med Eng).

Blake

Origin/meaning: Old English 'pale' or 'black'.
An English family name not uncommon as a first name in the US perhaps because of its short 'masculine' sound.

Blase

Origin/meaning: Latin 'stammerer' or possibly French 'from Blois'.
This name seems to go back to the martyr St Blaise, d.316. He was the patron saint of wool carders. The popularity of his name in Medieval England may well be due to the great importance of the wool industry at that time.

Variations and abbreviations: Biagio (It), Blaise (Fr), Blas (Sp), Blasien (Ger), Blasius (Ger/Latin), Blayze, Blaze.

Boris

Origin/meaning: Old Slav 'fighter', 'warrior'.
A popular Russian name, short for Borislav.

Brad

Origin/meaning: a short form of many family names e.g. Bradford, Bradley. Used, in the US especially, as a given name.

Bradley

Origin/meaning: Old English 'broad clearing'.
An English place-name used as a family name and used in the US as a given name. Also popular in Australia.

Abbreviation: Brad.

Brandon

Origin/meaning: Old English 'gorse hill'.
This old place name became a last name and then finally a first name. It is especially popular in the US.

Variations and abbreviation: Brand, Branden.

Brayden

Origin/meaning: Old English 'wide valley'.
This name is popular in the US.

Variation: Braydon.

Brendan

Origin/meaning: Old Irish 'dweller by the flame' or 'dweller by the beacon'.
An Irish name, correctly pronounced without the d. St Brendan was a 6th-century Irish saint and according to legend the first discoverer of America.

Variations: Brandan, Brandon, Brendin, Brenainn (Ir Gaelic), Brennan.

Brett

Origin/meaning: Old English/Old French 'Breton'.
Particularly popular in the US.

Brian

Origin/meaning: Celtic (probably Old Irish) from the word 'strength' or 'hill'. A Celtic name introduced to England from Brittany at the time of the Conquest.

Variations: Briano (It), Briant, Brien, Brion, Bryan, Bryant, Bryon.

Broderick

Origin/meaning: Old Welsh 'son of Roderick'.
A family name used, particularly in the US, as a first name.

Brook

Origin/meaning: Old English 'brook'.
A common last name used as a first name, particularly in the US.

Variation: Brooks.

Brooklyn

Origin/meaning: Place name, borough of New York City.
England soccer star David Beckham and his wife Victoria named their first child in honour of where he was conceived – Brooklyn in New York. As a result Brooklyn has emerged as a fashionable given name.

Bruce

Origin/meaning: a place name, Braöse/Brieuse (modern) in Normandy.
This was brought over to Britain as a last name – de Braöse or de Bruce – at the time of the Norman Conquest. The family was very influential and widespread.

Variation: Brucie.

Bruno

Origin/meaning: Old German/Old English 'brown'.
Used in the Middle Ages to honor St Bruno, 1033–1101, the founder of the Carthusian Order of Monks.

Bryn

Origin/meaning: Old Welsh 'hill'.
Rare outside Wales.

Bud

Origin/meaning: US familiar term for 'brother'.
Usually a nickname but sometimes used as a given name.

Variations and abbreviations: Budd, Buddie, Buddy.

Byron

Origin/meaning: Old English 'at the cowsheds'.
A place name from the North of England from which the name of Lord Byron, the English Romantic poet, derived.

Variations: Byram, Byrom.

Cadell

Origin/meaning: Old Welsh/Old Scots 'spirit of battle'.
Found as a first name in Wales and a family name in Scotland.
Variation: Cadel.

Cai (pron. Kay)

Origin/meaning: from the Roman family name Gaius which is derived from the verb 'to rejoice'. This Roman name is still used today in Wales. It is more familiar in England as Kay q.v. who was one of the Knights of the Round Table.

Variations and abbreviations: see Kay.

Calum

Origin/meaning: Latin/Scottish 'dove'.
Calum is a form of the old Latin name Columba. Its recent popularity may be linked to Calum Best, celebrity son of former soccer star George Best.

Variations and abbreviation: Callum, Cally.

Calvin

Origin/meaning: Latin 'bald'.

John Calvin, 1509–1564, the religious reformer, was a hero figure among Puritans, especially those who went to America.

By the 18th century his last name was being used as a first name.

Variations and abbreviations: Cal, Calv, Vin, Vinny.

Cameron

Origin/meaning: Old Scots 'crooked nose'.
A Scottish clan-name used as a first name.

Abbreviation: Cam.

Carl

Origin/meaning: Old German 'man'.
This is a German form of Charles q.v. now used as a separate name in its own right.

Variations: Karl, Carlo (It).

Carlos

Origin/meaning: Old German 'man'.
The Spanish and Portuguese form of Charles that has become prevalent in the US.

Variation and abbreviation: Carlo.

Carson

Origin/meaning: origin unknown.
A name from Scotland and Northern Ireland that was used in the 13th century as a last name.

Cary

Origin/meaning: Old English place name from the Somerset area.
As a first name, it was popularized by film star Cary Grant.

Casimir

Origin/meaning: Polish 'command of peace'.
The English and French version of a Polish name.
Variations: Casimiro (It), Kasimir (Ger), Kazimierz (Pol), Kazmer.

Caspar

Origin/meaning: uncertain, possibly Persian.
Sometimes, because of the legend of the three wise men, said to mean 'treasurer'.
Variations and abbreviations: Casper, Cass, Cassie, Kaspar (Ger), Kasper. See also Jasper.

Cassius

Origin/meaning: Latin 'vain'.
Cassius is the name of one of the men who plotted against Julius Caesar in Shakespeare's play.
Variations and abbreviations: Cass, Cassie, Cassy.

Cecil

Origin/meaning: Latin – Caecilius – one of the patrician families of Rome. Probably from the Latin word for 'blind'.
One of many aristocratic family names (in this case of the Marquis of Salisbury) used as a masculine first name from the 19th century.

Cedric

Origin/meaning: uncertain. Possibly Old Welsh 'war chief'.
Used by Sir Walter Scott for one of his characters, Cedric the Saxon in 'Ivanhoe', 1820.
Its use for the hero of Frances Hodgson Burnett's popular book 'Little Lord Fauntleroy', 1886, reinforced its popularity.

Ceredig

Origin/meaning: a character from Welsh legend. Ceredig was the son of Cunedda.
He gave his name to the area Ceredigion.

Chandler

Origin/meaning: Old French/English 'candle maker'.

An old family name that came from an occupation, it has been given a new lease of life thanks to the character Chandler Bing, played by Matthew Perry, in the TV comedy 'Friends'.

Charles

Origin/meaning: Old German 'man'.

This was the name of the Holy Roman Emperor Charlemagne – 742–814. The German form of the name was Karl, Latinized in documents as Carolus. In France it developed into Charles, the name of many French kings.

Variations and abbreviations: Carl, Carlo (It), Carlos (Sp), Carrol, Carroll, Cary, Caryl, Charley, Charlie, Chick, Chuck, Karel, Karl, Karol (Pol).

Chase

Background: Norman 'huntsman'.

Far more common as a first name in the US than in Britain.

Chester

Origin/meaning: Latin/Old English 'fortified camp'.

A place name which became a common family name now found, mainly in the US, as a given name.

Abbreviation: Chet.

Chris

Origin/meaning: Latin 'Christian' or 'Christ bearer'.
A short form of Christian, Christopher or Christine q.v., sometimes used as an independent name.

Variations: Cris, Kris.

Christian

Origin/meaning: Latin 'Christian'.
Especially popular in Denmark which has had several Kings of that name.

Variations and abbreviations: Chrétian (Fr), Chris, Chrissy, Christiano (It/Sp), Kristian (Sp).

Christopher

Origin/meaning: Greek 'Christ bearer'.
This is one of the earliest Christian names. It was applied to a legendary saint who was supposed to have carried the infant Christ across a river. St Christopher thus became the patron saint of all travelers.

Variations and abbreviations: Chris, Chrissie, Chrissy, Christie, Christoffer (Dan), Christoforo (It), Christoph, Christophe (Fr), Christophonis (Ger), Christy, Chrystal, Cris, Cristóbal (Sp), Cristoforo (It), Cristoval (Sp), Kester, Kit, Kristoff (Scand).

Chuck

Origin/meaning: 'man'.
US familiar form of Charles q.v.

Clarence

Origin/meaning: Latin 'bright', 'famous'.
An English Royal title. Lionel, son of Edward III, was given the title Duke of Clarence in 1362, because his wife was heiress of the Clare family.

Clark

Origin/meaning: Old French 'scholar'.
A common English last name which has become a first name, particularly in the US.

Variations: Clarke, Clerk.

Claud

Origin/meaning: Latin 'lame'. The name of a patrician Roman family.
Introduced to England from France in the 16th century.

Variations: Claude (Fr), Claudian, Claudianus (Ger), Claudio (It/Sp), Claudius (Ger/Dut), Klaudius (Ger). See also Antony, Cecil.

Clem

Origin/meaning: Latin 'gentle', 'merciful'.

A short form of Clement sometimes found as an independent name, particularly in the US.

Cliff

Origin/meaning: Old English 'ford at a cliff'.

Short form of Clifford, the family name of Baron Clifford of Chudleigh, and occasionally of other last names. Frequently used as an independent name.

Clinton

Origin/meaning: Old English 'from the headland farm'.

An English last name used as a given name.

Abbreviation: Clint.

Clive

Origin/meaning: Old English 'at the cliff'.

The last name of Robert Clive, 1725–1774, the Englishman largely responsible for annexing India for the East India Company. His last name became popular as a first name.

Cody

Origin/meaning: Old English 'cushion'.

Has become a widely-used name in the US, probably in honor of the Wild West hero William Frederick Cody, better known as Buffalo Bill.

Variation: Codie.

Colan

Origin/meaning: Old Cornish 'dove'.

Colan is the Old Cornish version of the Latin Columba.

Colin

Origin/meaning: Greek/Old French 'victory of the people' or Old Scots 'young man'.

The name came to England from France in the Middle Ages as a diminutive of Nicholas.

The Scottish name is sometimes considered another variation on the name Columba, 'dove'.

Variations and abbreviations: Cailean (Scot), Col, Colán (Ir), Cole, Collin.

Colum

Origin/meaning: Latin 'dove'.

This Irish name is one of several Celtic forms of Columba. Their popularity resulted from the great prestige of St Columba among people in Celtic areas.

Variations and abbreviations: Col, Cole, Colm. See also Colan, Colin, Malcolm.

Conan (pron. Cóe-nan; Irish, Connáwn)

Origin/meaning: Old Irish 'high', 'mighty' or 'intelligent'.

A widely found Celtic name.

Variations and abbreviations: Con, Conal, Conn, Conny, Kynan.

Connor

Origin/meaning: Old Irish 'high desire'.

An extremely popular Irish name.

Variations and abbreviations: Con, Connaire (Ir), Conn (Ir), Conor.

Conrad

Origin/meaning: Old German 'bold counselor'.

Variations and abbreviations: Con, Conn, Connie, Conrade (Fr), Corrado (It), Corradino (It), Cort (Dan), Curt, Koenraad (Dut), Konrad (Ger/Scand), Kurt.

Conway

Origin/meaning: Old Welsh 'holy water' or Old Irish 'hound of the plain'.

The name possibly originated from the place-name Conway in Wales. Generally a last name, it is now a regularly used first name.

Variations and abbreviations: Con, Conn, Connie, Conny.

Cormac

Origin/meaning: Old Irish 'charioteer'.

An Irish last name and first name, it features in many of the pagan Irish myths and legends.

Variations and abbreviations: Cormack, Cormick, Mac.

Cornelius

Origin/meaning: the Cornelius family, one of the great families of Ancient Rome.

The name may come from the Latin 'horn' which implied kingship. There were several saints of the name.

Variations and abbreviations: Con, Conn, Connie, Connor, Conny, Cornel, Cornelis (It/Sp), Cornell, Corny, Cory.

Cosmo

Origin/meaning: Greek 'order', 'harmony', 'the universe'.

SS Cosmas and Damian were, according to legend, twin brothers, who practiced as doctors without charging money. The Medici family, Dukes of Florence, adopted the form Cosimo as a family name which popularized it further.

Variations and abbreviations: Cos, Cosimo (It/Sp), Cosmé (Fr).

Courtenay

Origin/meaning: either Old French 'short nose' or de Courtenay, an aristocratic family from Courtenay in France.
The family name of the West Country Earls of Devon. It was particularly successful in the US.

Variations and abbreviations: Court, Courtnay, Curt.

Craig

Origin/meaning: Old Scots/Old Welsh 'crag'.
One of the most common Scots last names, based on several place names and popular as a given name.

Crispian/Crispin

Origin/meaning: Latin 'curled'.
Crispinianus and Crispinus were two shoemakers who were both martyred, probably in the 3rd century. They became the patron saints of shoemakers.

Cruz

Origin/meaning: Spanish 'cross'.
England soccer star David Beckham and wife Victoria named their third son Cruz, a Spanish name, while the baby's father was playing for Real Madrid.

Curt

Origin/meaning: a short form of names like Conrad, Courtney, Curtis. Used as a given name, particularly in the US.
Variation: Kurt.

Cyril

Origin/meaning: Greek 'lordly'.
St Cyril, 827–869, with his brother, took Christianity to the Slavs. They were aided by their knowledge of Slav languages. They devised a script to write these languages down, known as Cyrillic, which is still used today for the Russian language.
Variations: Cirille (Fr), Cirillo (It), Cirilo (Sp), Cyrill (Ger), Cyrillus (Dut), Kyrill (Ger), Kyrillus (Ger).

Cyrus

Origin/meaning: Persian/Greek 'throne'.
Cyrus the Great, 560–629, first Persian king and a powerful ruler, surrounded by fable and legend. The name is popular in the US.
Variations and abbreviations: Ciro (It/Sp), Cirus, Cy, Russ.

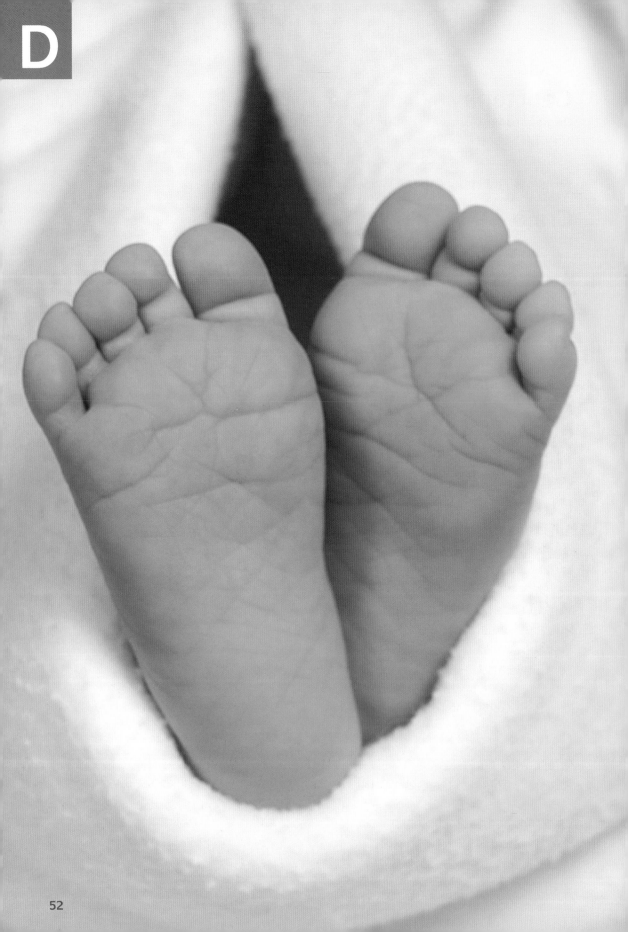

Dai

Origin/meaning: Hebrew 'darling', 'friend'.
A popular Welsh short form of David q.v. from Dewi and Dafydd.

Dale

Origin/meaning: Old English 'from the valley'.
An English last name used as a first name, usually for boys.

Variations and abbreviations: Dael, Dal.

Damian

Origin/meaning: Greek 'tamer'.
Damian and Cosmas were two early Christian martyrs who probably died in Syria.

Variations and abbreviations: Dami, Damiano (It), Damien (Fr), Damyan.

Daniel

Origin/meaning: Hebrew 'God has judged' or Old Irish 'dark-haired'.
Daniel was a Hebrew prophet who was delivered from the lions' den where he had been thrown by the Persian king Darius. The 17th-century Puritan liking for Biblical names gave it an extra boost.

Variations and abbreviations: Dan, Daniele (It), Danilo (Slav), Danni, Dannie, Danny, Deiniol (Wel).

Darby

Origin/meaning: Old Irish 'free from envy' or English 'from Derby'.
The use of Darby in the phrase 'Darby and Joan', meaning an inseparable old married couple, dates back to 1735.

Variation: Derby.

Darcy

Origin/meaning: Old French 'from Arcy', Old Irish 'dark man'.
This is a name that came to England as a last name with William the Conqueror. It became an Irish first name after a branch of the family settled there in the late Middle Ages.

Variations: D'Arcy, Darsey, Darsy.

Darren

Origin/meaning: uncertain. Sometimes given as Old Irish 'little one' or Greek 'from Doris'
This appeared in the 1960s and 70s and is a last name used as a first name.

Variations: Daren, Daron, Darrin.

Daryl

Origin/meaning: Old English 'little dear', 'darling'.

A very old name still used occasionally today.

Variations and abbreviations: Darrel, Darrell, Darryl, Daryll.

Daud

Origin/meaning: Arabic 'beloved'.

A widespread Muslim name similar to David q.v.

Variations: Daudi (E Africa), Dauvud.

David

Origin/meaning: Hebrew 'darling' or 'friend'.

King David, who slew Goliath and is reputed to have written the Psalms, is one of the outstanding characters in the Bible. The 6th-century Welsh saint Dewi (David) founded many monasteries, chief among them being at Mynyw, now known as St David's. The Scots had their own St David, 1084–1153, who was also their king, David I.

Variations and abbreviations: Dai (Wel), Dafydd (Wel), Dave, Davidde, Davide (Fr/It/Sp), Davie, Davin, Davy, Deio (Wel), Dewey (Wel).

Dean

Origin/meaning: 'from the valley'.

An English last name used as a first name.

Variations: Deane, Dene, Dino.

Declan

Origin/meaning: origin unknown.

This old Irish name has recently become extremely popular though it is often shortened to Dec. Declan is the real first name of singer Elvis Costello.

Abbreviation: Dec.

Denis

Origin/meaning: Latin/Greek 'follower of Dionysos'.

The Greek name Dionysius was common because of the popularity of the god of fertility and wine. A St Dionysius, who took Christianity to France, was beheaded at Montmartre in Paris in 258. He was adopted as the patron saint of France and known as St Denys.

Variations and abbreviations: Den, Denness, Dennet, Denney, Dennis, Denny, Denys (Fr), Dion, Dionisio (It/Sp), Dionys (Ger), Dionysius (Ger).

Denzil

Origin/meaning: uncertain, possibly Latin/Greek 'follower of Dionysos'.

A Cornish last name used as a first name since the 17th century.

Variation: Denzell.

Derek

Origin/meaning: Old German 'ruler of the people'.

This name is from the Old German Theodoric. In the late Middle Ages trade with Holland introduced the Dutch forms Diederick and Dirk, from which the 20th-century Derek evolved.

Variations and abbreviations: Dedrik, Deric, Deryk, Derrick, Diederich (Ger), Diederick (Dut), Dietrich (Ger), Dirk.

Dermot

Origin/meaning: Old Irish 'free from envy'.
This is an Anglicized form of the Irish Diarmaid. Diarmaid in Irish legend ran off with Grainne, Queen of Tara. Her husband forced Diarmaid to fight with a wild boar which killed him.
Variations: Darby, Derby, Dermott, Diarmid, Diarmit.

Desmond

Origin/meaning: Old Irish 'from South Munster'.
This is an Irish last name which came into general use as a first name in the 19th century.
Abbreviation: Des.

Dexter

Origin/meaning: Old English 'dyer'. Sometimes given as Latin 'right-handed', 'dexterous'.
An English last name sometimes used as a first name.

Dhruva (pron. Dhroov)

Origin/meaning: this is the Hindu name for the pole star.
Dhruva is a character from Indian mythology. Rejected by his father, King Uttanpada, he went into the forest and gradually achieved spiritual perfection through meditation. On his death the gods transformed him into Dhruva-Loka, the pole star.

Digby

Origin/meaning: Old English 'settlement by a ditch'.
An English place name which became a last name and has been occasionally as a first name.

Diggory

Origin/meaning: French 'lost', 'strayed'.
An old-fashioned name, possibly Cornish, rare nowadays.

Dillon

Origin/meaning: Old Irish 'faithful' or Old German 'destroyer'.
An Irish last name sometimes used as a first name.

Dinesh

Origin/meaning: Hindi/Gujerati 'helper of the poor'.

Dion

Origin/meaning: Latin/Greek 'follower of Dionysus'.
A form of Denis q.v.

Dirk

Origin/meaning: Old German 'ruler of the people'.

A Dutch form of Theodoric. It has been found in England since the late Middle Ages when England was engaged in the wool trade with Holland.

Variations: Dierk (Ger), Derk.

Dominic

Origin/meaning: Latin 'of the Lord'.

A name either intended to dedicate a child to God or to indicate he was born on a Sunday, the Lord's day. It gained wider use in the Middle Ages when it was given to honor St Dominic, 1170–1221, founder of the Dominican Order of Friars.

Variations and abbreviations: Dom, Domenic, Domenico (It), Domingo (Sp), Dominick, Dominique (Fr), Nick, Nickie, Nicky.

Donald

Origin/meaning: Old Scots 'world ruler'.

The name of six Scottish kings, Donald is, not surprisingly, one of the commonest Scottish names. The short form Don/Donen can have the independent meaning 'dark', and is found in several last names which are sometimes used as given names, such as Donovan, Donnelly and Donahue.

Variations and abbreviations: Don, Donal (Ir), Donalt, Donn, Donnie, Donny.

Donovan

Origin/meaning: Old Irish 'dark warrior', 'brown warrior'.
Abbreviation: Don.

Dorian

Origin/meaning: Greek 'from Doris' (one of the famous areas of classical Greece).

This is the male version of Doris q.v. Made famous by Oscar Wilde's novel 'The Picture of Dorian Gray', 1891.

See also Dylan.

Dougal (pron. Doogal)

Origin/meaning: Old Irish 'dark stranger'.

Used by the Irish as a term for Scandinavian invaders it became a general Celtic term used by Irish, Scots and Bretons for strangers.

Variations and abbreviations: Doug, Doyle (Ir), Dug, Dugald, Duggie.

Douglas

Origin/meaning: Old Irish/Scots 'from the dark water'.
A common descriptive place or river name. The famous Scottish clan Douglas developed as a first name within the family, when used as a name to both male and female children.
Variations and abbreviations: Doug, Dougie, Douglass, Dougy, Dug, Duggie.

Drew

Origin/meaning: Old German 'bearer' or Old French 'vigorous'.
This is the Medieval English form of the name Drogo, by way of the French form Dru. Drogo lost its popularity after the 17th century but Drew survives, in the US particularly.
Variations: Drogo, Dru.

Duane (pron. Dwayne)

Origin/meaning: Old Irish 'small and dark'.
A 'new' first name popular in the US in the 1950s and 60s perhaps because of the guitarist Duane Eddy and also its similarity to another 60s favourite, Wayne.
Variation: Dwayne.

Dudley

Origin/meaning: Old English 'Dudda's clearing'.
Dudda was a Saxon nobleman, and Dudley is a town in the English West Midlands. The Dudley family was one of the fastest rising families in Tudor England, eventually granted the Earldom of Leicester. Dudley was not used as a first name until the 19th century.
Abbreviation: Dud.

Duncan

Origin/meaning: Old Irish 'brown headed'.
Like many names of Irish origin this was quickly adopted by Scotland whose language was so similar. There were two Scottish kings of that name, the first of whom is the Duncan, 1034–1040, murdered by Macbeth and well known from Shakespeare's play.
Abbreviations: Dun, Dunc, Dunk.

Dwight

Origin/meaning: uncertain, possibly Old French 'from the Isle of Wight' or Old Flemish De Witt, 'from Witt'. It became a first name in the 19th century particularly in North America.

Dylan (pron. Dúllan)

Origin/meaning: Old Welsh 'dark' often given as 'from the sea'.
A character from Welsh legend whose father was the God of the Sea.
Variations and abbreviations: Dill, Dillan, Dillon, Dullan.

Eamon

Origin/meaning: Old English 'prosperous protector'.
The Irish form of Edmund q.v.

Variation: Eamonn.

Earl

Origin/meaning: Old English 'nobleman' or 'warrior'.
This is an English last name which probably indicates an ancestor was in the service of an earl. Since the 19th century this family name has been used in the US as a first name.

Variations: Earle, Erle.

Ebenezer

Origin/meaning: Hebrew 'stone of help'.
This is a Biblical place name referred to in the first Book of Samuel. It was popular among the 17th-century Puritans. It declined in popularity, partly because of the unattractive character Ebenezer Scrooge in 'A Christmas Carol' by Charles Dickens.

Variations and abbreviations: Benezer, Eben.

Ebner

Origin/meaning: Hebrew 'father of light'.

Eden

Origin/meaning: Hebrew 'delight' or Old English 'rich'.
The second meaning refers to Eden when used as a form of Ede and Edith q.v. during the Middle Ages.

Edgar

Origin/meaning: Old English 'rich spear'.
Edgar (Eadgar) was one of the names used by the royal house of Wessex. Its royal usage together with hopes of a Saxon revival, may account for the survival of the name for several centuries after the Norman Conquest.

Variations and abbreviations: Eadgar, Ed, Edgard (Fr).

Edmund

Origin/meaning: Old English 'rich guardian'.
As in Edward, Edgar and Edith the first syllable of this name indicates it was used by the royal house of Wessex before the Conquest.

Variations and abbreviations: Eamon (Ir), Ed, Eddie, Edmond (Fr), Edmondo (It), Edmundo (Sp), Ned, Nedely, Ted, Teddy.

Edward

Origin/meaning: Old English 'rich guardian'.

Like most names beginning with Ed- this is closely connected with the royal house of Wessex. Edward the Martyr, 963–978, succeeded his father King Edward and was murdered by his stepmother Elfrida. Edward the Confessor, 1003–1066, was the last of the Anglo-Saxon kings. He founded Westminster Abbey and was made a saint shortly after his death.

Variations and abbreviations: Duarte (Port), Ed, Eddie, Eddy, Edouard (Fr), Eduard (Ger/Dut), Eduardo (It/Port/Sp), Edvard (Scand), Ned, Neddie, Neddy, Ted, Teddie, Teddy.

Edwin

Origin/meaning: Old English 'rich friend'.

Edwin, King of Northumbria, 585–633, eventually gained overlordship over most of England. Northumbria at that time extended into Scotland and Edwin gave his name to Edinburgh. He was a convert to Christianity and was canonized after his death in battle.

Variations and abbreviations: Ed, Eddie, Eddy, Eduino (It/Sp), Edwyn, Ned, Neddie, Neddy, Odwin, Otwin, Ted, Teddie.

Elijah

Origin/meaning: Hebrew 'Jehovah is God'.

Elijah was a Hebrew Prophet who lived about 900 bc. He was fed by ravens at the brook Cherith and miraculously brought back to life the son of Zeraphath.

Elliot

Origin/meaning: Hebrew, Greek 'The Lord is my God'.

This widely-used name, especially in the US, comes from the same roots as Elias and Elijah q.v.

Variations: Eliot, Eliott, Elliott.

Ellis

Origin/meaning: Hebrew, Greek 'The Lord is my God'.

A last name that became a first name, Ellis comes from the same roots as Elijah q.v.

Elmer

Origin/meaning: Old English 'noble and famous'.

An English last name which developed from the Old English name Aylmer. It has been popular as a first name in the US, sometimes attributed to the Elmer brothers who were prominent in the American Revolution.

Elvis

Origin/meaning: Old Norse 'all wise'.

Recent use is almost totally due to the fame of the US singer Elvis Presley.

E

Emanuel

Origin/meaning: Hebrew 'God with us'.
A name used in the Old Testament to describe the promised Messiah (Isaiah ch.7 v.14).
This is the Greek/Latin form of Immanuel.

Variations and abbreviations: Emanuele (It), Emmanuel (Fr), Immanuel (Ger), Mannie, Manny, Manoel (Port), Manuel (Sp).

Emile

Origin/meaning: Latin: from the Roman clan name, Aemilius. Meaning sometimes given as 'zealous' or 'bronze beater'. This is the masculine equivalent of Emily q.v. It is rare in English-speaking countries but frequently used in Germany and France.

Variations and abbreviations: Aemilius, Emil (Ger), Emilio (It/Sp), Emlyn (Wel).

Emlyn

Origin/meaning: Latin: from the Roman clan name, Aemilius. Meaning sometimes given as 'zealous' or 'bronze beater'.
This is the Welsh form of the name which is found in Europe as Emile or Emil.

Emrys

Origin/meaning: Greek 'divine' or 'immortal'.
The Welsh form of Ambrose q.v. Ambrosius Aurelianus was a legendary 5th-century Welsh king whose resistance to the Saxons may have given rise to the legends of King Arthur.

Enoch

Origin/meaning: uncertain. Possibly Hebrew 'mortal' or 'skilled'.
Enoch was a Hebrew patriarch, father of Methuselah (who was said to have lived 969 years) and grandfather of Noah (Genesis ch.5).

Variation: Enos (Greek).

Ephraim

Origin/meaning: uncertain. Sometimes given as Hebrew 'very fruitful'.
This is a Biblical name. Ephraim was the grandson of Jacob and gave his name to one of the tribes of Israel. It was used by 17th-century Puritans, particularly those living in New England.

Variations: Efrem, Ephraem, Ephrem.

Erasmus

Origin/meaning: Greek 'beloved'.
This name was used in the Netherlands and Germany in the Middle Ages. St Erasmus, a 4th-century martyr, was the patron saint of sailors.

Variations and abbreviations: Asmus, Elmo, Erasme (Fr), Erasmo (It), Telmo.

Eric

Origin/meaning: Old Norse usually given as 'ever ruling'.

This is a popular Scandinavian name and was brought to England and Scotland by the Scandinavian invaders who followed the fall of Roman rule.

Variations and abbreviations: Aic, Erich (Ger), Erick, Erico (It), Erik (Swed/Dan), Eirik (Nor), Jerik (Dan), Rick, Rickie, Ricky.

Ernest

Origin/meaning: Old German 'earnestness' or 'vigor'.

This was introduced into Britain in the 18th century by the Hanoverian royal family. Oscar Wilde used the name in his play 'The Importance of Being Earnest', 1895.

Variations and abbreviations: Earnest, Ern, Ernesto (It), Ernestin (Fr), Ernestus, Ernie.

Errol

Origin/meaning: Old English/Old Norse 'army power'.

A variation of the name Harold q.v. one of its earliest forms, Eral. A popular US first name.

Esmé

Origin/meaning: French/Latin 'beloved'.

Used both as a masculine and a feminine name. Like the masculine Amyas it is a variation of the more popular Amy.

Variations: Aimé, Amyas.

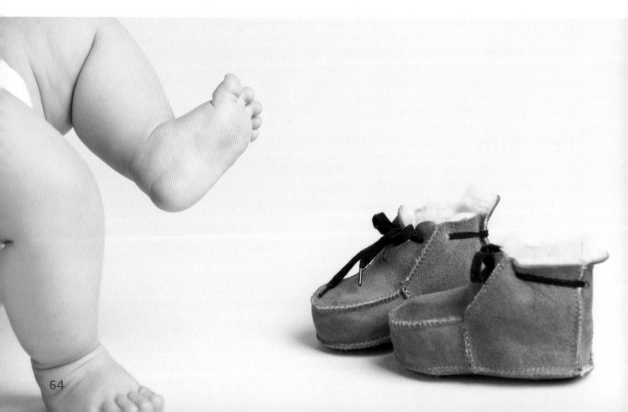

Esmond

Origin/meaning: Old English 'grace protection'.
This Old English name had more or less died out as a first name by the end of the 14th century but survived as a comparatively unusual last name. In the 19th century, Thackeray's highly successful novel 'The History of Henry Esmond', 1852, brought the name back into currency as a personal name.

Ethan

Origin/meaning: Hebrew 'long-lived'.
This name's recent popularity is probably due in part to the actor Ethan Hawke, though it has been a widely-used name in the US for some time.

Etienne

Origin/meaning: Greek 'wreathed', 'crowned'.
A French form of Stephen q.v.

Euan/Ewan

Origin/meaning: Old Scots/Irish 'young warrior'.
This is probably from the same root as the common Welsh name Owen q.v.
Variations: Evan, Owain (Wel), Owen.

Eugene

Origin/meaning: Greek 'noble', 'well-born'.

This name was used in the Middle Ages to honor St Eugenius, a pope, but was popularized among the British and their allies by the exploits of Prince Eugene of Savoy, 1663–1736. The name was popular in the US especially in its short form Gene.

Variations: Eugen (Ger), Eugène (Fr), Eugenio (It/Sp), Eugenius (Ger/Dut), Yevgeny (Rus).

Eustace

Origin/meaning: Greek 'fruitful'.

St Eustace was a Roman general. He was converted to Christianity while out hunting, by a vision of a stag with a luminous cross between its antlers. The soldier was later martyred and became one of the patron saints of huntsmen. The name came to England with the Normans.

Variations and abbreviations: Eustache (Fr), Eustachius (Ger), Eustasius (Ger/Dut), Eustatius (Dut), Eustazio (It), Eustic, Stacy.

Evan

Origin/meaning: Old Scots/Old Irish 'young warrior'.

An English form of the Scots name Euan q.v. and the Welsh names Owen q.v. and Ifan.

Evelyn (pron. Eevlyn)

Origin/meaning: diminutive of the Old German name Avi, or Old French 'hazel tree' or Old Celtic 'pleasant'.

Evelyn has been used as a masculine first name since the 16th century. It was used as a first name in families which had married into families with the last name Evelyn.

Everard

Origin/meaning: Old German 'strong as a boar'.

Introduced into England by the Normans.

Variations: Everett, Ewart.

Ezra

Origin/meaning: Hebrew 'help'.

Ezra was a prophet who lived in the 5th century bc. His name was given to one of the Books of the Old Testament.

Variation: Esra (Ger).

Farquhar (pron. Fárkar)

Origin/meaning: Old Scots 'friendly man'.

This is used as a first name and, more commonly, as a last name in Scotland. Fearchur was an early Scottish king.

Felix

Origin/meaning: Latin 'fortunate'.

This is the name of over 50 saints, not all of whom are well documented. It is still used today although it is rather unusual.

Variations: Félicité (Fr), Félix (Fr), Felice, Feliciano (It).

Fergus

Origin/meaning: Old Irish/Old Scots 'choice of men'.

This is generally considered a Scottish name, although there is an Irish version. It gave rise to the Scottish last name Ferguson and is the name of ten saints.

Variations and abbreviations: Fergie, Feargus (Ir).

Finbar

Origin/meaning: Irish 'fair haired'.

A traditional Irish name that has recently become more widely used.

Variations: Finbarr, Fionnbharr.

Finlay

Origin/meaning: Scottish 'fair haired warrior'.

An old Scottish name, it has become more common in recent years.

Variation: Finley.

Fletcher

Origin/meaning: Old French 'arrow-maker'.

This is a family name sometimes used as a first name.

Floyd

Origin/meaning: Old Welsh 'grey'.

This is an English adaptation of the common Welsh name Lloyd. It is sometimes used as a first name derived from the family name.

Variation: Lloyd.

Forbes

Origin/meaning: Scottish 'field'.

Forbes is an old Scottish local name and last name that can now be found as a first name.

Francis

Origin/meaning: Old German 'a Frank'. Medieval Latin 'from France' or 'free'.
The Franks were a Teutonic race who took their name from the franca, a type of javelin.

Variations and abbreviations: Chico (It), Ffransis (Wel), Fran, Francesco (It), Francisco (Sp/Port), François (Fr), Frank, Frankie, Frannie, Frans (Swed), Frants (Dan), Franz (Ger), Franziskus (Ger), Pancho (Sp).

Franklin

Origin/meaning: Old German 'a Frank'. Medieval English 'free citizen'.
The Frankish tribes prided themselves on their liberty and independence. Their name became a Latin word for free (francus) and Franklin, a diminutive of Frank, was the medieval word for a free man.

Variations and abbreviations: see Francis.

Franz

Origin/meaning: Old German 'a Frank' or 'free'.
A German familiar form of Francis (Franziscus) used frequently as an independent name.

Fraser

Origin/meaning: French 'strawberrier'.
This common Scottish last name comes from the Norman last name de Fresel, a place in France.

Variation: Frazer.

Fred

Origin/meaning: Old German 'peace'.
A short form of names beginning or ending with Fred, e.g. Frederick q.v. or Alfred q.v.

Frederick

Origin/meaning: Old English/Old German 'peace-rule'.
The -rick part of this name is the same word that is found in Richard and in words like rex (the Latin word for king), and reich (the German word for kingdom).

Variations and abbreviations: Federico (It), Federigo (Sp), Ferry (Med Eng), Fred, Freddie, Freddy, Frédéric (Fr), Frederic, Frederich, Frederik (Dan/Dut), Fredric, Fredrick, Friedrich (Ger), Fritz (Ger), Rick, Rickie, Ricky, Rik.

Frodo

Origin/meaning: Old Norse 'wise'.
This is the invented name of the hero of the epic novel and film trilogy 'The Lord of the Rings'. However, there is a real Scandinavian name Frode.

Gabriel

Origin/meaning: Hebrew 'strong man of God'.
Gabriel, with Michael and Raphael is one of the three archangels named in the Bible.
Variations and abbreviations: Gabby, Gabe, Gabriele (It), Gavrilo (Russ).

Galahad

Origin/meaning: uncertain. Given as Welsh 'battle hawk' to tie in with Gawain q.v.
Sir Galahad was the son of Elaine and Sir Lancelot.
Variation: Galaad.

Ganesh (pron. Ganess)

Origin/meaning: Sanskrit 'head of the Ganas'. (The Ganas are demi-gods who wait on Shiva.)
This is a very popular name in India because the god it honors is the god of wisdom and
patron of the arts, more or less the equivalent of the Greek goddess Athena.
Variations: Ganapati, Ganesha.

Gareth

Origin/meaning: either Old German 'hard-spear' (from Gerard) or Welsh 'gentle'.
Gareth is a character from the tales of King Arthur and his Knights of the Round Table.
Variations and abbreviations: Garrett, Garth, Gary, Gerard.

Garth

Origin/meaning: Welsh 'high-land' or a form of Gareth q.v.
This is the name of several mountains in Wales and is used as a Welsh name. It may also be
a modern short form of Gareth q.v. It was the name of a comic strip hero who appeared for
many years in the 'Daily Mirror'.

Gary

Origin/meaning: Old German 'spear'.
A short form of Gerald and Gerard q.v. through the form Garret. Also used as a form of
Gareth q.v.

Gavin

Origin/meaning: uncertain. Usually given as Welsh 'hawk of the plain'.
A medieval form of Gawain q.v.

Gawain

Origin/meaning: uncertain. Usually given as Welsh 'hawk of the plain' or 'little hawk'.
Possibly also Old German 'tribute' or 'partition of land'.
Variations: Gauvaine, Gavin, Gawayne, Gawen, Gawin, Gwion.

Gaylord

Origin/meaning: Old French 'merry', 'high-spirited'.
This is derived from the French word gaillard. In the US it is an established first name.

Gene

Origin/meaning: Greek 'noble', 'well-born'.
This is the usual short form of Eugene q.v. in the US, where it is frequently found as an independent name.

Variations and abbreviations: see Eugene.

Geoffrey

Origin/meaning: Old German. Uncertain. Probably 'district peace'. Sometimes given as 'traveler peace'.
A common medieval name. The alternative spelling is Jeffrey. Its early popularity is evident from the many last names such as Jeffreys, Jepherson and Jeeves, which derive from it.

Variations and abbreviations: Geoff, Geoffroi (Fr), Geoffroy (Fr), Jeff, Jeffrey.

George

Origin/meaning: Greek 'farmer'.
St George was a Roman officer martyred at Lydda in 303 for his adherence to the Christian faith. He is the patron saint of Greece as well as England and the centre of his cult was in Palestine where he was martyred.

Variations and abbreviations: Dod, Doddy, Geordie, Georg (Ger), Georges (Fr), Georgie, Georgy, Giorgio (It), Jöran (Swed), Jorge (Sp), Jörgen (Dan), Seiorse (Ir), Siôr (Wel), Yorick, Yuri (Russ).

Geraint (pron. Gerrighnt or Jerrighnt)

Origin/meaning: Greek 'old'.
Like several other Welsh names this is based on a Roman name. The original is probably the Roman name Gerontius.

Gerald

Origin/meaning: Old German 'spear-rule'.
This name was adopted by the Normans who introduced it into England.

Variations and abbreviations: Gary, Gearalt (Ir), Gerallt (Wel), Géralde (Fr), Gerold (Ger), Gerrie, Gerry, Giraldo (It), Giraud (Fr), Jerold, Jerrie, Jerry.

Gerard

Origin/meaning: Old German 'spear-hard'.
This is a similar name to Gerald and was more popular in the Middle Ages, giving rise to several last names including Garrard and Garret.

Variations and abbreviations: Gary, Garry, Garret, Gearard (Ir), Geraud (Fr), Gerardo (Sp/It), Gerhard (Ger/Scand), Gerhardt (Ger), Gerrard, Gearoid, Gerry, Jerry.

Gershom

Origin/meaning: Hebrew 'bell'. Sometimes given as 'stranger'.
A Biblical name given to the first born child of Moses and Zipporah. Nowadays it is used mainly by Jewish people.

Variation: Gersham.

Gervase

Origin/meaning: uncertain. Possibly Old German 'spear' plus Celtic 'servant' (as in vassal).
St Gervase was an early martyr.

Variations: Gervais, Gervaise (Fr), Gervasio (It), Gervaso (It), Gervasius (Ger), Jaruis.

Gideon

Origin/meaning: Hebrew 'destroyer', 'tree feller'.
A Biblical name of one of the Judges of Israel.

Variations: Gedeon, Gédéon (Fr), Gedeone (It).

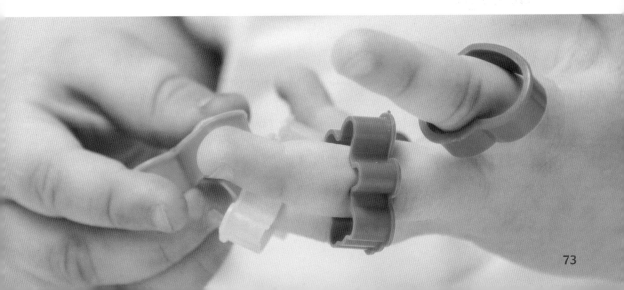

Gilbert

Origin/meaning: Old German 'bright pledge'.

The Normans introduced this name into England and gained popularity in the Middle Ages.

Variations and abbreviations: Bert, Bertie, Berty, Gib, Gibb, Gil, Gilberto (It), Gilbrecht (Ger), Gill, Giselbert (Ger), Giselbrecht (Ger).

Giles

Origin/meaning: uncertain. Usually given as Greek 'kid' therefore 'youthful'.

The Latin name Aegidius was said to be taken from the Greek word for kid.

Variations and abbreviations: Aegidius, Egide (Fr), Egidio (It), Egidius (Dut), Gide, Gil (Sp/Ger), Gill (Ger), Gilles (Fr), Gyles.

Giorgio

Origin/meaning: Greek 'farmer'.

A prevalent Italian form of George, for example, the fashion designer Giorgio Armani.

Glenn

Origin/meaning: Celtic 'valley', 'glen'.

It began as a family name in the US, more recently to honor John Glenn, the astronaut.

Variations: Glen, Glyn (Wel), Glynn.

Glyn

Origin/meaning: Welsh 'valley' or possibly a short form of Glyndwr (Glendower).

A popular Welsh name now also fairly common outside Wales.

Variations: Glenn (Scot/Ir), Glynn.

Godfrey

Origin/meaning: Old German/Old English 'God's peace'.

Introduced by the Normans in the 11th century.

Variations: Godefroi (Fr), Godofredo (Sp), Golfredo (It), Gottfrid (Scand), Gottfried (Ger).

Gordon

Origin/meaning: uncertain. Possibly Scots Gaelic 'by the great hill'.

The name of one of a famous Scottish clan, the Gordons.

Variations and abbreviations: Gorden, Gordie, Gordy.

Goronwy (pron. Gorónwee)

Origin/meaning: Welsh 'hero'.

A popular Welsh first name.

Variations and abbreviations: Gronow, Gronw, Ronw.

Graham

Origin/meaning: Old English 'gravelly homestead' or 'from Grantham'.
This name was taken to Scotland in the Middle Ages by an Anglo-Norman nobleman. It came into use as a first name in the 19th century.
Variations and abbreviations: Graeme, Grahame, Grame.

Grant

Origin/meaning: French 'tall'.
This is a last name which came into use as a first in the 19th century. In the US it was used to honor General Ulysses S. Grant, 1822–1885, the 18th President and hero of the Civil War.

Gregory

Origin/meaning: Greek 'watchman'.
A name which has many associations with the Orthodox and Catholic churches. In the Western church there were sixteen Pope Gregorys. The best known in England is the first, St Gregory the Great, 540–604, who sent St Augustine to England to convert the Anglo-Saxons.
Variations and abbreviations: Greer (Eng), Greg, Gregg, Grégoire (Fr), Gregor (Scot/Ger), Greggor (Dut), Gregorio (Sp/It), Gregorius (Dut/Ger), Grigori (Russ).

Griffith

Origin/meaning: Old Welsh 'lord'.
This is the English spelling of the Welsh Gruffudd. Often found as a last name outside Wales, it has also become usual as a first name.
Variations and abbreviations: Griff, Griffin.

Guy

Origin/meaning: Old German, uncertain, possibly 'wood' or 'wild'.
Guy, Earl of Warwick was a legendary hero of the Middle Ages. Guy Fawkes' attempt to blow up James I in the Houses of Parliament placed the name firmly out of fashion in Britain.
Variations and abbreviations: Guido (Fr/Ger/It/Sp), Vito (It), Vitas, Wido (Ger).

Gwilym

Origin/meaning: Old German 'helmet of resolution'.
The Welsh form of William q.v.

Gwyn

Origin/meaning: Welsh 'white/fair' or 'good'.
A short form of names like Gwynfor or an independent name.
Variations: Gwynn, Gwynne, Wynne.

Habib

Origin/meaning: Arabic 'beloved'.
A name found in all Muslim countries.

Hal

Origin/meaning: Old German 'home-ruler'.
This was the most usual pet form of Henry for many hundreds of years. King Henry VIII was known to his people as Good King Hal.
Variations and abbreviations: see Henry.

Hamish

Origin/meaning: uncertain. Usually given as 'supplanter'.
The English spelling of Seumas, the Scottish form of James q.v.
Variations and abbreviations: see James.

Hanif

Origin/meaning: Arabic 'true believer'.
This is a Muslim name, found in North Africa.

Hank

Origin/meaning: Old German 'home ruler'.
A familiar form of Henry confined almost entirely to the US.
Variations and abbreviations: see Henry.

Harold

Origin/meaning: Old English/Old Norse 'army power'.
After King Harold was killed by William the Conqueror's invaders at the battle of Hastings the name died out in England. It survived in its other native land, Norway.
Variations and abbreviations: Araldo (It), Errol (Eng), Harald (Scand), Harry, Herold (Dut).

Haroun

Origin/meaning: Arabic 'exalted'.
A common Muslim name in North Africa.
Variation: Harun.

Harrison

Origin/meaning: English 'son of Harry'.
A last name that has become much used as a first name thanks to the fame of Hollywood actor Harrison Ford.
Variation and abbreviation: Harry.

Harry

Origin/meaning: Old German: 'home-ruler'.

In the last 100 years this has been used as a familiar form of Henry and in the last few years Harry has again been used in England as an independent name and not as a pet name.

Variations and abbreviations: see Henry.

Harvey

Origin/meaning: Celtic French 'battle worthy' or Old German 'warrior in battle'.

This is a name introduced by the Normans, but is similar to the Saxon name Harvig. Harvey developed most successfully as a last name. In the 19th century it was one of many last names which were revived as first names.

Variations: Herve (Fr), Hervey, Herwig (Ger).

Hasan

Origin/meaning: Arabic 'handsome'.

A version of this name is found in all Muslim countries.

Variations: Hasani, Husani (E Africa).

Hayden

Origin/meaning: English 'hedged valley'.

More common as a last name, but now often used as a given name as well.

Variations: Haden, Hadyn.

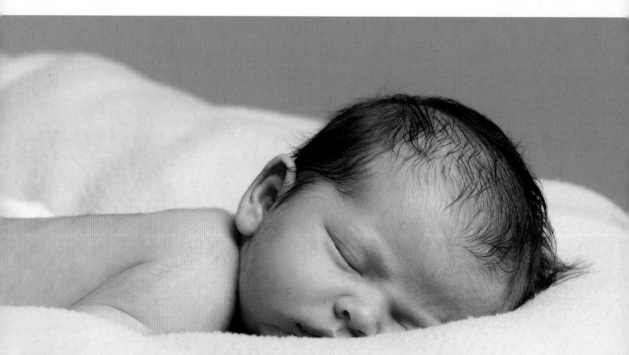

Hector

Origin/meaning: Greek 'steadfast'.

Hector was a Trojan hero, the son of Priam and Hecuba. He was killed by the Greek Achilles, who added insult to injury by dragging his body three times round the walls of Troy.

Variations: Ector (Fr), Ettore (It).

Henry

Origin/meaning: Old German 'home-ruler'.

This name was introduced into England by the Normans in the form Henri. In England Henry and Harry developed simultaneously but although Harry was probably more used, Henry is usually assumed to be the slightly more formal version.

Variations and abbreviations: Arrigo (It), Enrico (It), Enrique (Sp), Hal, Hank, Harry, Heindrick, Heinrich (Ger), Heinz (Ger), Hendrik (Dut/Scand), Henne (Scand), Henri (Fr), Henrik (Scand).

Herbert

Origin/meaning: Old English/Old German 'bright army'.

This Saxon name was a favorite of the Normans who brought over their own version of it after the Conquest. Like many early names it was rediscovered in the 19th century.

Variations and abbreviations: Aribert (Fr), Ariberto (It), Bert, Bertie, Berty, Erberto (It), Harbert, Haribert, Hebert, Herb, Herbiberto (Sp), Herbie.

Hew

Origin/meaning: Old German 'understanding' or 'thought'.

A form of Hugh q.v.

Hilary

Origin/meaning: Medieval Latin 'cheerful'.

The masculine and feminine forms of this medieval name are the same. The feast day of St Hilary (Hilaire) of Poitiers, 315–367, is January 14th and because of this the first law and university term of the calendar year became known as the Hilary term in the UK.

Variations: Hilaire (Fr), Hilar (Ger), Hilario (Sp/Port), Hilarius (Dut/Ger/Scand), Ilario (It).

Hiram

Origin/meaning: uncertain. Sometimes given as Hebrew 'my brother is high'.

Hiram was the king of Tyre, the Lebanese sea-port. Lebanon was famous for its cedars which Hiram supplied to King David and King Solomon, to build the temple in Jerusalem.

Abbreviations: Hi, Hy.

Homer

Origin/meaning: Greek 'pledge' or 'hostage'.

The name of the Greek epic poet, author of the 'Odyssey' and the 'Iliad', is occasionally used as a first name.

Variations: Homère (Fr), Homerus (Dut/Ger), Omero (It).

Horace

Origin/meaning: Latin, from Horatius, the name of a famous Roman clan.

This French form of Horatius became an alternative form of the name in England, together with Horatio.

Horatio (pron. Horáysheeo)

Origin/meaning: Latin, from Horatius, the name of a famous Roman clan.

Horatio probably arrived in England from Italy in about the 16th century. Shakespeare has a character called Horatio in his play 'Hamlet', 1600.

Variations and abbreviations: Hod, Horace (Fr/Eng), Horacid (Sp/Port), Horas, Horatius, Horaz (Ger), Horry, Orazio (It).

Howard

Origin/meaning: either Old German 'brave thought' or Middle English 'hayward' (the guardian of the animal enclosure). This name developed in the Middle Ages into a last name, most notably of the Earls of Norfolk, hereditary Earls Marshal of England.

Variations and abbreviations: Howey, Howie.

Hubert

Origin/meaning: Old German/Old English 'bright thought'.

A popular medieval name, perhaps because of St Hubert, d.727, who, according to legend, was converted to Christianity by finding a stag with a cross between its antlers.

Variations and abbreviations: Bert, Bertie, Berty, Hubertus (Dut/Ger), Huberto (Sp/It), Hugbert (Ger), Oberto (It), Uberto (It).

Hugh

Origin/meaning: Old German 'understanding' or 'thought'.

This was a name introduced by the Normans into Britain, although a similar Celtic name, Huw q.v. already existed. The English Hugh is pronounced like the Medieval French but the spelling reflects the German/Latin Hugo.

Variations: Hew, Huey, Hughie, Hugo (Ger/Latin), Hughes (Fr), Huw (Wel), Ugo (It).

Hugo

Origin/meaning: Old German 'understanding' or 'thought'.

This German Latin form of Hugh was used in England in the Middle Ages and is coming back into favor.

Hunter

Origin/meaning: English 'hunter'.

An old occupational last name that became well known as a first name thanks to the controversial American journalist and writer Hunter S. Thompson.

Huw

Origin/meaning: Celtic 'fire'.

This Welsh name is now usually assumed to be the same as the Old German Hugh q.v. although their origins and meanings are really separate.

Hyman

Origin/meaning: Hebrew 'life'.

This is primarily a Jewish name. It is the English form of Chaim.

Variations and abbreviations: Chaim, Hayyim, Hy, Hymie, Mannie, Manny.

Hywel (pron. Howell)

Origin/meaning: Welsh 'eminent'.

A popular Welsh first name. Hywel Dda (Hywel the Good), d.950, was one of the most famous Welsh Kings. During his reign Welsh law was first codified. Hywel has given rise to several last names. One of these, Powell, a contraction of Ap Hywel, meaning son of Hywel.

Variations: Hoel (Celtic Fr), Howel (Eng), Howell (Eng), Powell.

I

Iago

Origin/meaning: uncertain. Possible Hebrew 'supplant'.
The Spanish and Welsh form of Jacob/James q.v. from the Latin version Jacobus. Iago causes the destruction of Othello in Shakespeare's play.

Iain/Ian

Origin/meaning: Hebrew 'Jehovah has favored'.
The Scots form of John. Iain is regarded as the slightly more authentic spelling and is the version still found mainly in Scotland.

Variations and abbreviations: see John.

Idris

Origin/meaning: Old Welsh 'fiery lord'.
Id- is a part of many Welsh names and it means lord. Idris is one of the most popular Welsh names but it does not have an English form.

Ifor (pron. Eevor)

Origin/meaning: Old Celtic 'lord'.
A name related to other Welsh names beginning with Id- or ending with -udd, both of which mean lord in Welsh. The Cornish saint Ifor gave his name to the little town of Saint Ives.

Variations and abbreviations: Ifar, Ives, Ivor (Eng).

Ignatius

Origin/meaning: uncertain. Possibly Latin 'fiery'.
This was originally a Greek name which may have been interpreted as fiery because of the similarity to the Latin word 'ignis' – 'fire'. In the Eastern Church it was popular because of St Ignatius, Bishop of Antioch who was martyred about ad 114.

Variations and abbreviations: Enesco, Enego, Ignace (Fr), Ignacio (Sp), Ignaz (Ger), Ignazio (It), Inigo.

Imran

Origin/meaning: Arabic 'strong'.
A well-known Muslim name in Britain thanks to the great Pakistani cricket all-rounder Imran Khan.

Indiana

Origin/meaning: English 'land of the Indians'.
The name of a US state, Indiana has become used as a first name thanks to the fictional character Indiana Jones played in a series of Hollywood films by Harrison Ford.

Variation and abbreviation: Indy.

Ingmar

Origin/meaning: Old Norse/Old German 'famous Ingvi'.
A Scandinavian name, one of many containing the name of the hero-god Ing or Ingvi.
He was a hero of the Teutonic (Germanic) tribes who spread throughout Northern Europe
including Britain.

Variations and abbreviations: Ingemar, Ingo.

Inigo

Origin/meaning: uncertain. Possibly Latin 'fiery'.
A form of Ignatius q.v. familiar because of the first great English architect Inigo Jones,
1573–1652, who introduced the Palladian style of architecture into England.

Iolo

Origin/meaning: uncertain, possibly Greek 'downy', i.e. 'unbearded', 'youthful'.
Commonly assumed to be the Welsh form of Julius.

Irving

Origin/meaning: uncertain. Possibly Old English 'sea friend' or 'green river'.
A last name derived from an English place-name. It has become a popular 20th-century first
name in the US, particularly among Jewish people.

Isaac

Origin/meaning: uncertain. Possibly a non-Hebrew name. Usually given as Hebrew
'laughter'.
Abraham's wife Sarah was past the age of child-bearing when she gave birth to Isaac her
first child. The name is usually supposed to refer to her laughter of joy.

Variations and abbreviations: Ike, Ikey, Isaak (Ger/Dut), Isacco (It), Izak, Izaak.

Ivan

Origin/meaning: Hebrew 'Jehovah has favored'.
The Russian form of John q.v. used by six notable Russian Grand Dukes and Tsars.

Variations and abbreviations: see John.

Ivor

Origin/meaning: Old Welsh 'lord'.
The English version of the Welsh Ifor q.v. a name found, in several forms, in all Celtic areas.

Variations: Ifar (Wel), Ifor (Wel), Ivar, Iver, Ives, Yvor.

Jack

Origin/meaning: Hebrew 'Jehovah has favored'.
This is a long established familiar form of John from the medieval form Jankin. In the 20th century it has been much used as an independent name.
Variations and abbreviations: Jackie, Jacko (Scot), Jacky.

Jacob

Origin/meaning: uncertain. Possibly Hebrew 'supplanter'.
Both James and Jacob come from the same Hebrew name Aqob. The patriarch Jacob tricked his father Isaac into giving him the elder son's blessing intended for Esau.
Variations and abbreviations: Cob, Cobb, Giacobbe (It), Giacobo (It), Giacopo (It), Jacobo (Sp), Jake, Jakie, Jakob (Ger).

Jackson

Origin/meaning: English 'son of Jack'.
Though best known as a last name, it is used in the US as a given name.

Jake

Origin/meaning: uncertain. Possibly Hebrew 'supplanter'.
A Medieval English form of Jacob/James possibly from the French form Jacques, which the English pronounced Jakes.
Variation: Jaikie.

James

Origin/meaning: Possibly Hebrew 'supplanter'.

James is a form of the Hebrew name Aqob. It was brought back by pilgrims who had visited the famous shrine at Compostella in Spain where the remains of the apostle St James the Great were said to be buried.

Variations and abbreviations: Diego (Sp), Giacomo (It), Hamish (Anglo-Scot), Iago (Sp/Wel), Jacques (Fr), Jago (Cornish), Jaime (Sp), Jake, Jamey, Jamie, Jay, Jayme (Sp), Jem, Jemmy, Jim, Jimi, Jimmie, Jimmy, Seamus (Ir), Seumas (Scot), Shamus (Anglo-Ir).

Jamie

Origin/meaning: uncertain. Possibly Hebrew 'supplanter'.

A Scottish familiar form of James q.v.

Jarvis

Origin/meaning: Old German 'spear' plus Celtic 'servant'.

A form of Gervase q.v. usually found as a last name but sometimes used as a first name.

Jason

Origin/meaning: uncertain. Sometimes given as Greek 'healer'.

This is a Biblical name, which came into use in the 17th century. It is a rendering of the name Eason which occurs in Acts 17 vs.5–9 and St Paul's Epistle to the Romans ch.16. The English form was presumably influenced by the name of Jason the Greek mythological hero.

Jasper

Origin/meaning: uncertain. Possibly Persian.
Sometimes given as 'treasurer' because of the legend of the three wise men.
Variations: Caspar, Gaspar (Sp), Gaspard (Fr), Gaspare (It), Jesper (Scand).

Javed

Origin/meaning: Arabic 'immortal'.
The former Pakistan cricket captain Javed Miandad helped make this name more common.

Jay

Origin/meaning: Old French 'jay'.
The name of this common European bird has been used as an English last name since the Middle Ages.

Jayden

Origin/meaning: Hebrew 'God has heard'.
Popular in the US.
Variation: Jaden.

Jed

Origin/meaning: Hebrew 'beloved of the Lord'.
This is a short form of the Biblical name Jedidiah, a name used for King Solomon.

Jeevan

Origin/meaning: Sanskrit 'life'.
A popular name in India.

Jefferson

Origin/meaning: English 'son of Jeffrey'.
The name is sometimes given in honor of the great statesman and 3rd US president Thomas Jefferson, 1743–1826.

Jeffrey

Origin/meaning: uncertain. Probably Old German 'district peace'. Sometimes given as 'traveler peace'. An alternative spelling of Geoffrey q.v. a common medieval name which is again popular today.

Jehangir

Origin/meaning: Sanskrit 'conqueror of the world'.
A Muslim name. Jehangir, 1569–1627, was the third Mogul Emperor of India.
Variation: Jahangir.

Jem

Origin/meaning: uncertain. Possibly Hebrew 'supplanter'.

An old short form of James from a medieval form Jeames.

Variation: Jemmy. See also James.

Jeremy

Origin/meaning: Hebrew 'God is high'.

This is the native English form of the name of the prophet Jeremiah. It developed in the Middle Ages from the Greek/Latin Jeremias.

Variations and abbreviations: see Jeremiah.

Jermyn

Origin/meaning: Latin 'a German'.

Jerome

Origin/meaning: Greek 'sacred name'.

Jerome is the English form of the Greek name Hieronymous. This became an acceptable Christian name in the Middle Ages because of St Eusebius Sophronius Hieronymous.

Variations and abbreviations: Gerome, Geronimo (It), Gerrie, Gerry, Hieronymous (Dut/Ger), Jérôme (Fr), Jerry.

Jesse (pron. Jessy)

Origin/meaning: Hebrew 'Jehovah exists'.

This is a Biblical name brought into general use after the Reformation.

Variations and abbreviations: Jess, Jessie.

Jethro

Origin/meaning: Hebrew 'pre-eminence'.

This Hebrew name may well have begun as a title (cf. English names Earl and Prince). The name is found in the Old Testament as the father-in-law of Moses.

Jevan

Origin/meaning: Hebrew 'Jehovah has favored'.

This is one of several Anglo-Welsh forms of John. The true native Welsh form of John is Siôn.

Variations: Evan, Owen.

Jim

Origin/meaning: uncertain. Possibly Hebrew 'supplanter'.

The most usual modern short form of James q.v.

Variations: Jimi, Jimmie, Jimmy. See also James.

Jocelyn

Origin/meaning: Old German 'a man of the Goths'.
Jocelyn was one of many Teutonic names brought to England by the Normans and in the Middle Ages Jocelyn was not an unusual name.

Variations: Jocelin, Joscelin, Joss.

Joe

Origin/meaning: Hebrew 'May Jehovah increase'.
The usual English short form of Joseph q.v. Sometimes used as an independent name.

Variations: Jo, Joey. See also Joseph.

Joel

Origin/meaning: Hebrew 'Jehovah is God'.
A Biblical name. Joel was a minor Hebrew prophet in the 5th century bc. A Book of the Old Testament contains his prophecies.

John

Origin/meaning: Hebrew 'Jehovah has favored' (via the Latin form Johannes).
An important Christian name since almost a hundred early saints were called John.

Variations and abbreviations: Evan (Anglo-Wel), Ewan (Anglo-Scot), Ewen, Giovanni (It), Hans (Ger), Iain (Scot), Ian, Jack, Jacky, Jan (Dut/Slav), Janesi, Jean (Fr), Jens (Dan), Jevan (Anglo-Wel), Jock (Scot), Jocko, Johan, Johann, Johannes (Ger), Johnnie, Johnny, Jon, Jonn, Juan (Sp), Owen (Anglo-Wel), Sean (Ir), Shaughn (Ir), Shaun, Shawn (Anglo-Ir), Siôn (Wel), Zane.

Jolyon

Origin/meaning: from the Roman family name Julius possibly meaning 'downy'.
A north country English form of Julian given wider currency by John Galsworthy (1867–1933) in his novel sequence 'The Forsyte Saga', 1920–1934.

Jon

Origin/meaning: Hebrew 'Jehovah has favored' or Hebrew 'Jehovah gave'.
A short form of either John or Jonathan.

Jonah

Origin/meaning: Hebrew 'dove'.
Jonah was the name of a Hebrew prophet.

Variation: Jonas.

Jonathan

Origin/meaning: Hebrew 'Jehovah gave'.
Jonathan was the son of Saul and friend of David.

Variations and abbreviations: Gionata (It), Jon, Jonathon, Jonty. See also Nathaniel, Theodore.

Jordan

Origin/meaning: Hebrew 'flowing down'.
Jordan has been used as a masculine and feminine name since the Crusaders brought back the name of this river from the Holy Land in the Middle Ages.

Joseph

Origin/meaning: Hebrew 'may Jehovah increase'.
Joseph was the favorite son of Jacob and Rachel whose brothers, envying the coat of many colors which was a sign of their father's favor, sold him into captivity in Egypt.

Variations and abbreviations: Beppo (It), Giuseppe (It), Iossif (Russ), Iossip (Russ), Jo, Joe, Joey, José (Sp), Josef (Ger), Josephus.

Joshua

Origin/meaning: Hebrew 'Jehovah saves'.
Joshua was the successor of Moses. Joshua was much loved as a name by Puritans on both sides of the Atlantic in the 17th and 18th centuries.

Variations and abbreviations: Giosué (It), Josh, Josua (Ger), Josué (Fr).

Jude

Origin/meaning: Hebrew 'praise of the Lord'.
The Anglicized form of the Jewish name Judah.

Variations and abbreviations: Jud, Judah, Judas, Judd, Yehudi.

Julian

Origin/meaning: from Julius, a Roman family name, possibly meaning 'downy'.
Julian's popularity was due in part to the great number of saints who bore the name.

Variations and abbreviations: Jolyon, Jules, Julyan.

Justin

Origin/meaning: Latin 'just'.
A name borne by two 5th-century Byzantine Emperors.

Variations and abbreviations: Giustino (It), Giusto, Justinian, Justino (Sp), Justinus, Justus, Yestin (Wel).

Kai

Origin/meaning: origin uncertain, possibly from the Roman name Caius, 'rejoice'.
The name may be related to Kay or perhaps have its own roots in Scandinavian languages,
in which case its original meaning might be 'hen'.

Kamuzu

Origin/meaning: Nguni 'medicinal'.
This name comes from the South of Africa.

Variation: Kamazu.

Kane

Origin/meaning: Gaelic Irish 'little battle'.
An Anglicized form of an old Irish name.

Kant

Origin/meaning: Sanskrit 'lover'.
This is found as a name in its own right, and also as a typical masculine suffix to a name
ending in a, i or e, e.g. Suryakant.

Kanti (pron. Kantee)

Origin/meaning: Sanskrit 'sun's rays' or 'beauty'.
Found throughout India but less popular than it used to be.

Karl

Origin/meaning: Old German 'man'.
A form of Charles q.v.

Variation: Carl.

Kashyapa

Origin/meaning: unknown.
This is the name of one of the ancient Hindu saints of India.

Kay

Origin/meaning: from the Roman name Gaius or Caius, 'rejoice'.
This is the English spelling of the Welsh name, Cai. Sir Kay was one of the characters
from the Tales of King Arthur and his Knights of the Round Table, who was known for his
boastfulness.

Variations: Cai (Wel), Caius, Gaius, Kai, Kaye, Key.

Keith

Origin/meaning: Scots Gaelic 'wood'.

This is a Scots last name taken from several Scottish places which have the name. It came into use as a first name in the
19th century when last names became popular as first names.

Kenneth

Origin/meaning: Scots Gaelic 'handsome'.

This is primarily a Scots name although there are native forms in other Celtic areas. Kenneth I (Coinneach) MacAlpine of Scotland was a 9th-century king who kept the Danes out of Scotland.

Variations and abbreviations: Canice (Ir), Cennydd (Wel), Ken, Kenny. See also Kevin.

Kentigern

Origin/meaning: Old Welsh 'head chief'.

St Kentigern, d.612, also known by his nickname Mungo, was a Scot who brought Christianity to his native area of Lothian. He is the patron saint of Glasgow and his symbols, a ring and a fish, appear on the city's coat of arms.

Kevin

Origin/meaning: Old Irish 'handsome at birth'.

This name is similar in meaning to the Scots name Kenneth q.v. St Kevin, d.618, was, according to tradition, a Leinster nobleman who founded a monastery at Glendelough. He is said to have died at the age of 120.

Variations and abbreviations: Kev, Kevan.

Khan

Origin/meaning: Sanskrit 'king', 'lord' or 'ruler'.

Khan added to Muslim names indicates respect as for the Aga Khan. Genghis Khan, 1162–1227, changed his name from Temujin to Genghis Khan which means 'very mighty ruler'.

Kian

Origin/meaning: Irish 'ancient'.

A variant of an old Irish name Cian that has become popular.

Variation: Keane.

Kieran

Origin/meaning: Old Irish 'black-haired'.

This is a diminutive of an Old Irish name Ciar, meaning black or black-haired. The Irish place-name Kerry means the home of Ciar's people or the home of dark-haired people.

Kim

Origin/meaning: Old English 'cyne' – 'royal'. From the last name Kimball 'royal hill' or Kimberley 'royal meadow'.

This name became popular for boys after the publication in 1901 of Rudyard Kipling's book 'Kim'. It has now become equally popular for girls.

Kingsley

Origin/meaning: Old English 'from the king's wood'.

An English last name that came into use as a first name in the 19th century. It may have been given to honor Charles Kingsley, 1819–1875, the popular Victorian novelist, author of 'The Water Babies'.

Kirk

Origin/meaning: Old Norse 'church'.

Kirk is a common last name in the areas of Scotland and the North of England which were invaded by the Vikings. Kirk is now used as a first name.

Variation: Kirke.

Krishna

Origin/meaning: Hindu.

Krishna is regarded by Hindus as the greatest and most complete incarnation of the god Vishnu. He is found in many stories and poems, most notably the 9th-century 'Bhagavata Purana'. Krishna was a defender of justice and slew many wrongdoers and evil demons.

Kurt

Origin/meaning: Old German 'bold counselor'.
An alternative spelling of Curt, a short form of Conrad q.v.

Variations and abbreviations: see Conrad.

Kusum-chandra

Origin/meaning: Sanskrit 'flower'.
The equivalent of the feminine Kusum with the addition of the typical male suffix –
chandra. The a at the end should not be pronounced or it becomes the female name
meaning 'moon'.

Kwame

Origin/meaning: Akan 'born on Saturday'.
Similar names are Kwasi – born on Sunday; Kwakoa – born on Wednesday.

Kyle

Origin/meaning: English 'narrow channel'.
A name that originally came from a Scottish last name and place name, Kyle is now widely
used as a first name.

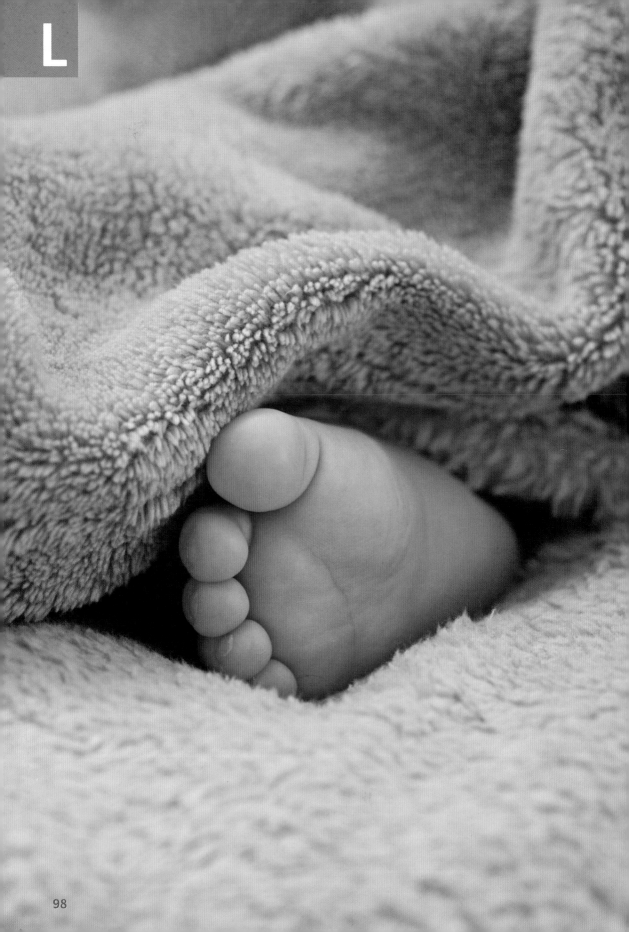

Lachlan (pron. Loklan)

Origin/meaning: Scots Gaelic 'from the lake (fiord) land' i.e. 'a Viking'.
This is a Scots first name and last name.

Lance

Origin/meaning: Old German 'land'.
The original French name from which Lancelot (little Lance) developed.

Variations and abbreviations: see Lancelot.

Lancelot

Origin/meaning: Old German 'land'.
This is a French diminutive of the name Lance and means 'little Lance'. The tale of Lancelot's illicit love for Guinevere, King Arthur's wife, became one of the best known stories of the Arthurian romance.

Variations and abbreviations: Lance, Lancelin, Lancelyn, Lando (Ger), Lanslet, Launce, Launcelot.

Latif

Origin/meaning: Arabic 'pleasant'.
A common Muslim name.

Variation: Lateef (E Africa).

Laurence

Origin/meaning: Latin 'from Laurentium' (the city of laurels).
This name probably became popular because laurel leaves were the victor's traditional crown. It was rare in England before the Norman Conquest. In English-speaking countries the spellings Laurence and Lawrence are equally valid.

Variations and abbreviations: Lanty (Ir), Larry, Lars (Swed), Lauren, Laurenz (Ger), Laurens (Dut), Laurent (Fr), Laurentius (Ger/Dut), Laurien, Lauritz (Dan), Lauro (It), Lawrence, Lawrie, Lawry, Lonnie, Lonny, Loren, Lorens, Lorenzo (Ger/Dut), Lorenzo (It), Lorin, Lorrie, Lorry.

Lawrence

Origin/meaning: Latin 'from Laurentium' (the city of laurels).
An alternative English spelling of Laurence q.v. It is the spelling most often used as a last name.

Variations and abbreviations: see Laurence.

Leabua

Origin/meaning: Sotho 'you speak'.
This name is much used in the South of Africa.

Leander

Origin/meaning: Greek 'lion-like'.
A name occasionally used because of the Greek legend of Hero and Leander.

Lee

Origin/meaning: Old English 'meadow'.
An English last name adopted in the 19th century as a first name. Originally a masculine name it is now used equally for girls.
Variations: Lea, Leigh.

Leo

Origin/meaning: Greek/Latin 'lion'.
A pre-Christian name, it was adopted as a Christian name because of the Roman St Leo the Great, 390–461. Also a short form of names beginning with Leo.

Leon

Origin/meaning: Greek 'lion'.
The original Greek form of the Latin word leo.
Variations: Léon (Fr), Léonce (Fr), Leone (It), Leonz (Ger), Lyon.

Leonard

Origin/meaning: Latin, Old German 'lion-bold'.
In the Middle Ages St Leonard was much loved, particularly among Crusaders, who regarded him as the patron saint of prisoners.
Variations and abbreviations: Leander (Ger), Len, Lenard, Lennard, Lennart (Scand), Lennie, Lenny, Leo, Leon, Léonard (Fr), Leonardo (It), Leonerd, Leonhard (Ger), Leinhard (Swiss). See also Leander, Leo, Leon, Lionel, Singh.

Leopold

Origin/meaning: Old German 'people-bold'.
A German name, Leopold was used in 19th-century Britain, because of Queen Victoria's uncle, Leopold I, 1790–1865, King of the Belgians. A sensible moderate man, he was much respected and Queen Victoria named one of her own sons after him.
Variations and abbreviations: Leo, Leobold, Léopold (Fr), Leopoldo (It), Luitpold.

Leroy

Origin/meaning: French 'king'.
This name is common in the US where it may have been taken from the Northern French last name Le Royer, which means 'wheelmaker'. However it is undoubtedly intended to mean 'le roi' – king.

Leslie

Origin/meaning: Scots Gaelic 'garden by the pool'.
The usual spelling of the Scottish last name when used as a masculine name. It came into use as a personal name in the 19th century, helped along by its aristocratic connections, being the last name of the Earls of Rothes.
Variations and abbreviations: Lee, Les, Lesley, Lezlie.

Lester

Origin/meaning: Old English 'Leicester'.
This is an English last name derived from the place-name. It has become well established as a personal name since the 19th century.

Levi

Origin/meaning: Hebrew 'associated' or 'joined'.
An old Biblical name that is more often found in the US than Britain.

Lewis

Origin/meaning: Welsh 'lion-like' or from the name of the Celtic god Luel.
This is an Anglicized form of Lewys, a short form of the Welsh name Llywelyn. It is quite unconnected with the English version of the French Louis.

Liam

Origin/meaning: Old German, English 'determined protector'.
A short version of a Gaelic form of William – Uilliam – that has become extremely popular as a first name, for example the lead singer of the band 'Oasis', Liam Gallagher.

Lindsay

Origin/meaning: Old English. Uncertain, possibly 'Lincoln's island'.
A Scottish aristocratic last name adopted as a male and female first name.
Variations and abbreviations: Lin, Lindsey (Eng), Linsay, Linsey, Lyn, Lynsey.

Linus

Origin/meaning: Latin 'flaxen-haired'.
Possibly a name derived from the Latin word for flax. It is well known because of the Peanuts cartoons in which the character Linus appears.

Lionel

Origin/meaning: Latin/French 'little lion'.
The French diminutive of Leon q.v. it has been used in Britain since the Middle Ages.
Variations: Lionello (It), Lyonel. See also Leo, Leon, Leonard.

L

Lloyd

Origin/meaning: Welsh 'gray' or 'brown'.

This is a common Welsh last name occasionally used as a first name.

Variation: Floyd.

Llyr

Origin/meaning: Welsh mythology. Llyr was a sea god. He was the father of Branwen. Lear, used by Shakespeare for his play 'King Lear', 1607, is thought to be based on it.

Variations: Lear, Leir.

Llywelyn (pron. Chloowellin)

Origin/meaning: uncertain. May be Welsh 'like a lion' or a reference to the Celtic god Luel. This is one of the most popular Welsh names perhaps because it was borne by two famous Welsh princes, Llywelyn ap Iorwerth, d.1240, and his nephew Llywelyn ap Gruffydd, d.1282, the last Welsh Prince of Wales.

Variations and abbreviations: Flewelin, Fluellen, Leoline (Eng), Lewellings, Lewis (Eng), Llelo, Llew, Llewelin, Llowelin, Lyn, Wellings.

Logan

Origin/meaning: Scottish 'little hollow'.

A place name turned last name that is now widely used as a given name.

Louis (pron. Lóuee or Lóuiss)

Origin/meaning: Old German 'glorious battle'.

The original Teutonic form of this name was Chlodovech. Chlodovech, 465–511, was the first Merovingian king of the Western Franks (France). In Latin documents Chlodovech was known either as Clovis or Ludovicus. Ludovicus developed into the French name Louis.

Variations and abbreviations: Aloys (Provençal), Aloysius, Lew, Lewes, Lewis (Eng), Lodewig (Ger), Lou, Louie, Louis (Fr/Scot), Lovis, Lowes (Med/Eng), Lowis, Lodovico (It), Ludovic (Scot), Ludovico (It), Luigi (It).

Luca

Origin/meaning: Greek 'from Lucania', a region of southern Italy.

This Italian form of Luke is now used in the English-speaking world.

Lucas

Origin/meaning: Greek 'from Lucania'.

This is a Latin form of the name better known in England as Luke. In France and Germany Lucas is a common form of Luke.

Variations and abbreviations: see Luke.

Lucian (pron. Lóosean or Lóoshan)

Origin/meaning: Latin 'light'.
St Lucian, d.312, was a theologian from Antioch who revised the Greek version of the Old Testament and the gospels.
Variation: Lucien (Fr).

Lucius

Origin/meaning: Latin 'light'.
This name was a pre-Christian Roman name, probably used for a child born at first light of day. The English feminine form Lucy is very popular.
Variations: Lucian, Luciano (It), Lucien (Fr), Lucillio (It), Lucio (It), Luzian, Luzius (Ger).

Ludovic

Origin/meaning: Old German 'glorious battle'. This is a variation of the name Lewis q.v. through one of its Latin forms, Ludovicus.
Variations and abbreviations: Lodowick (Eng), Lodovico (It), Ludo, Ludovico (It), Ludwig (Ger). See also Lewis.

Luke

Origin/meaning: Greek 'from Lucania'. Sometimes given as 'wolf'.
This is the name of one of the four Evangelists, and author of the Acts of the Apostles. He was a Greek and a doctor, called by St Paul 'our beloved Luke, the physician'. He is the patron saint of doctors.
Variations and abbreviations: Loukas (Gr), Luc (Fr), Luca (It), Lucano (It), Lucas (Fr/Eng/Ger), Lucio (Sp), Luck (Eng), Lukas (Ger/Scand).

Lyall

Origin/meaning: French 'from Lyons' ('the hillfort') or French 'little lion'.
An English last name not infrequently used as a first name.

Lyn

Origin/meaning: uncertain. Possibly Welsh 'like a lion' or a reference to the Celtic god Luel. A Welsh male name. A short form of Llewelyn q.v. now used as an independent name.

Lyndon

Origin/meaning: Old English 'from the lime tree hill'.
An English place-name which became a last name.
Variation: Lindon.

Madhukar (pron. Madtookarr)

Origin/meaning: Sanskrit 'bee'.

The masculine equivalent of Madhuri q.v.

Magnus

Origin/meaning: Latin 'great'.

This adjective became a name in its own right.

Variation: Manus (Ir).

Malcolm

Origin/meaning: Old Scots 'servant of Columba'.

A popular Scottish name for hundreds of years because of the influence of St Columba who brought Christianity to a large part of Scotland.

Abbreviation: Mal.

Malik

Origin/meaning: Arabic 'the king'.

A popular Muslim name.

Manfred

Origin/meaning: Old German 'man-peace'.

A pre-Conquest name adopted by the Normans and introduced by them into England. Byron wrote a drama 'Manfred', 1819.

Variations: Manfredo (It), Manfried (Ger).

Marcel

Origin/meaning: Latin 'little Marcus' from 'Mars' (the Roman god of war) i.e. 'warlike'. The French form of the Latin Marcellus, a diminutive of Marcus.

Variations: Marcello (It), Marcellus, Marzellus (Ger). See also Mark.

Marcus

Origin/meaning: Latin 'of Mars' (the Roman god of war), i.e. 'warlike'.

This is the Roman name which developed into the Christian name Mark q.v.

Variations and abbreviations: see Mark.

Marius

Origin/meaning: Latin, from the name of the Roman Marius family, probably connected with Mars, god of war.

Marius was one of many classical names re-introduced during the 16th-century renaissance.

Variation: Mario (It). See also Marcus, Mark, Martin.

Mark

Origin/meaning: Latin 'of Mars' (the Roman god of war), i.e. 'warlike'.
This name comes from the popular Roman name Marcus. It became an established Christian name because of St Mark who wrote one of the four gospels. St Mark is closely associated with the city of Venice for in 829, his body was brought there after his martyrdom.

Variations: Marek (Slav), Marc (Fr), Marcel (Fr), Marco (It), Marcos (Sp), Marcus, Marko, Markus (Ger/Dut/Scand), Marks, Marx.

Marlon

Origin/meaning: origin unknown, possibly Old French 'little Mark'.
A name whose original popularity was due almost entirely to the great actor Marlon Brando.

Martin

Origin/meaning: Latin 'of Mars' (the Roman god of war), i.e. 'warlike'.
This was a popular name in the Middle Ages when it was given to honor St Martin of Tours, 315–397. A young Roman officer,
he gave half his cloak to a poor beggar whom he later recognized as Christ.

Variations and abbreviations: Mart, Martainn (Scot), Marten, Martie, Martinet (Fr), Martino (It/Sp), Marton, Marty, Martyn, Merten, Morten (Dan). See also Marcus, Mark.

Mason

Origin/meaning: English 'mason'.
An occupational last name that is now used as a given name.

Masud

Origin/meaning: Arabic 'fortunate'.
This is a common Muslim name found in all Muslim countries.

Variations and abbreviations: Mansur, Masood, Massur.

Matsimela

Origin/meaning: Sotho 'roots'.
This name comes from the African state of Lesotho, formerly known as Basutoland, in South Africa.

Matthew

Origin/meaning: Hebrew 'gift of Jehovah'.
In England the name developed from Mattheu, which was introduced by the Normans. It was given to honor St Matthew, the Apostle and Evangelist.

Variations and abbreviations: Mat, Mateo (Port/Sp), Mathias, Matias, Matt, Matteo (It), Matthaeus, Matthäus (Swiss), Mattheus, Matthias (Ger), Matthieu (Fr), Mattias, Mattie, Matty.

Maurice

Origin/meaning: Latin 'a man from Mauretania' (Morocco).

This Roman name was introduced as a Christian name because of the 3rd-century St Maurice (Mauritius). He was said to have been the commanding officer of a legion of Christian Roman soldiers who refused to obey orders to take part in heathen rituals.

Variations and abbreviations: Maur (Fr/Ger), Mauricio (Port/Sp), Maurie, Maurise, Mauritius (Ger), Maurits (Dut), Mauriz, Maurizio (It), Mauro (It), Maurus (Ger), Maury, Morie, Moritz (Swiss), Moriz, Morris, Morry.

Mawulawde (pron. Mahwoolawdáy)

Origin/meaning: Ewe 'God will provide'.

This name comes from Ghana in West Africa.

Mawuli (pron. Máhwoolee)

Origin/meaning: Ewe 'there is a God'.

A popular name in Ghana.

Max

Origin/meaning: Latin 'greatest'.

A short form of Maximilian or Maxwell. It has become popular since the end of the19th century as an independent name.

Variations and abbreviations: see Maximilian.

Maximilian

Origin/meaning: Latin 'greatest'.

This is derived from the Latin word maximus. The name became popular in Germany because of the highly successful and popular Emperor Maximilian I, 1459–1519.

Variations and abbreviations: Mac, Massimiliano (It), Massimo (It), Max, Maxime (Fr), Maximilien (Fr), Maximus.

Maxwell

Origin/meaning: Scots/Old English 'Magnus's well'.

This is a Scottish place-name which became a last name. It has been used consistently since the 19th century as a first name.

Variations and abbreviations: Mac, Max.

Mayur

Origin/meaning: Sanskrit 'peacock'.

One of Shiv's sons, Kumara or Skanda, the six-headed god of war, is usually depicted riding on a peacock.

Melvin

Origin/meaning: French/English 'town on a hill' or Old English 'sword friend'.

An English last name which has been established as a personal name since the 19th century.

Variations and abbreviations: Mel, Melville, Melvyn.

Merlin

Origin/meaning: Old Welsh 'sea hill'.
This name is still used occasionally in Wales. It is widely known as King Arthur's magician.
Variation: Merlyn.

Mervyn

Origin/meaning: Old English 'famous friend' or Celtic 'fair sea'.
This last name has English and Welsh forms and the two may be quite separate.
Variations and abbreviations: Merfyn (Wel), Merv, Mervin. See also Morgan, Murdoch, Murray.

Michael

Origin/meaning: Hebrew 'Who is like the Lord?'
Michael is the name of the archangel who led the angels into battle to cast out Satan.
Variations and abbreviations: Meikle, Micah, Michal, Michel (Fr), Michele (It), Mick, Mickey, Mickie, Micky, Miguel (Sp/Port), Mikael (Scand), Mike, Mikel, Mikey, Mikhail (Russ), Mikkel (Dan), Mischa (Russ), Mitch, Mitchell.

Mihir

Background: Sanskrit 'sun'.
A popular Indian name.

Miles

Origin/meaning: Old German. Uncertain, possibly 'merciful' or Latin 'soldierly'.
A popular medieval name, which was successfully revived in the 19th century.
Variations and abbreviations: Milo (Ger/Ir), Myles.

Milo

Origin/meaning: origin uncertain, possibly Latin 'soldierly'.
This variation of Miles has become increasingly widespread in its own right.

Mitchell

Origin/meaning: Hebrew 'Who is like God?'
A last name that came from Michael and that is now used as a first name.
Variation and abbreviation: Mitch.

Mohammed

Origin/meaning: Arabic/Swahili 'praised'.
Mohammed is a religious title that prefixes the personal name.
Variations: Mehemmet, Muhammed.

Mohan

Origin/meaning: a Hindu name for Krishna q.v.
This was Gandhi's first name, used with the addition of the typical male suffix -das, i.e. Mohandas Gandhi.

Morgan

Origin/meaning: Old Welsh 'sea bright'.
Morgan was a 7th-century Welsh prince who gave his name to the area of South Wales known as Glamorgan.
Variation: Morgen.

Moses

Origin/meaning: Egyptian 'saved from the water', Hebrew 'law-giver'.
Moses was chosen by God to lead the Israelites out of slavery in Egypt to the Promised Land (see the 2nd Book of Moses – Exodus).
Variations and abbreviations: Moshe (Hebrew), Moss, Moyse, Mozes.

Moyo (pron. Móyo)

Origin/meaning: Ngoni 'good health'.
This name comes from the Central African state of Malawi.

Mungo

Origin/meaning: Gaelic 'lovable', 'most dear'.
This was an adjective used to describe St Kentigern, d.612. It came to be used as an alternative name for him and then as a first name.
Variation: Munghu.

Murdoch

Origin/meaning: Scots Gaelic 'man of the sea'.
A Scots first name that developed as a last name and is now used as a first name again.
Variation: Murtagh (Ir).

Murray

Origin/meaning: Scots Gaelic 'sea settlement'.
This is a Scottish place-name (Moray is a Scots county) which became a last name.
Variation: Moray. See also Murdoch, Morgan, Mervyn.

Mwai (pron. M'wáhee)

Origin/meaning: Ngoni 'good fortune'.
A name from the Central African state of Malawi.

Nasim

Origin/meaning: Arabic 'discipliner'.

A Muslim name.

Variation: Nizam.

Nassor

Origin/meaning: Swahili 'victorious'.

A name found in Tanzania in East Africa.

See also Victor.

Nathan

Origin/meaning: Hebrew 'gift'.

This is the name of an Old Testament prophet. It is also used as a short form of Nathaniel q.v.

Variation and abbreviation: Nat.

Nathaniel

Origin/meaning: Hebrew 'God has given'.

This is the first name of the Apostle who is better known by his family name, Bartholomew.

Variations and abbreviations: Nat, Nataniel (Sp), Nataniele (It), Nathan, Nathanael, Nathaneal, Natty. See also Theodore and Jonathan.

Nazir

Origin/meaning: Arabic 'victorious'.

This is a Muslim name.

Variations: Nasser, Nassor (E Africa), Nasr.

Neal(e)

Origin/meaning: Old Irish 'champion'.

This is one of the many spellings of the name Neil, which is a form of Niall (Irish) and Nigel q.v.

Variations and abbreviations: see Nigel.

Neil (pron. Neeal)

Origin/meaning: Old Irish 'champion'.

This is a form of the Irish name Niall, which developed from the word 'niadh' and is the direct equivalent of Nigel q.v.

Variations and abbreviations: see Nigel.

Neville

Origin/meaning: French 'new city' (Neuville is a place in Normandy.)

This is a Norman French last name which came over to England at the time of the Conquest in the form of de Nevil. The Nevilles were an important aristocratic family in the Middle Ages.

Variations: Nevel, Nevil, Nevill.

Niall (pron. N´ye-all)

Origin/meaning: Old Irish 'champion'.

A modern Irish name, the equivalent of the English Nigel. Both names stem from the Old Irish 'niadh' meaning champion. The form Neil is also common in Ireland.

Variations and abbreviations: see Nigel.

Nicholas

Origin/meaning: Greek 'victory of the people'.

This pre-Christian Greek name was adopted as a Christian name because of the veneration for St Nicholas, a 4th-century bishop of Myra in Asia Minor.

Variations and abbreviations: Claus (Ger), Cole, Colet, Colin, Klaas (Dut), Klaus (Ger), Niccolo (It), Nick, Nickie, Nicko, Nicky, Nicol (Med Eng), Nicolas (Fr), Nikita (Russ), Niklaus (Ger), Nikolai (Russ), Nikolaus (Ger).

Nicol

Origin/meaning: Greek 'victory of the people'.

This is one of the earliest English forms of Nicholas. It was used for boys and girls.

Variations and abbreviations: see Nicholas.

Nigel

Origin/meaning: Old Irish 'champion'.

This name developed from the Irish Celtic 'niadh' meaning champion.

Variations and abbreviations: Neal, Neale, Neel, Nele, Neil, Neill, Neils (Scand), Nels (Scand), Nial, Niall, Niel, Niels (Scand), Nils (Scand).

Ninian

Origin/meaning: uncertain, possibly a Celtic corruption of the Latin 'vivianus' (Vivian) – 'full of life'.

This was the name of an early British missionary, St Ninian, d.432, who converted the Southern Picts of Scotland to Christianity.

Variations: Ninias, Ninnidh (Ir), Nynia.

Nkrumah

Origin/meaning: Akan 'ninth born'.

This is a Ghanaian name.

Noël

Origin/meaning: Latin/Old French 'birth day', i.e. 'Christmas'.

This French word for Christmas has been used as a name for children born at the Christmas season since the early Middle Ages.

Variations: Natale (It), Noel, Nowel (Eng), Nowell.

Norman

Origin/meaning: Old English/Old German 'north man'.

This is a pre-Conquest name. It developed in England to describe the many invaders from Scandinavia, to the North of the British Isles, who repeatedly invaded the country after the departure of the Romans.

Variations and abbreviations: Norm, Normand, Normann (Ger).

Norris

Origin/meaning: Old French 'northerner'.

This is a family name occasionally used as a first name.

Nural

Origin/meaning: Arabic 'born in daylight'.

A popular Arabic name.

Variation: Nuru (E African).

Oberon

Origin/meaning: Old German 'little elf-ruler'.

An alternative spelling of Auberon q.v. which was used by Shakespeare as an appropriate name for the king of the fairies in 'A Midsummer Night's Dream'.

Octavius

Origin/meaning: Latin 'eighth'.

A name given to an eighth son or child. Octavius was the brother-in-law of Julius Caesar. His son, Octavianus, became the Emperor Augustus.

Odysseus

Origin/meaning: uncertain. Possibly Etruscan 'wanderer' – sometimes given as 'hater'.

The original Greek version of Ulysses q.v.

Okechuku (pron. Okehchóoku)

Origin/meaning: Yoruba 'God's gift'.

A Nigerian name.

Okpara (pron. Okpára)

Origin/meaning: Ibo 'first son'.

This name comes from Nigeria.

Olaf

Origin/meaning: Old Norse 'ancestor-inheritance/remains'.

The Danes who invaded Britain brought the name with them but it died out after the Norman Conquest. It probably survives as the English Oliver q.v. and French Olivier.

Oliver

Origin/meaning: uncertain. Possibly Old Norse 'ancestor-inheritance/remains', from Anleifr. Sometimes given as 'olive tree'.

The name is likely to have the Old Norse meaning of the Scandinavian name Olaf q.v. Oliver was the form used in England in the Middle Ages.

Variations and abbreviations: Noll (Med Eng), Nolly, Olaf (Scand), Olav (Scand), Oliverio (Sp), Olivier (Fr), Oliviero (It), Ollie, Olly.

Olu

Origin/meaning: Yoruba 'pre-eminent'.

This name comes from Nigeria.

Omar

Origin/meaning: Arab (and Swahili) 'highest'.

Omar, 581–644, was the second Khalif. He was the father of one of Mohammed's nine wives.

Variations: Omari (Swahili), Umar.

Orlando

Origin/meaning: Old German 'fame-land' usually given as 'famous man of the land'.

This is the Italian form of the English Rowland and French Roland q.v. It was found in England during the Renaissance period and Shakespeare used it in his play 'As You Like It'.

Orson

Origin/meaning: Latin 'bear'.

This is the English form of the Italian name Orso.

Orville

Origin/meaning: Old French 'golden town'.

A rare name familiar because of the US aviation pioneer Orville Wright, 1871–1948.

Osakwe (pron. Osárkway)

Origin/meaning: Benin 'God agrees'.

A Nigerian name. The word Os – God, appears in many Nigerian names, for example Osahar – 'God hears', Osayaba – 'God forgives' and Osaze – 'liked by God'.

Osbert

Origin/meaning: Old English 'god-famous'.

One of several Old English names e.g. Oscar, Osborn, which contain the word Os, God. It was found in Northumbria where Viking influence was strong and it has a Old Norse equivalent.

Osborn

Origin/meaning: Old English 'god-warrior' or Old Norse 'god-bear'.

A pre-Conquest name which developed primarily as a last name in the Middle Ages, now found as a personal name again.

Variations and abbreviations: Osborne, Osbourne, Ossy.

Oscar

Origin/meaning: Old Norse 'god spear', i.e. 'divine spear'.

A Scandinavian name which was introduced into Britain by the Viking invaders, although the Anglo-Saxon equivalent may well have existed.

Variations and abbreviations: Asger (Dan), Ansgar, Osgar (Ir), Oskar (Ger/Scand), Ossie, Ossy, Ozzie, Ozzy.

O

Osgar

Origin/meaning: Old Norse 'sea-spear', i.e. 'divine spear'.
The Irish form of Oscar q.v.

Osmond

Origin/meaning: Old English/Old Norse 'god-protection', i.e. 'divine protection'.
Like Osbert, Oswald and Oscar, this name developed in several countries simultaneously. It
survived the Conquest because the Normans had already adopted it.

Variations and abbreviations: Osmonde, Osmund, Ozzy.

Oswald

Origin/meaning: Old English 'god-power'.
Another Old English Northumbrian name, like Osbert q.v., which is very similar to an Old
Norse name.

Variations and abbreviations: Ossy, Oswell, Ozzy, Waldo.

Otto

Origin/meaning: Old German 'of the fatherland' or 'rich'.

The version of the Old German name Odo which has survived most successfully into the 20th century.

Variations and abbreviations: Odo, Oddo, Odilo, Othello, Otho.

Owen

Origin/meaning: uncertain. Possibly Old Scots/Irish 'young warrior' or Welsh 'lamb' or Old Welsh 'well born'.

One of the most common Welsh names both as a first name and as a last name.

Variations: Eugene, Ewen (Scot), Owain (Wel), Ywain (Old Wel).

Paddy

Origin/meaning: Latin 'patrician'.

An Irish familiar form of Patrick q.v. and occasionally of the feminine form Patricia.

Variation: Patty

Pádraig (pron. Pórreg)

Origin/meaning: Latin 'patrician'.

The native Irish form of Patrick q.v.

Variation: Pádraic.

Paris

Origin/meaning: Greek/English, legendary character of Troy.

Paris was the son of Priam and the man who fell in love with the already-married Helen.

Parker

Origin/meaning: English 'park keeper'.

Originally an occupation name, and still more usual as a last name.

Patrick

Origin/meaning: Latin 'patrician' i.e. aristocratic.

This is a name long associated with Ireland, St Patrick is, of course, the patron saint of Ireland.

Variations and abbreviations: Paddie, Paddy, Pádraic, Pádraig, Padrig (Wel), Pat, Patric, Patrice (Fr), Patrizio (It), Patrizius (Ger/Dut), Patsy, Patty.

Paul

Origin/meaning: Latin 'small'.

Just as Timothy and Euphemia were long-established Greek personal names adopted as Christian names as they appear in the Bible, so Paul (Paullus) is an established Roman name.

Variations: Paavo (Finn), Pablo (Sp), Paolo (It), Paolino (It), Paulinus, Paulus, Pavel (Russ), Poul (Dan).

Perceval

Origin/meaning: French 'from Percheval' a village in Normandy.

This is a Norman French last name occasionally used as a first name in England and France since the Middle Ages. The short form Percy soon became a separate last name right.

Variations and abbreviations: Perce, Percival, Percy.

Peregrine

Origin/meaning: Latin 'foreigner', 'traveler', 'pilgrim'.

A rare name, it is used since the Middle Ages to honor St Peregrinus, the patron saint of Modena.

Variations and abbreviations: Pellegrino (It), Peregrin (Ger), Perry.

Peter

Origin/meaning: Greek 'stone'.

In John I, v.42, Jesus renamed Simon saying, 'Thou art Simon, the son of Jona: thou shalt be called Cephas, which is by interpretation, a stone'.

Variations and abbreviations: Pär (Swed), Parry, Peadar (Ir), Pearce, Peder, Pedro (Sp), Peer (Norway), Per (Swed), Perkin (Med Eng), Perry, Pete, Pierce, Pierre (Fr), Pieter (Dut), Piero (It), Pietro (It), Pyotr (Russ), Pyrs (Wel).

Phelim

Origin/meaning: Old Irish 'ever good'.

A popular Irish name. Sometimes 'translated' to Felix by English speakers.

Variations: Feiolim (Celt), Felim, Felimy.

Philip

Origin/meaning: Greek 'lover of horses'.

This is the name of one of the Apostles and was therefore much used in the Middle Ages when saints' names were popular.

Variations and abbreviations: Felipe (Sp), Filip (Scand), Filippo (It), Lippo (It), Phil, Philipp (Ger), Philippe (Fr), Philippus(Ger/Dut), Pip.

Phineas

Origin/meaning: uncertain. Sometimes given as Hebrew 'oracle' or Egyptian 'negro'.

This is a Biblical name adopted by 17th-century Puritans, especially in New England.

Variation: Phinehas.

Piers

Origin/meaning: Greek 'stone'.

The form of Peter q.v. introduced into Britain by the Normans in 1066.

Variations and abbreviations: see Peter.

Placido (pron. Plassido)

Origin/meaning: Latin 'calm'.

An adjective occasionally used as a name, made famous by Spanish singer Placido Domingo.

Purushotam (pron. Pooróosotam)

Origin/meaning: Sanskrit 'best of men'.

The name of a Hindu god. Found throughout India.

Quentin

Origin/meaning: Latin 'fifth'.
Quintus was a Roman forename and also the name of a famous tribe, the Quintii, renowned for their exemplary behavior.

Variations and abbreviations: Quinn, Quint, Quintilio (It), Quintin, Quinto (It), Quinton, Quntus (Ger).

Quincy

Origin/meaning: Latin/Old French 'from the fifth place', 'from the fifth son's estate'.
There are several places called Quincy in France and settlers in England at the time of the Conquest brought the name with them.

Variations and abbreviations: Quin, Quincey, Quinn.

Quinn

Origin/meaning: Old Irish 'counsel' or (sometimes) Latin 'fifth'.
A common Irish last name used as a first name. It is sometimes found as a short form of Quintin or Quincy.
Variation: Quin.

Quintin

Origin/meaning: Latin 'fifth'.
An alternative spelling of Quentin q.v.

Rafe

Origin/meaning: Old Norse/Old English 'wolf counsel'.
A variation of Ralph q.v. which is spelt according to the pronunciation.

Rajan

Origin/meaning: Sanskrit 'king'.
This is the Gujerati version of the name. The Sikh version uses the typical Sikh addition Singh, which means 'lion'.
Variation: Rajinder, Singh (Sikh).

Raksha

Origin/meaning: Sanskrit 'protected'.
This is the name of a Hindu festival (usually in August) when brothers are reminded of their duty to protect their sisters.

Ralph (pron. Rafe. Modern pron. Ralph)

Origin/meaning: Old Norse/Old English 'wolf counsel'.
This (sometimes in the form Radulf) was a pre-Conquest English name. It was also popular with the Normans so it did not die out in England after the Norman Conquest.
Variations and abbreviations: Rafe, Ralf, Raoul (Fr).

Ranald

Origin/meaning: Old German/Old English 'power-might'.
An uncommon spelling of Ronald, the Scottish equivalent of Reynold and its variation Reginald. Unlike Ronald, Ranald has remained distinctively Scottish.

Randal

Origin/meaning: Old English 'shield wolf'.
One of two medieval forms of this pre-Conquest name, the other being Ranulf. Randal has survived into the 20th century as well as giving rise to several last names, including Randle, Ransom, Rankin etc.
Variations and abbreviations: Rand, Randall, Randell, Randolf, Randolph, Randy, Ranulf, Ranulph. See also Ralph.

Randolph

Origin/meaning: Old English 'shield wolf'.
The 18th-century 'classical' version of the old name Ranulf, more commonly found today in the medieval form Randal q.v.

Raphael
Origin/meaning: Hebrew 'God has healed'.
One of the three named archangels in the Bible, together with Gabriel and Michael.
Variations and abbreviations: Rafael, Raffaele (It), Raffaello (It), Raphaël (Fr), Rafe, Ray.

Ravi
Origin/meaning: Sanskrit 'sun'.

Ravindra (pron. Ravindr)
Origin/meaning: Sanskrit 'sun-king of heaven'.
Variations: Rabindra, Ravinder Singh (Sikh).

Raymond
Origin/meaning: Old German 'strength protection' or 'counsel protection', i.e. 'strong'.
A name found in Britain since it was introduced by the Normans in 1066. It is found in various forms throughout Europe and is also a last name.
Variations and abbreviations: Raimondo (It), Raimund (Ger), Raimundo (Sp), Ramón (Sp), Ray, Raymund, Reamonn (Ir), Reimund (Ger).

Reginald
Origin/meaning: Old German/Old English 'power-might'.
This is a late medieval version of the name Reynold from the form which appeared in Latin manuscripts 'Reginaldus'.
Variations and abbreviations: Reg, Reggie, Reginaldo (It), Reginauld (Fr), Rex, Reynold.

Reuben
Origin/meaning: uncertain. Sometimes given as 'behold, a son'. Possibly Hebrew 'renewer'.
This is a Biblical name. Reuben was one of the sons of Jacob and gave his name to one of the tribes of Israel.
Variations and abbreviations: Rube, Rubén (Sp), Rubin.

Rex
Origin/meaning: Latin 'king'.
A name which appears in the early years of the 20th century presumably to honor the accession of a king (Edward VII) after the long reign of Queen Victoria.

Rhys (pron. Rees)
Origin/meaning: Welsh 'fiery'.
An old name that has become popular in recent times.
Variations: Reece, Rees.

Richard

Origin/meaning: Old English 'rule hard', i.e. 'strong king'.
An Anglo-Saxon name, used by a Kentish king who went as a monk to Europe.

Variations and abbreviations: Diccon (Med Eng), Dick, Dickie, Dicky, Reichard (Ger), Ric, Ricard, Ricardo (Sp), Riccardo (It), Rich, Richardt (Ger), Richart (Dut), Richie, Richy, Rik, Riocard (Ir), Ritchie.

Ridley

Origin/meaning: English 'clearing in the reeds'.
This old place name and last name is best known as the given name of celebrated Hollywood film director Ridley Scott.

Riley

Origin/meaning: English 'clearing in the rye'.
An old place name that is sometimes found as a given name.

Rob

A popular short form of Robert and Robin q.v.

Robert

Origin/meaning: Old German 'fame-bright'.
This name, originally Hrodebert, was the name of a Saxon bishop of the 8th century.

Variations and abbreviations: Bert, Bertie, Bob, Bobbie, Bobby, Rab, Rabbie, Riobard (Ir), Rob, Robbie, Robby, Roberto (It), Robin, Robrecht (Ger), Rupert.

Robin

Origin/meaning: Old German 'fame-bright'.
An originally French diminutive of Robert. The ending implies affection.

Rocco

Origin/meaning: Old German 'rest'.
This Italian name, equivalent of the English Rock, has become especially popular after pop star Madonna and Guy Ritchie used this name for their son.

Rock

Origin/meaning: Old German 'crow'/'jay' or Old English 'rock'.
A short form of several obsolete names beginning with Roch, such as Rochbert.

Variations and abbreviations: Rocco (It), Roch (Fr), Rochus (Ger/Dut), Rocky.

Roderick

Origin/meaning: Old German 'fame ruler'. Usually given as 'famous ruler'.
One of the most lasting and widespread of the Old German names.

Variations and abbreviations: Rod, Rodd, Roddie, Roddy, Roderich (Ger), Roderigo, Rodrigo (Sp/It/Port), Rodrigue (Fr), Rory, Rurik (Scand/Russ), Ruy (Sp).

Roger

Origin/meaning: Old English/Old German 'fame spear'. Usually given as 'famous spearman'.
An ancient name found in its original form – Hrothgar – in 'Beowulf', the Old English poem.

Variations and abbreviations: Rodge, Rodger, Rog, Rogerio (Sp), Rüdiger (Ger), Ruggiero (It), Rutger (Dut), Ruttger.

Roland

Origin/meaning: Old German 'fame land', usually given as 'famous man of the land'.
This is the French version of the name which was brought to England by the Normans in 1066.

Roman

Origin/meaning: Latin, Russian 'Roman'.
This name remains very popular in parts of Eastern Europe and Russia.

Romeo

Origin/meaning: Latin, Italian 'pilgrim to Rome'.
The name was made famous by Shakespeare in 'Romeo and Juliet'.

Variation: Romeus.

Ronald

Origin/meaning: Old German/Old English 'power-might'.
Like the English Reginald q.v. this Scottish name is a development of Reynold.

Variations and abbreviations: Ranald, Reginald, Reynold, Ron, Ronnie.

Rory

Origin/meaning: Gaelic 'red-haired' or Old German 'famous ruler'.
The original Celtic name Ruaridh (Scots) and Rhuadhri (Irish) became Roderigh or, more familiar, Rory.

Variations and abbreviations: Rorie, Roderick, Roger, Roy.

Ross

Origin/meaning: Old Scots 'of the promontory' or Old German 'fame'.
A common Scots last name which has gained popularity in the 20th century as a first name.

Rowan

Origin/meaning: Old Norse 'rowan tree'.

A last name used as a first name, perhaps influenced by the similarity to Rowland.

Rowland

Origin/meaning: Old German 'fame-land', usually given as 'famous man of the land'.

This spelling was the most usual in England from the late Middle Ages until the 18th century.

Variations and abbreviations: Orlando (It), Roland (Fr/Ger), Rolando (It/Port/Sp), Roldan (Sp), Rolland, Rollo, Rolly, Rowley, Rowly, Ruland (Ger).

Rudolph

Origin/meaning: Old German 'fame-wolf'.

A modern German form of a pre-Conquest name.

Variations and abbreviations: Rodolf, Rodolphe (Fr), Rolph, Rodolf, Rodolfo (It), Rodolphe (Fr), Rudolf, Rudy.

Rufus

Origin/meaning: Latin 'red-haired'.

This originated as a nickname and was used by the Romans. An early example is William the Conqueror's son who was known as William Rufus, because of his red hair.

Variations and abbreviations: Rory, Roy.

Rupert

Origin/meaning: Old German 'fame-bright'.

This comes from Rupprecht, the German version of a Saxon name.

Variations: Ruppert, Rupprecht, Ruprecht.

Russell

Origin/meaning: French 'little red head'.

An aristocratic last name (it is the family name of the Duke of Bedford) it came into use as a first name in the 19th century.

Variations and abbreviations: Russ, Rusty.

Ryan

Origin/meaning: origin unclear, possibly Gaelic 'king'.

A very common Irish and English last name that is widely used now as a first name in the English-speaking world.

Sacha

Origin/meaning: Ancient Greek 'defender of mankind'.

A French form of Sasha, this name is now becoming popular in the English-speaking world.

Sachin

Origin/meaning: Sanskrit 'affectionate'.

A much-used name in India thanks to the huge profile of the great Indian batsman Sachin Tendulkar, one of the best cricketers in the world.

Sadiq

Origin/meaning: Arabic 'faithful'.

A popular Muslim name.

Variation: Sadiki (E African).

Said (pron. Séye-eed)

Origin/meaning: Arabic 'happy' or 'fortunate'.

A traditional Muslim name.

Variations: Saeed, Sayed.

Salim

Origin/meaning: Arabic 'peace'.

A popular Muslim name. The feminine version is Salama. 'Peace' is a traditional Muslim greeting.

Variation: Selim.

Samson

Origin/meaning: Hebrew 'child of Sham' (the sun god).

The Biblical hero Samson, with his immense strength, was the scourge of the Philistines. Delilah seduced him into revealing that his strength came from his hair, and then cut it off while he slept. The name was introduced into England at the Norman Conquest.

Variations and abbreviations: Sam, Sammy, Sampson, Sansom, Sanson (Sp), Sansone (It), Simson.

Samuel

Origin/meaning: Hebrew 'name of God'. Possibly 'Sham is God' – see Samson. Occasionally 'summer traveler', i.e. 'Viking'.

Samuel was the great prophet whose life and work is covered by the ninth and tenth books of the Old Testament.

Variations and abbreviations: Sam, Sammy, Samuele (It).

Sandy
Origin/meaning: Greek 'defender of men' or 'red-haired'.
This is a familiar form of Alexander q.v. or a nickname, usually given to someone with red hair.

Sanjay
Origin/meaning: Sanskrit 'victorious'.
Sanjay Gandhi was the son of former Indian prime minister Indira Gandhi. He was killed in a plane crash in 1980.

Scott
Origin/meaning: Old English 'Scottish'.
A last name used as a first name.
Variations and abbreviations: Scot, Scotty.

Seamus (pron. Shaymus)
Origin/meaning: uncertain, possibly Hebrew 'supplanter'.
The Irish version of James or Jacob q.v.
Variations: Seumus (Scot), Shamus.

Sean (pron. Shawn)
Origin/meaning: Hebrew 'Jehovah has favored'.
An Irish form of John q.v. through the French form Jean. It is increasingly used by non-Irish people.
Variations: Shaun, Shawn. See also John.

Sebastian
Origin/meaning: Greek 'venerable' and Latin 'from Sebastia'.
St Sebastian was particularly well known because the manner of his death (he was shot with arrows and then cudgeled to death) made a striking subject for many paintings.
Variations and abbreviations: Bastian, Bastien, Seb, Sebastiano (It), Sébastien (Fr), Sebastianus (Ger).

Selwyn
Origin/meaning: Old English 'friend of the house'.
An Old English name which developed as a last name. In the 19th century it came into use as a first name, perhaps influenced by the name of Bishop Selwyn who founded Selwyn College, Cambridge. It is most commonly found in Wales.
Variation: Selwin.

Sergius

Origin/meaning: uncertain. Possibly Etruscan 'fisherman'.

A popular name in Russia and other areas of the Orthodox Church because of two saints, one a Roman martyr, d.303, whose cult was very strong, and the second St Sergius of Radonegh, 1314–1392, a Russian abbot and mystic.

Variations and abbreviations: Serge, Sergé (Fr), Sergei (Russ), Sergio (It).

Seth

Origin/meaning: Hebrew 'substitute'.

This was the appropriate name given to the son born to Adam and Eve after the murder of their second son Abel, by his brother Cain.

Shane

Origin/meaning: Hebrew 'Jehovah has favored'.

An Anglicized spelling of Sean q.v. the Irish version of John.

Variation: Shan.

Shankar (pron. Sankar)

Origin/meaning: Hindu. Another name for Shiv q.v.

Shankar was a famous Hindu saint who helped defend India against Muslim invaders.

Shashi

Origin/meaning: Sanskrit 'moon'.

This can be turned into a girl's name with the addition of the suffixes -bai or -ben.

Shaun

Origin/meaning: Hebrew 'Jehovah has favored'.

An English phonetic spelling of Sean q.v.

Variation: Shawn.

Shiv (pron. Seev)

Origin/meaning: Hindu 'destruction'.

Shiv is the Lord of all creatures who supports the world by his constant meditation. Paradoxically he is also the god of death.

Shuresh (pron. Suress)

Origin/meaning: Hindu 'supreme god'.

This is an alternative name for Indra (pron. Indr). In early Hindu mythology he was the warrior king of the gods.

Variations: Surinder-Singh (Sikh), Surendra (Gujerati).

Sidney

Origin/meaning: Latin/Greek 'follower of Dionysios'.
This aristocratic last name is a contraction of St Denis, a French place name. As a first name it had the additional boost to its popularity of being the last name of the much admired Elizabethan poet Sir Philip Sidney, 1554–1586.
Variations and abbreviations: Sid, Syd, Sydney.

Siegfried

Origin/meaning: Old German 'victory peace'.
A popular German name used occasionally in Britain since the end of the 19th century. This was the direct result of the influence of Richard Wagner's opera cycle 'The Ring', in which the hero's name is Siegfried.

Silas

Origin/meaning: Latin. From Silvanus, the Roman god of uncultivated land or woodland. Silas is close in origin to the name Silvester.
Variations and abbreviations: Si, Silvain (Fr), Silvan, Silvano (It), Silvanus (Ger/Dut), Silverio (It/Sp), Silvio (It/Sp), Sylvain (Fr), Sylvanus.

Silvester

Origin/meaning: Latin 'of the woodland'.
A name similar to Silas q.v. This was a reasonably widespread name in the Middle Ages, probably because there were three Popes who used the name.
Variations: Silvanus, Silverius, Silvestro (It), Silvius, Sylvester, Sylvestre (Fr).

Simba

Origin/meaning: Swahili 'lion'.
A name familiar to the West because it was often given to lions in captivity and in literature.

Simeon

Origin/meaning: uncertain. Usually given as Hebrew 'hearkening' but may be a non Hebrew name adopted by the Israelites. This is the usual Old Testament form of the Hebrew name Shim'on given as Simon in the New Testament.

Simon

Origin/meaning: uncertain. Usually given as Hebrew 'hearkening'. Being the Greek influenced version of the name Shim'on or Simeon it may also incorporate the Greek word meaning 'snub-nosed'.
Variations and abbreviations: Semjon (Russ), Si, Sim, Simeon, Siméon (Fr), Simmie, Simone (It), Simpkin, Symon, Symond (Med Eng), Ximines (Sp).

Sinclair

Origin/meaning: French. A contraction of St Clair, a town in Normandy.

This is an aristocratic last name popular as a first name in the 19th century. It is the family name of the Earls of Caithness.

Singh

Origin/meaning: Sanskrit 'lion'.

This is a Sikh name from the Punjab region. It is not used on its own but is added to other male names as a form of politeness.

See also Leo and Simba.

Siôn (pron. Sheón)

Origin/meaning: Hebrew 'Jehovah has favored'.

This is the native Welsh form of John q.v.

Variation: Sionyn (dim). See also John.

Siôr (pron. Shaw)

Origin/meaning: Greek 'farmer'.

This is the Welsh form of George q.v.

Variation: Shaw.

Solomon

Origin/meaning: Hebrew 'little man of peace'.

A Biblical name referring to David's son, King Solomon, who was famous for his wisdom.

Variations and abbreviations: Salomo, Salomon (Fr/Ger), Salomón (Sp), Salomone (It), Selim (Arab), Sol, Solly, Soloman, Sulaiman (Arab). See also Salome.

Spencer

Origin/meaning: Old French 'steward' or 'butler'.

The steward was the 'dispenser' of household supplies. Used as a first name in families connected with the Spencer family and the Spencer-Churchill family (the Dukes of Marlborough), it became more widespread in the 19th century.

Variation: Spenser.

Stanley

Origin/meaning: Old English 'stony meadow'.

An aristocratic last name, the family name of the Earls of Derby, it has been used as a first name since the 19th century.

Abbreviation: Stan.

Stephen

Origin/meaning: Greek 'wreathed' or 'crowned'.

This name comes from the wreath or crown of laurel leaves given to a victorious athlete in ancient Greece. St Stephen was the first known Christian martyr who died c.35. The name was introduced into England at the Norman Conquest. Steven is an alternative spelling.

Variations and abbreviations: Etienne (Fr), Esteban (Sp), Estevan, István (Hung), Stefan (Ger/Pol), Stefano (It), Steffan (Wel), Stephan, Stéphan (Fr), Stephanus, Steve, Steven, Stevie, Stevy, Stevyn (Med Eng), Ystffan (Wel).

Stuart

Origin/meaning: Old English 'animal keeper' or 'steward'.

This Scottish last name is particularly famous as the name of the Scottish royal family. It was 1371 when one of the hereditary stewards of Scotland came to the throne as Robert II. In the 19th century Scottish last names, like aristocratic names, became generally popular.

Variations and abbreviations: Steuart, Stew, Steward, Stewart, Stu. See also Bruce, Cameron, Douglas, Graham.

Sudhakar (pron. Soothoh-kar)

Origin/meaning: Hindu 'treasure of nectar'.

The masculine equivalent of Sudha q.v.

Sulaiman

Origin/meaning: Arabic 'peaceful'.

This is a Muslim name closely related to Salim, another popular Muslim name. It is the same name as Solomon q.v.

Sven

Origin/meaning: Old Norse 'boy'. A Scandinavian name that is now used in the English-speaking world. In Britain it is best known as the first name of the soccer manager Sven-Göran Eriksson.

Tad

Origin/meaning: uncertain, possibly Hebrew 'praise'.

A short form of Thaddeus q.v.

Tam

Origin/meaning: Aramaic 'twin'.

Scottish form of Thomas, as in Robert Burns' poem 'Tam O'Shanter'. It is sometimes given as an independent name.

Tancred

Origin/meaning: Old German 'grateful counsel'.

The Normans brought the name over to England in 1066, and into another of their kingdoms in Southern Italy.

Variations: Trancrède (Fr), Trancredi (It), Tankred (Ger).

Tariq

Origin/meaning: uncertain. Possibly Arabic 'conqueror'.

Tariq was a Muslim general who led the Moorish invasion of Southern Spain.

Variation: Tarik.

Tate

Origin/meaning: Old German/Old English 'glad' or 'dear'.

An early name which developed principally as a last name, sometimes used as a first name.

Tau

Origin/meaning: Tswana 'lion'.

A name from Botswana.

Teague (pron. Theeg)

Origin/meaning: Old Irish 'poet'.

In Ireland this name developed as an easier way of saying the Old Gaelic Tadhgh. Once considered typically Irish rather as Paddy is today.

Variations and abbreviations: Teige, Thaddeus, Thaddy, Timothy.

Terence

Origin/meaning: from Terentius, the name of an ancient Roman tribe. Meaning obscure. Also Old Irish 'tower of strength'.

A Roman name, which like several others was used by the Irish to translate a native name.

Variations and abbreviations: Terencio (Sp), Terenziano (It), Terenzio (It), Terrence, Terry.

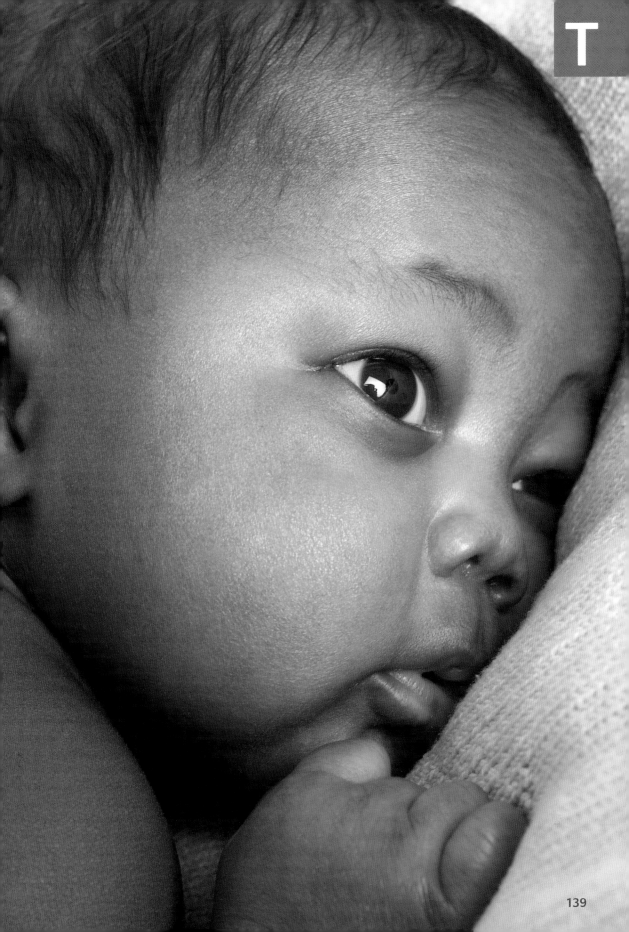

Tewdwr (pron. Tudor)

Origin/meaning: The Welsh version of Theodore q.v. usually given the English spelling Tudor.

Thaddeus

Origin/meaning: uncertain, possibly Hebrew 'praise'.

In Matthew's gospel, it is given as the last name of one of the Apostles, Lebbaeus.

Variations and abbreviations: Fadej (Russ), Tad, Tadd, Taddeo (It), Tadeo (Sp), Tadeusz (Pol), Thad, Thaddoeus, Thaddäus (Ger), Thaddés (Fr), Thady.

Theobald

Origin/meaning: Old German/Old English 'bold folk'.

The medieval version of this pre-Conquest name was pronounced Tibald/t. An example of this is Tybalt, one of the characters in Shakespeare's 'Romeo and Juliet'. The common cat's name, Tibby or Tibbles, refers back to a cat named Tybalt in the medieval folk-tale cycle, 'Reynard the Fox'.

Variations and abbreviations: Dietbold (Ger), Tebaldo (It), Teobaldo (It/Sp), Thebault (Fr), Theo, Thibaud (Fr), Thibaut (Fr), Tibald, Tibold (Ger), Tiebout (Dut), Tybalt.

Theodore

Origin/meaning: Greek 'gift of God'.

Theodore Roosevelt, 1858–1919, helped to popularize the name in the US where the typical short form is Teddy. It was from Roosevelt that the Teddy bear got its name.

Variations and abbreviations: Fedor (Russ), Fyodor (Russ), Ted, Teddy, Tewdr (Wel), Teodoro (It), Theo, Théodore (Fr), Tudor (Wel). See also Jonathan, Matthew, Nathaniel.

Thomas

Origin/meaning: Aramaic 'twin'.

It was the name of one of the Apostles. The name's popularity was boosted by the reverence for St Thomas Becket. An Archbishop of Canterbury, he was killed in 1170 at the instigation of Henry II.

Variations and abbreviations: Tam, Tamas, Tammie, Tammy, Thom, Tom, Tómas (Sp), Tomas (Ir), Tomaso (It), Tompkin, Tommie, Tommy.

Thurstan

Origin/meaning: Old Norse/Old English 'Thor's stone'.

A last name from East Anglia which is also used as a first name. Sometimes said to be the origin of the name Tristram q.v.

Variations: Thurston, Tristram.

Timothy

Origin/meaning: Greek 'honor to God'.

This is a Greek name pre-dating Christianity. It was the name of St Paul's companion in the Acts of the Apostles.

Variations and abbreviations: Tim, Timmie, Timmy, Timoteo (It/Sp), Timothée (Fr), Timotheus (Ger/Dut).

Titus

Origin/meaning: uncertain, possibly Greek 'honored'.

A Latin name, derived from the Greek.

Variation: Tito (It).

Tobias

Origin/meaning: Hebrew 'God is good'.

The more familiar English form is Toby q.v. Tobias was the son of Tobit in the Book of Tobit (Apocrypha).

Toby

Origin/meaning: Hebrew 'God is good'.

The English form of Tobiah, generally more popular than the Greek form, Tobias q.v.

Variations and abbreviations: Tobia (It), Tobiah, Tobias (Ger), Tobie (Fr), Tobin, Tobit.

Tom

Origin/meaning: Aramaic 'twin'.

A common short form of Thomas, often used as an independent name.

Tony

Origin/meaning: Latin Antonius – the name of one of the great Roman families.

The most popular short form of Antony q.v. sometimes given as an independent name.

Torquil

Origin/meaning: obscure, possibly Old Norse 'Thor's cauldron'.

This is the Gaelic version of an Old Norse name introduced into Scotland and the North of England by the Vikings from the 8th–11th centuries.

Variations: Thorkill, Thorketill, Torcull.

Travis

Origin/meaning: Old French 'toll collector'.

An occupation name now used as a first name. Its popularity has been boosted by the success of pop group Travis.

Trevor

Origin/meaning: Old Welsh 'large settlement'.

This is a Welsh place name which is found as a given name or last name as far back as the 10th century. The Welsh form is Trefor.

Abbreviation: Trev.

Trey

Origin/meaning: Old English 'three' or 'third born'.

Mostly found in the US.

Tristan

Origin/meaning: uncertain. Either Old Welsh 'herald', Latin/French 'sad' or Old Norse 'Thor's stone'.

Variation: Tristano (It).

Tristram

Origin/meaning: uncertain. Either Old Welsh 'herald', Latin 'sad' or Old Norse 'Thor's stone'.

There may be an element of all these definitions in Tristram for the name seems to have developed independently in several countries. Tristram and Iseult (Tristan and Isolde) is an Arthurian romance which may date back as far as the 6th century.

Variations: Thurstan, Tristan (Fr), Tristano (It), Tristran, Trystram.

Troy

Origin/meaning: Old Irish 'foot soldier' or a place name after Troy in Asia Minor or Troyes in France.

Town names from the ancient Greek world were often given to settlements in North America after the civil war as if to emphasize the influence of Greek democracy. For the same reason these city names were sometimes used as personal names.

Truman

Origin/meaning: Old German, Old English 'true man'.

A name largely found in the US and whose use was boosted by the example of US president Harry S. Truman, 1884–1972.

Variation: Trueman.

Ty

Origin/meaning: a short form of names beginning with Ty. Most are last names used as first names, e.g. Tyler, Tynan.

Tyler

Origin/meaning: English 'roof tiler'.

This occupational name is very popular now, especially in the US. It is also used as a name for girls.

Variations: Ty, Tyla.

Tyrone

Origin/meaning: Old Irish 'land of Owen'.

This is an Irish place name (County Tyrone), and an aristocratic last name – the Earl of Tyrone is the elder son of the Marquess of Waterford.

Ulysses

Origin/meaning: uncertain, possibly Etruscan 'wanderer'. Sometimes given as 'hater'. In Ireland 'mind reward'.

This is the Latin form of Odysseus, the name of a Geek hero of the Trojan wars whose journeyings are described in Homer's epic poem 'The Odyssey'. In Ireland it was used to translate the native names Ulrick and Uileos. The Irish writer James Joyce used it as the title of one of his novels published in 1922. In the US it has been used to honor Ulysses S. Grant.

Variations and abbreviations: Uileos, Uillioc (Ir), Ulick (Ir), Ulises (Sp), Ulisse (It).

Umar

Origin/meaning: Arabic 'highest'. Sanskrit 'husband of Uma'.

This is another name for Shiv q.v. (Lord Shiva) as Uma was a reincarnation of Parvati q.v., Shiva's wife.

Uni

Origin/meaning: Yao 'life'.

A name from Malawi in Central Africa.

Uriah

Origin/meaning: Hebrew 'light of Jehovah'.

This is a Biblical name used occasionally by Puritans after the 16th-century Protestant Reformation.

Valentine

Origin/meaning: Latin 'strong', 'healthy'.

Well known because of St Valentine the Roman martyr, whose feast day (February 14th) coincided with a pagan festival in which young people chose partners. This tradition was retained by the new Christian religion.

Variations and abbreviations: Val, Valentijn (Dut), Valentin (Fr/Ger/Scand/Sp), Valentine (It).

Vere

Origin/meaning: 'from Ver' (an area of Normandy).

A last name introduced at the Conquest. Its aristocratic connections made it an ideal candidate for adoption as a first name during the 19th century.

Vernon

Origin/meaning: Latin 'springlike' or Old French 'little alder grove'.

Either a masculine form of the Latin word Verna or a typical 19th-century adoption of an aristocratic last name.

Variations and abbreviations: Vern, Verne, Verney.

Vidal

Origin/meaning: Latin 'vital' or 'belonging to life'.

A Spanish form of the rare English name Vitalis. A more current English equivalent of Vivian q.v.

Vijay

Origin/meaning: Sanskrit 'victory'.

Variation: Viajay.

Vikram/a (the final a is not pronounced)

Origin/meaning: Sanskrit 'a record-breaker'.

Vikram, whose full title was Vikramaditya (Vikram of the eternal) was a legendary Indian Raja (king) possibly based on the real King Chandragupta II, 375–415.

Vinay

Origin/meaning: Hindu 'courtesy'.

Vincent

Origin/meaning: Latin 'conquering'.

This name was used in Medieval England to honor St Vincentius of Saragossa who was martyred by the Emperor Diocletian at the beginning of the 4th century.

Variations and abbreviations: Vicente (Sp), Vin, Vince, Vincente, Vincenzo (It), Vinny, Vinzent, Vinzenz (Ger).

Vishnu

Origin/meaning: Hindu. The name of one of the greatest of the Hindu gods. According to the Hindu religion Vishnu is probably the greatest of all the gods, although he himself acknowledged the supremacy of Shiva. At crucial points in the cycle of time Vishnu is incarnated and comes to earth.

Vivian

Origin/meaning: Latin 'full of life'.
A rare masculine name which, as Vivianus, dates back to the early Middle Ages.

Variations and abbreviations: Viv, Vivien (Fr), Viviano (It), Vyvyan.

Vladimir

Origin/meaning: Slavic 'famous prince'.
Prince and saint, Vladimir, 955–1015, is credited with the definite conversion of European Russia to Christianity.

Walid

Origin/meaning: Arabic 'new born'.
This is a Muslim name.
Variation: Waleed.

Wallace

Origin/meaning: Old Scots 'from Wales' or 'Welsh'.
A famous Scottish last name initially used as a first name in the 19th century when aristocratic last names were fashionable.
Variations and abbreviations: Wal, Wally.

Walter

Origin/meaning: Old German/Old English 'rule-people'.
The Norman version of this name was very popular. One of the most popular short forms Wat, indicates that in the Middle Ages the pronunciation was Water.
Variations and abbreviations: Gauthier (Fr), Gautier, Gaulterio (Sp), Gualtiero (It), Gwaleter (Wel), Wally, Walt, Walther (Ger), Wat.

Waqar

Origin/meaning: Arabic 'dignity'.
A popular name in Pakistan.
Variation: Waqaar.

Warren

Origin/meaning: probably Old German 'of the Verini tribe'. Sometimes listed as 'defender'.
Warren developed almost exclusively into a last name in the Middle Ages. Its use as a first name has been
revived in the last 100 years, particularly in America.

Wasim

Origin/meaning: Arabic 'handsome'.
Wasim Akram was an extremely talented Pakistani cricketer in the 1980s and 1990s.
Variation: Waseem.

Washington

Origin/meaning: Old English 'home of the Wassa folk'.
Washington in County Durham gave its name to the family of George Washington, first President of the US. As a result this last name has periodically been popular as a first name in the US.

Wayne

Origin/meaning: Old English 'wagon'.

A last name, sometimes a short form of Wainwright (wagon-mender). Frequently found as a first name in the US because of film actor John Wayne and the hero of the Revolution General Anthony Wayne.

Wilbur

Origin/meaning: either Old German 'resolute defence' or Dutch 'wild farmer'.

This name, so popular in the US but rare in other English-speaking countries, may have either or both of the above meanings. In both cases it derives from a last name.

Variations and abbreviations: Will, Wilber.

Wilfred

Origin/meaning: Old English 'will peace', i.e. 'determined for peace'.

This Old English name usually found before 1066 as Wilfrith, did not survive the competition of the new names which arrived with the Conquest. It was revived in the 19th century.

Variations and abbreviations: Fred, Wilf, Wilfrid, Will.

William

Origin/meaning: Old German 'will helmet', i.e. 'helmet of resolution'.

One of the most consistently popular names in England since it was introduced in the old forms Wilhelm and Guillamo by William the Conqueror in 1066.

Variations and abbreviations: Bill, Billie, Billy, Guglielmo (It), Guillaume (Fr), Guillermo (Sp), Gwylim (Wel), Liam (Ir), Vilhelm (Scand/Slav), Wilhelm (Ger), Will, Willem (Dut), Willie, Willis.

Winston

Origin/meaning: Old English 'friend's farm' (the name of a small village in Gloucestershire).

The family name of the grandmother of John Churchill, 1st Duke of Marlborough, and it is still a regularly used name in the Churchill family. Sir Winston Churchill was a grandson of the 7th Duke of Marlborough.

Variations and abbreviations: Win, Winnie, Winny.

Wolfgang

Origin/meaning: Old German 'approach of the wolf'.
A South German/Austrian name world famous because of the Austrian composer Wolfgang Amadeus Mozart, 1756–1791.

Variations and abbreviations: Volfango (It), Wolf, Wolfe, Wolfie, Wolfy, Wulf.

Wyatt

Origin/meaning: Old English 'battle strong'.
The best-known bearer of this name was the famous US lawman Wyatt Earp.

Wynne

Origin/meaning: Welsh 'white/fair'.
A form of Gwyn q.v. It is found as part of many Welsh names as well as being a name in its own right.

X

Xavier (pron. Sp Havierr, Eng Zayvier).

Origin/meaning: Arabic 'bright' or 'splendid'.

The last name of the Spanish missionary St Francis Xavier, 1506–1552. It is a popular name among Catholics, particularly of course in Spanish-speaking countries.

Variations: Javier, Xaver (Ger).

Ximenes (pron. Sp Hímehnehth, Eng Ziminez)

Origin/meaning: Hebrew 'hearkening'.

A Spanish form of Simon q.v.

Yaqub

Origin/meaning: Arabic 'supplanter'.

This is the same name as the Hebrew Jacob and English James.

Yehudi

Origin/meaning: Hebrew 'praise of the Lord'.

A Jewish form of Jude q.v. as is Judah.

Variations and abbreviations: see Jude.

Yestin

Origin/meaning: Latin 'just'.

The Welsh version of Justin.

Variation: Iestin.

Yogesh (pron. Yogess)

Origin/meaning: Sanskrit/Gujerati 'expert at yoga'.

Yusuf

Origin/meaning: Arabic 'he shall add (to his power)'.

This is the Muslim form of the Hebrew name Joseph q.v.

Yves (pron. Eve)

Origin/meaning: Old German 'yew'.

The French version of the English Ivo or Ives, common in Medieval France, particularly in Brittany, and still popular today.

Variation: Yvon.

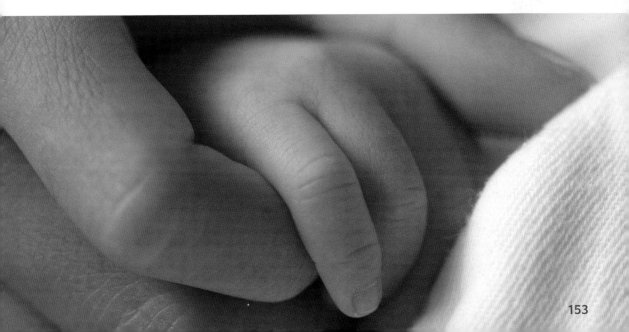

Zacchaeus

Origin/meaning: Hebrew 'the Lord has remembered'.
The Latinized version of the short form of Zachariah (see Zachary). Zacchaeus (Luke 19) was a small man, a publican, who climbed a sycamore tree to get a good view of Jesus.

Zachary

Origin/meaning: Hebrew 'the Lord has remembered'.
This is the English version of the Biblical name Zachariah or Zacharias. It is still found in the US, particularly in one of its short forms.
Variations and abbreviations: Zacarias (Sp), Zaccaria (It), Zacharias, Zachariah, Zacharian, Zacharie (Fr), Zack, Zacky, Zak, Zechariah, Zeke.

Zaid

Origin/meaning: Arabic 'increase'.
A common Muslim name.
Variations: Zaeed, Zayed, Ziyad.

Zavier (pron. Záyvyer)

Origin/meaning: Arabic 'bright'.
One of the Anglicized versions of Xavier q.v.
Variation: Zaver.

Zebedee

Origin/meaning: Hebrew 'gift of the Lord'.
Zebedee was the father of the Apostles James and John (Mark ch.1:19).
Variations and abbreviations: Zeb, Zebadiah, Zebediah.

Zeke

Origin/meaning: Hebrew 'the Lord has remembered' or Hebrew 'God is strong'.
A short form of Zachary or Ezekial, found as an independent name in the US.

Girls' Names

Aakash (pron. Akass)
Origin/meaning: Hindu 'sky'.
Found throughout India but considered rather unusual.

Aarti
Origin/meaning: Hindu.
The name of a prayer made with a candle. This name comes from West India.

Abbey, Abby
Origin/meaning: Hebrew 'father of joy'.
Popular North American contraction of Abigail q.v. used as a name in its own right.

Abebi
Origin/meaning: Yoruba 'asked for child'.
A Nigerian name. Abeje and Abeke have similar meanings.

Abigail
Origin/meaning: Hebrew 'father's joy' or 'father (source) of joy'.
One of the wives of King David. In the 17th-century play 'The Scornful Lady' by Beaumont and Fletcher, Abigail was the handmaid and confidante of the heroine. As a result Abigail became synonymous with maid servant.
Variations and abbreviations: Abigael, Abagail, Abaigael (Ir), Abbe, Abbi, Abbie, Abby, Abbye, Abigael, Gael, Gail, Gale, Gayel, Gayle.

Acacia
Origin/meaning: Greek 'guileless, innocent', 'acacia tree'.
The acacia tree is said to symbolize the resurrection and therefore immortality.
Variations and abbreviations: Cacia, Cacie, Casey.

Ada

Origin/meaning: Old German Eda, Etta and Old English Eadda, 'happy'.
Popular in Britain in the 18th and 19th centuries. Byron's first daughter, the mathematician, b.1816, was christened Ada.

Adela

Origin/meaning: 'noble' from the Old German 'adal'.
Adela was brought over to England at the time of the Norman Conquest. It enjoyed a period of popularity in the 19th century partly because of the fashionable French version Adèle.

Variations and abbreviations: Ad, Adel, Adèle (Fr), Adella, Adelle, Addie. See also Adelaide, Adeline, Alice.

Adelaide

Origin/meaning: Old German 'nobility'.
The original Old German version was Adalheid. Old French corrupted Adalheid to Adeliz from which we get Alice q.v.

Variations and abbreviations: Ada, Adalheid, Addi, Addie, Adel, Adelaida (Ital), Adelheid (Ger), Della, Heidi (Ger). See also Adela, Adeline, Alice.

Adeline

Origin/meaning: Old German 'nobility', 'noble maiden'.
This has the same root, 'adal' – 'noble', as Adela and Adelaide. They were all brought to Britain with the Norman Conquest.

Variations and abbreviations: Addi, Addy, Adel, Adelena, Adelene, Adelina (Ital), Aline q.v., Edelina, Edolina.

Adeola

Origin/meaning: Yoruba 'crown has honor'.
A Nigerian name. One of several similar names such as Adedagbo – 'happiness is a crown', and Adeleke – 'crown achieves happiness'.

Aditi

Origin/meaning: Hindu. Meaning obscure.
In mythology Aditi was one of the wives of the Hindu saint Kasnyapa. She gave birth to all the gods.

Adriana/Adrienne

Origin/meaning: Latin 'from Adria'.

Feminine versions of Adrian, q.v.

Variations and abbreviations: Adria, Adriane (Ger), Adrianna, Adrianne, Hadria.

Aduke (pron. Adóokay)

Origin/meaning: Yoruba 'much loved child'.

A name from Nigeria.

Afiya

Origin/meaning: Swahili 'health'.

An East African name.

Afra

Origin/meaning: obscure. May be Latin 'African', an abbreviation of Greek, Aphrodite, or Hebrew 'house of dust'. There is a 4th-century saint called Afra, whose feast day is August 5th.

Variations: Aphra, Ayfara, Aphry.

Agatha

Origin/meaning: Ancient Greek 'good'.

The name of a 3rd-century Sicilian Saint, Agatha was a popular medieval name. William the Conqueror gave it to one of his daughters.

Agnes

Origin/meaning: Greek 'pure', chaste.

This was an extremely popular name during the Middle Ages and was found in a variety of forms. One of these, Annis, shows us how it used to be pronounced.

Variations and abbreviations: Aggi, Aggie, Agna, Agnella, Agnese (Ital), Agneta (Scand), Agnete (Ital), Annis (Med Eng), Annys, Ines (Sp), Inez, Nezza, Nessie, Nesta (Wel), Ynes, Ynez. See also Senga.

Aida (pron. Ayéeda)

Origin/meaning: Arabic 'benefit'.

This name is quite separate from Aida, a version of Ada q.v.

Aileen

Origin/meaning: Greek 'light' or 'bright'.

The Irish version of the immensely popular name Helen.

Variations: Ailene, Aleen, Ailene, Eileen, Ilene, Ileana.

Ailsa

Origin/meaning: uncertain. Possibly Hebrew 'God is my satisfaction' or Old German 'noble'. This is almost exclusively Scottish and may simply be a native Scottish name with no certain meaning.

Aithne (pron. Ethnee or Awnye)

Origin/meaning: Old Irish 'little fire', 'little fiery one'.

The feminine version of Aidan q.v. In Irish mythology Aine (pron. Awnye) Queen of the Fairies.

Variations and abbreviations: Aine (Old Celtic), Eithne, Ena, Ethne, Ina.

Aiyetoro (pron. Aryétoro)

Origin/meaning: Yoruba 'peace on earth'.

This name comes from East Africa.

Alanna

Origin/meaning: Celtic 'beautiful'.

The feminine form of Alan q.v.

Variations and abbreviations: Alaine, Alana, Alanda, Alane, Alayne, Alina, Allene, Allin, Allina, Allyn, Lana, Lanna.

Alba

Origin/meaning: Latin 'white', 'blonde'.

Variation: Alva.

Alberta

Origin/meaning: Old German 'nobly bright'.

Feminine version of Albert q.v.

Variations and abbreviations: Adalberta (Old Ger), Albertina (Ital), Albertine (Fr), Ally, Elberta, Elbertina, Elbertine, Berta, Bartie.

Alcina

Origin/meaning: Greek 'sea-maiden'.

Variations: Alcine, Alcinia.

Alethea

Origin/meaning: Greek 'truth'.

Like other virtues, Faith, Hope, Prudence etc., Alethea was a popular name in the Puritan England of the 17th century and among Puritan settlers in America.

Variations and abbreviations: Alatheia, Aleta, Aletea (Sp), Alethia, Aletia, Aletta, Alithia.

Alexandra

Origin/meaning: Greek 'defender of men'.
The feminine form of Alexander q.v.

Variations and abbreviations: Alejandra (Sp), Alessandra (Ital), Alex, Alexa, Alexandria, Alexandrina, Alexina, Alexine, Alexis, Ali, Alix, Alla, Alli, Lexi, Lexine, Sandi, Sandie, Sandra, Sandy, Sondra, Zandra, Zandria.

Alguni

Origin/meaning: Hindu: the name of the 5th month of the year.
In this month there is a big religious festival in West and North India, which celebrates the arrival of Spring.

Alice

Origin/meaning: Old German 'nobility' or Greek 'truth'.
It comes from the Norman French version of Adelaide – Adelize. When this name was translated into Latin in documents it became Alesia from which Alice eventually developed.

Variations and abbreviations: Adelice, Adelize, Ali, Alicea, Alis, Alisa, Alison, Allison, Allyce, Allys, Alyss, Alyssa.

Aline

Origin/meaning: Old German 'nobility' from adal 'noble'.
Short form of Adeline q.v. Often used as an independent name. Sometimes confused with Aileen, the Irish form of Helen.

Variations: Alena, Alene, Alina, Alyna, Arleen, Arline.

Alison

Origin/meaning: Old German 'nobility'.
A diminutive form of Alice q.v. which is itself a derivation of Adelaide q.v. It is now an independent first name.

Variations and abbreviations: Alicen, Allison, Alyson, Elsie.

Allegra

Origin/meaning: Italian 'cheerful'.
An Italian name. Given to Lord Byron's daughter by his mistress Claire Clairmont.

Alma

Origin/meaning: Latin 'kind' or Italian 'soul'.
This name enjoyed a vogue after the Battle of Alma, 1854, which was an incident in the Crimean War.

Almeria

Origin/meaning: Arabic 'princess'.

Almira

Origin/meaning: Arabic 'truth'.

Variation: Elmira.

Alphonsine

Origin/meaning: Old German 'noble and ready'.

A French feminine form of Alphonse, comparatively recent in origin.

Variations: Alfonsina (Ital), Alfonsine, Alonsa, Alonza.

Althea

Origin/meaning: Greek 'wholesome'.

Aluna (pron. Alóona)

Origin/meaning: 'come here'.

A name used in Kenya.

Alyssa

Origin/meaning: Greek 'sane', 'wise'; also the name of a yellow rock plant, alyssum.

This may be an independent name or it can be regarded as a form of Alice q.v.

Amanda

Origin/meaning: Latin 'lovable'.

Another of the many names which originate from the Latin verb 'amare' – 'to love'.

Variations and abbreviations: Manda, Mandie, Mandy.

Amarylis (pron. Ammahr´yllis)

Origin/meaning: Ancient Greek 'fresh stream'.

Used by the Greek and Roman poets as a name for a fresh country girl.

Amber

Origin/meaning: Arabic/French. The name given to a translucent yellow resin used as a semi-precious stone.

This name was only rarely used before the book 'Forever Amber' by Kathleen Winsor, which was a best-seller in the 1950s.

Amelia

Origin/meaning: Old German 'hard work', 'industrious'.
The original Old German name Amalburga became Amelie in France.

Variations and abbreviations: Amalea, Amalia (Ital), Ameliarane, Amalie (Ger), Amelie (Fr), Amilia (Scot), Amiline, Emilia, Emelina, Emiline, Emily, Emmeline.

Amina

Origin/meaning: Arabic 'honest', 'faithful'.
A very popular Muslim and North African name.

Variation: Aminah. See Sati.

Amrita

Origin/meaning: Sanskrit 'immortal'.
In the Hindu texts, the ocean is churned to create ambrosia – from which the name Amrita derives – which when drunk allows the gods to defeat the demons.

Amy

Origin/meaning: Latin/French 'beloved'.
Amy became popular because of the 13th-century St Amata.

Variations: Aimée (Fr), Aimie, Amata (Ir/Sp), Ame, Ami, Amia, Amya, Amye, Anwyl (Wel), Esmé.

Anastasia

Origin/meaning: Greek 'resurrection'.
The name of a 4th-century saint who was martyred in Yugoslavia. Anastasia has always been more popular in Greece and Russia than in the West.

Variations and abbreviations: Amstice, Ana, Anastasie (Fr), Anstice, Nastasia (It), Nastasya (Russ), Stace, Stacey, Stacie, Stacy.

Andrea

Origin/meaning: Greek 'manly', 'brave'.
A Latinized feminine form of Andrew (which was originally used for girls as well as boys).

Angela

Origin/meaning: Greek 'messenger'.
Angel was the word used to translate the Hebrew word for messenger of God and it was occasionally used as a masculine name.

Variations: Angèle (Fr), Angelia, Angelica.

Angharad

Origin/meaning: Old Welsh 'much loved'.

Anila

Origin/meaning: Sanskrit 'air, wind'.

The feminine form of Anil. In the Hindu text, Vedas, Anil is the name of the wind god (also known as Vayu) who drove a golden chariot pulled by a thousand horses.

Anita

Origin/meaning: Hebrew 'graceful', 'little graceful one'.

A Spanish and Italian diminutive form of Ann q.v.

Variation and abbreviation: Nita.

Anju

Origin/meaning: Sanskrit 'one who lives in heart'.

Ann, Anne

Origin/meaning: Hebrew 'graceful'.

Ann and its variations are all based on the Hebrew name Hannah q.v. St Anne was popularly supposed to be the mother of the Virgin Mary.

Variations and abbreviations: Ana, Anette, Anja (Russ), Anita (Sp/It), Anna (Ger/It/Dut/Scand), Annetta, Annette (Fr), Anni, Annie, Anny, Anouska (Russ), Anya (Russ), Nan, Nana, Nancy, Nannie, Nita.

Anna

Origin/meaning: Hebrew 'graceful'.
A Latin form of Ann which became popular in England in the 18th century.

Annabel

Origin/meaning: Latin/French 'lovable'.
This name is Scottish and dates from the 12th century.

Variations and abbreviations: Annabella (It), Annabelle, Annabla (Ir), Bella, Belle. See also Arabella.

Annunciata

Origin/meaning: Latin 'bearer of news'.
This is a name which refers to the occasion when the Virgin Mary was told by an angel that she was to be the Mother of Jesus, celebrated in the Catholic Church on March 25th.

Variations: Annunziata (It), Annunciacion (Sp), Maria Annunciata (It).

Anthea

Origin/meaning: Greek 'flowery'.
One of the 17th-century literary names created to give characters names appropriate to their appearance or personality.

See also Flora, Fleur.

Antonia

Origin/meaning: from the Latin name Antonius, one of the Patrician families of Ancient Rome. Sometimes considered to mean 'inestimable' or 'priceless'.

Variations and abbreviations: Anthoine (Fr), Antoinette (Fr), Antonetta (Scand), Antonie (Ger), Antonietta (It), Antonina (It), Netta, Nettie, Netty, Toni, Tonia, Tonie, Tony.

Apple

Origin/meaning: English, the name of the fruit.
First known as a given name when used by Hollywood actress Gwyneth Paltrow for her daughter.

April

Origin/meaning: Latin 'opening', 'beginning of Spring'. The name of the fourth month of the year.

Variation: Avril (Fr).

Arabella

Origin/meaning: Latin 'lovable'.
This name was originally found only in Scotland and dates from the 12th century.

Araminta

Origin/meaning: Latin 'loving'.
This name was one of many made-up names found in 17th-century literature, which were taken up and used by real people.
Variation: Aminta.

Ardelle

Origin/meaning: Latin 'warm, enthusiastic'.
Variations and abbreviations: Arad, Ardelia, Ardella, Ardene, Ardine.

Ariadne

Origin/meaning: Greek 'very holy one'.
Originally the name of the daughter of the mythological King Minos of Crete.
Variations: Ariane (Fr/Ger), Ariana, Arianna (It).

Arianwen

Origin/meaning: Old Welsh 'silver white'.
See also Alba, Blanche.

Armine

Origin/meaning: Old German 'army person', 'a soldier'.
Rare feminine version of Armin, an English form of Armand. The variation Arminel is found in the Devon area of England.
Variations: Armina, Arminda, Arminel, Arminie, Armande (Fr).

Aruna

Origin/meaning: Sanskrit 'reddish-brown'.
The feminine form of Arun who, in Hindu texts, is the personification of dawn.

Arwa

Origin/meaning: Arabic 'mountain goats'.
A name popular in the Gulf States as well as Saudi Arabia and Jordan.

Asha

Origin/meaning: Sanskrit 'hope'.
In Hindu texts, Asha is the wife of one of the eight Vasus (demi-gods).

Asmita (pron. Asméeta)

Origin/meaning: Hindu 'self-respect'.
Found throughout India.

Astrid

Origin/meaning: Old Norse 'God's strength'.
Used by Scandinavian Royal families since the 11th century when it was the name of the wife of the Norwegian King and saint, Olaf.
Variations and abbreviations: Asta, Assa, Assi, Atti, Estrid.

Atalanta

Origin/meaning: Greek 'swift runner'.
In Greek mythology Atalanta was an athlete who would only marry someone who ran faster than she could. Suitors who lost the race were killed.
Variations: Atalante, Allante, Atlanta, Tala.

Athena

Origin/meaning: Greek 'wisdom'.
Athena was the Greek goddess of wisdom. Her symbol was an owl.
Variation: Athene (Fr).

Audrey

Origin/meaning: Old English 'noble strength'.
Audrey is a contraction of Ethelreda. After 1000 years Audrey became common as an independent name in the 16th century.
Variations and abbreviations: Audi, Audie, Audrie, Audry, Audrye, Dee. See also Adelaide, Alice.

Augusta

Origin/meaning: Latin 'venerable', 'majestic'. Title given to female relations of the Roman emperors.
Feminine version of Augustus q.v. The Hanoverians brought both the masculine and feminine versions to England in the 18th century.
Variations and abbreviations: Auguste (Dut/Fr/Ger/Scand), Augustina, Augustine, Austina, Austine, Gus, Gussie, Gussy, Tina.

Aurora

Origin/meaning: Latin 'dawn'.
In Roman mythology Aurora was the goddess of the dawn.
Variation: Aurore (Fr). See also Dawn, Roxane, Zarah.

Averil

Origin/meaning: Old English 'boar-battle'.

This name is now almost always feminine, despite its meaning, although it can be used for boys or girls. It is sometimes confused with Avril, the French form of April.

Variations: Averell, Averilla, Averyl, Everild, Everilda.

Avice (pron. Aviss)

Origin/meaning: Old German 'battle struggle'.

The original Old German name arrived in England at the time of the Conquest in the French form Havoise from which Avice derives.

Variations and abbreviations: Avicia, Avis. See also Hedwig.

Ayesha (pron. Ay'sha)

Origin/meaning: Arabic 'life' or 'alive'.

This popular Muslim name commemorates Ayesha, 610–677, the favorite of Mohammed's nine wives. He died on the 8th June, 632, with his head resting on her lap.

Variations: Aisha, Ashaas (Swahili), Ay'sha, Ayeshah.

Ayo

Origin/meaning: Yoruba 'joy'.

A Nigerian name. The word occurs in many other names such as Ayobami 'I am blessed with joy', Ayodele 'joy comes home', Ayoluwa 'joy of our people', Bayo 'joy is found', Dayo 'joy arrives', Nayo 'we have joy' and Olubayo 'highest joy'.

Aziza

Origin/meaning: Arabic 'precious'.

This is a common Muslim name.

Azra

Background: Arabic 'virgin'.

A long-established name given to of the mistress of Wamiq, a legendary lover who is found in Persian and Urdu poetry.

Babette

Origin/meaning: Hebrew 'God is my satisfaction'.
A short form of Elizabeth q.v. and occasionally of Barbara q.v.

Barbara

Origin/meaning: Greek 'stranger', 'foreigner'.
This was a popular medieval name in Europe given to girls in honor of a legendary St Barbara who was martyred by her own father.

Variations and abbreviations: Bab, Babbie (Scot), Babetta (It), Babette (Fr), Babita, Babs, Bar, Barbarina (It), Barb, Barbe (Fr), Barbie, Barbra (Dan), Barbro (Swed), Barby, St Barbe, Varina, Varinka, Varvara (Slav).

Bathsheba

Origin/meaning: Hebrew 'daughter of the oath' or 'voluptuous'.
King David sent Bathsheba's husband Uriah into the most dangerous area of battle so that he was killed. David was then able to marry her himself.

Variations and abbreviations: Bathshua, Batsheva, Sheba.

Beatrice (pron. Béeatriss)

Origin/meaning: Latin 'bringer of happiness'.
This is the Italian form of the name given to honor St Beatrice, an early Roman martyr.

Variations and abbreviations: Bea, Beat, Beate, Béatrice (Fr), Beatricia, Beatrisa, Beatrix (Lat/Old Eng/Ger/Dut), Beatriz (Sp), Bee, Beitris (Scot), Bettrys (Wel), Bice (It), Biche (Fr), Trix, Trixi, Trixie, Trixy.

Beatrix

Origin/meaning: Latin 'bringer of happiness'.
Old (Latin) form of Beatrice q.v.

Becky

Origin/meaning: Hebrew 'knotted cord' therefore 'faithful wife', or possibly 'heifer'.
A short form of Rebecca q.v.

Belinda

Origin/meaning: Old German 'snake-like', 'sinuous'.
The word 'linda' means snake. Snakes were regarded as magical or godlike by many communities including the Saxon peoples. This is therefore a complimentary name.

Variations and abbreviations: Bel, Belle, Linda.

Belle

Origin/meaning: French 'beautiful'.
Also a short form of names such as Anabel, Arabella, Belinda, Isabel etc.
Variations and abbreviations: Anwen (Wel), Bell, Bella. See also Shobha.

Benita

Origin/meaning: Latin 'blessed'.
A Spanish feminine form of the masculine name Benedict.

Berenice

Origin/meaning: Greek 'bringer of victory'.
As a Biblical name, Berenice was the daughter of King Agrippa (Acts 25–26).
Variations and abbreviations: Berenike (Ger), Bérénice (Fr), Berenice (It), Bernice, Bernie, Berny, Bunny.

Bernadette

Origin/meaning: Old German 'resolute as a bear'.
A French feminine form of Bernard q.v. Its great popularity in the 20th century particularly in Ireland and among Catholics.

Bernardine

Origin/meaning: 'resolute as a bear'.
Rare feminine equivalent of Bernard q.v.
Variations and abbreviations: Berna, Bernadene, Bernadetta (It), Bernadette (Fr), Bernadina, Bernadine, Bernarda, Bernarde (Fr), Bernardina (It/Sp), Berneta, Bernie, Berny.

Bertha

Origin/meaning: Old German 'bright'.
Bertha and Berta have been current in Europe since Saxon times. Because of its meaning the name was associated with the Feast of the Epiphany (January 6th).
Variations and abbreviations: Bert, Berta (Ger/It/Swed/Sp), Berte, Bertel (Ger), Berthe (Fr), Bertie, Bertina, Betty. See also Candida.

Beryl

Origin/meaning: Greek/Latin. A beryl is a precious stone, similar to an emerald, usually pale green, blue or white.
Variation: Berylla.

Bess

Origin/meaning: Hebrew 'God is my satisfaction'.
An English familiar form of Elizabeth q.v. often used for Elizabeth I who was popularly known as 'Good Queen Bess'.
Variations: Bessie, Bessy, Betsy.

Beth

Origin/meaning: Hebrew 'God is my satisfaction'.
English familiar form of Elizabeth q.v. sometimes used as an independent name.

Bethany

Origin/meaning: Aramaic 'house of poverty'.
A Biblical name (it was a small village near Jerusalem).

Bettina

Origin/meaning: Hebrew 'God is my satisfaction'.
An Italian short form of Elizabeth, popular in the 1960s, perhaps because of the famous model Bettina, wife of the Aly Khan.

Bettrys

Origin/meaning: Latin 'bringer of happiness'.
Welsh form of Beatrice q.v.
Variations: Beitiris (Scot Gaelic).

Betty

Origin/meaning: Hebrew 'God is my satisfaction'.
English familiar form of Elizabeth q.v. now often found as an independent name.

Variations: Beithidh (Gaelic), Betta (It), Bette, Betti (Ger), Bettie, Bettina (It), Betsey, Betsy.
See also Elizabeth.

Beulah

Origin/meaning: Hebrew 'married', 'matronly'.
Variation: Beula.

Beverley

Origin/meaning: Old English 'from the beaver stream'.
A last name derived from a place in Yorkshire, this has since been used as a first name.

Variations and abbreviations: Bev, Beverle, Beverlee, Beverly.

Bhavana (pron. Báunah)

Origin/meaning: Sanskrit 'conception', 'faith', 'love'.

Bianca

Origin/meaning: Italian 'white', 'fair'.
The Italian form of the French name Blanche q.v.

Variations: Biancamaria, Biancha (Med Eng), Bianka.

Billie

Origin/meaning: Old German 'helmet of resolution'.
A short form of feminine versions of William, e.g. Wilhelmina, Williamina. Sometimes given as an independent name.
Variations: Bill, Billee, Billi, Billy. See also Minnie.

Birgitta

Origin/meaning: Old Norse 'mountain stronghold' or Old Irish 'strong one'.
This is the Scandinavian form of Bridget q.v. The Swedish St Birgitta 1303–1373 was the wife of a nobleman and mother of eight children.
Variations and abbreviations: Berget, Birga, Birgit, Brig, Brigga, Brigitta, Brita, Britt, Britta, Gita, Gitta.

Blanca

Origin/meaning: Spanish 'white', 'fair'.
Blanca of Castile married Louis VIII of France, and became the mother of Louis IX, St Louis. The French translated her name directly into their own language as Blanche.

Blanche

Origin/meaning: French 'white' from Old German 'blaecan' to whiten.
A French name in its own right since the early Middle Ages, which was brought to England by the French wife of the Earl of Lancaster, a member of the royal family. It was one of the medieval names popularized in the 19th century.
Variations and abbreviations: Bianca (It), Blanca (Dan/Sp), Blanch, Blanchette (Fr), Blanchia, Blanka (Ger/Swed), Blaunch
(Med Eng), Blinnie, Blinny. See also Arianwen, Blodwen, Candida, Guinevere.

Blodwen

Origin/meaning: Old Welsh 'white flower'.
Rare outside Wales.
Variation: Blodwyn.

Blossom

Origin/meaning: Old English 'flower-like'.
A flower name that became popular, along with other flowers, in the 19th century.

Blythe

Origin/meaning: Old English 'gentle', 'cheerful'.
An unusual name, occasionally used as a boy's name.
Variations: Blithe, Blyth.

Bonita

Origin/meaning: Latin 'good', Spanish 'pretty'.

A Spanish name also used in the United States.

Variations and abbreviations: Bona (It), Bonnie, Nita.

Bonnie

Origin/meaning: Scots dialect 'pretty' perhaps derived from Latin bonus – good.

A name used as a familiar form of many names beginning with B.

Variations: Bonnee, Bonni, Bonny.

Branwen

Origin/meaning: Old Welsh 'beautiful raven', 'raven-haired'.

Rare outside Wales. In the collection of old Welsh tales 'The Mabinogion', Branwen was the beautiful daughter of the British King Llyr, who married the King of Ireland.

Variations: Brangwain, Brengwain. See also Bronwen.

Bree

Origin/meaning: Irish 'hill'.

An old name that has become better known recently due to a character in the US TV series 'Desperate Housewives'.

Brenda

Origin/meaning: Old Norse 'sword'.

This name comes from the Shetland Isles, which were settled by Viking invaders.

Briana

Origin/meaning: Old Irish 'strong'.

Modern feminine form of Brian q.v.

Variations: Brianne, Bryana.

Bridget

Origin/meaning: Old Irish 'strong one', 'mighty one' from the name of the Irish Celtic goddess of fire.

St Brigid of Kildare, 450–523, was the founder of the first convents in Ireland and she was greatly revered.

Variations and abbreviations: Bedelia, Beret, Berget, Biddie, Biddy, Birga, Birgit (Ger), Birgitta (Swed), Birte, Birtha, Brid (Ir), Bride, Bridie, Brietta, Brig, Brigga, Brighid (Ir), Brigid (Ir), Brigida (It/Sp), Brigide, Brigit (Ir), Brigitta (Swed/Ger), Brigitte (Fr/Ger), Brita, Britt (Swed), Britta (Swed), Bryde, Ffaod (Wel), Gita, Gitta.

Britt

Origin/meaning: Old Irish 'strong one', 'mighty one' or Old Norse 'mountain stronghold'.
A Swedish short form of Bridget q.v. from the form Brigitta.

Variations and abbreviations: Birte, Birtha, Brita, Britta. See Birgitta.

Bronwen

Origin/meaning: Old Welsh 'white breast'.
Common in Wales but rare elsewhere. It is a name which features in the collection of Welsh mythological tales 'The Mabinogion'.

Variations and abbreviations: Bron, Bronwyn.

Brooke

Origin/meaning: Old English 'brook'.
A common last name used as a first name, particularly in the US.

Variations: Brooks.

Brunhilda

Origin/meaning: Old German 'breast plate of battle', 'battle maid'.
The name of one of the Valkyrie, the twelve nymphs of Valhalla in ancient German and Norse legend. The name became known in English-speaking countries because of the popularity of Wagner's opera sequence 'The Ring of the Niebelung'.

Bryony

Origin/meaning: a climbing plant found in English hedgerows.

Buffy

Origin/meaning: Hebrew 'God is my satisfaction'.
A pet form of Elizabeth that has become known as a first name because of the TV series 'Buffy, the Vampire Slayer'.

Bunty

Origin/meaning: a term of endearment probably meaning plump or cuddly.
See also Bonnie.

Cadence
Origin/meaning: Latin 'rhythm'.
Variations: Cadena, Cadenza (Ital).

Caitlin
Origin/meaning: uncertain. Possibly Greek 'pure'.
An old Irish form of Kathleen.
Variation: Catlin (Eng), Kaitlin, Katelyn, Katlyn.

Callista
Origin/meaning: Greek 'most beautiful'.
Variations and abbreviations: Calesta, Calista, Callie, Calysta, Kalista.

Calypso
Origin/meaning: Greek 'concealer'.
In Greek myth Calypso was a nymph, Queen of the Isle of Ogygia (Gozo, near Malta) who kept Odysseus as her captive.

Camilla
Origin/meaning: Latin 'attendant at a sacrifice'.
Camilla was a female attendant. In the 18th-century Camilla became quite popular.
Variations and abbreviations: Cam, Camila (Sp), Camille (Fr), Cammie, Kamilla (Ger), Millie, Milly.

Camille
Origin/meaning: Latin 'attendant at a sacrifice'.
The French version of the Latin/Italian name Camilla q.v.

Candace (pron. Cánndiss)
Origin/meaning: Greek 'glittering', 'bright white'.
One of many names which mean white.
Variations and abbreviations: Candi, Candice, Candie, Candy, Kandace, Kandy.

Candida
Origin/meaning: Latin 'white', 'fair', 'pure'.
The name was given some currency in the last century by George Bernard Shaw's play 'Candida', 1898.
Variations and abbreviations: Candi, Candide (Fr), Candy, Kandida (Ger).

Cara (pron. Cárr-a)

Origin/meaning: either Latin 'beloved' or Old Irish 'friend'.
Only becoming popular in the 20th century in English-speaking countries.

Variations: Carina (It), Carita (It), Carrie, Carry, Kara (US) (Kara is also pron. Care-uh).

Carla

Origin/meaning: Old German 'man', meaning by association 'womanly'.
An Italian feminine form of Charles q.v.

Carlotta

Origin/meaning: Old German 'man', meaning by association 'womanly'.
An Italian feminine form of Charles q.v.

Carly

Origin/meaning: Old German 'man', meaning by association 'womanly'.
A pet form of feminine versions of Charles.

Variations: Carlie, Karlie, Karly.

Carmel

Origin/meaning: Hebrew 'garden'.
The name of the famous Mountain in Israel, Mount Carmel.

Variations and abbreviations: Carmela (It), Carmelina, Carmelita, Carmen (Sp), Carmencita, Carmina, Carmine, Carmita, Charmaine (Fr), Lita.

Carmen

Origin/meaning: Hebrew 'garden' or occasionally Latin 'song', 'poem'.
The Spanish form of Carmel q.v. The title of Bizet's opera.

Variations and abbreviations: Carma, Carmencita, Charmaine (Fr), Carmina.

Carol

Origin/meaning: Old German 'man', meaning by association 'womanly'.
A comparatively recent 20th-century name, Carol is connected to other feminine versions of Charles q.v. It may have begun as a shortened form of the 18th-century form Caroline.

Variations and abbreviations: Carola, Carole (Fr), Carroll, Carrie, Caryl, Carry, Karol, Karole, Karroll, Karoly.

Caroline

Origin/meaning: Old German 'man', meaning by association 'womanly'.
A feminine form of Charles introduced into England from Germany, when Caroline of Brandenburg-Anspach married the future George II.

Variations and abbreviations: Carlin, Carlina, Carlyn, Carlynn, Caro, Carolin, Carolina (It/Sp), Carolyn, Carolynn, Carolynne, Carrie, Karoline (Ger), Karolyn, Lyn.

Casey

Origin/meaning: Greek 'unheeded prophetess'.
The popular boy's name derives from the 19th-century hero train driver of the 'Cannonball Express' who saved the lives of passengers at the expense of his own.

Cassandra

Origin/meaning: Greek, uncertain, possibly 'disbelieved by men'.
Cassandra was a Trojan prophetess and the sister of their hero Hector.

Variations and abbreviations: Casandra (Sp), Cass, Cassandre (Fr), Cassandry, Cassie, Cassy, Sandie, Sandy.

Catharine/Catherine

Origin/meaning: uncertain; possibly Greek 'pure'.
A variant spelling of Katherine q.v.

Variations and abbreviations: Caitlin (Ir), Caitrin (It), Cass, Cassy, Catalina (Sp), Catarina (It), Cate, Caterina, Cath, Catharina, Catherina, Cathie, Cathleen (Ir), Cathlene, Cathrine, Cathryn, Cathy, Catie, Catriona (Scot). See also Katherine.

Catriona

Origin/meaning: uncertain, possibly Greek 'pure'.
Scottish form of Katharine q.v. Used by Robert Louis Stevenson as the title of one of his novels in 1893.

Variations and abbreviations: See Kathleen, Katharine.

Cecilia

Origin/meaning: Latin 'blind'.
Popular in the Middle Ages. St Cecilia was a martyr whose cult began in the 6th century and she became patron saint of music.

Variations and abbreviations: Caecilia, Celia, Cis.

Cecily (pron. Sissillee or Sessillee)

Origin/meaning: Latin 'blind'. From the Roman family Caecilius.
Introduced into Britain by William the Conqueror, who gave it to one of his daughters.

Variations and abbreviations: Cecil, Cécile (Fr), Cecilia, Celia, Cicely, Cissie, Cissy, Sheila, Shelagh (Ir), Sisley, Sissie, Sissy, Zazilie, Zilla.

Celeste

Origin/meaning: Latin 'heavenly'.
A French variation of Celia q.v.

Variations and abbreviations: Cele, Celesta, Celestia, Celestina (It), Celestine (Fr), Celestyn, Celestyna, Celina.

Celia

Origin/meaning: either 'heavenly' from the Ancient Roman family Caelius or 'blind' from the Ancient Roman family Caecilius.

Variations and abbreviations: Caelia, Celiana (It), Célie (Fr), Celeste (Fr), Celestine (Fr), Zilia.

Chandra (pron. Chandráh)

Origin/meaning: Sanskrit 'moon'.

Chantal (pron. Shontell)

Origin/meaning: A French place-name, Chantal or Cantal.
It honors St Jeanne Françoise de Chantal, 1572–1641, founder of a religious order.

Chardonnay

Origin/meaning: a white wine made from the grape of the same name.
First used as a given name when used as the name of a scheming female main character in the British TV drama series 'Footballers' Wives'.

Charis (pron. Káriss)

Origin/meaning: Greek 'grace', 'love'.
A 17th-century literary name. Also the origin of the word Charisma which means an ability to inspire devotion.

Variations and abbreviations: Carissa, Carrie, Charissa. See also Grace.

Charity

Origin/meaning: Greek 'grace', Latin 'affection', English 'charity', 'Christian love'.
One of the three virtues, spoken of by St Paul: 'And now abideth faith, hope, charity, these three; but the greatest of these is charity'.

Variations and abbreviations: Carita (It), Caritina (It), Chattie, Cherry. See also Charis.

Charlene

Origin/meaning: Old German 'man', meaning by implication 'womanly'.
A feminine form of Charles popular in the US.

Variations: Carleen, Carlene, Carline, Charleen, Karleen, Karlene, Sharleen, Sharline.

Charlotte (pron. Shárlott)

Origin/meaning: Old German 'man', meaning by implication 'womanly'.
One of many feminine forms of Charles.

Variations and abbreviations: Carlota, Carlotta (It), Charleen, Charlene, Charlie, Charlotta, Chatty, Karlotta, Karlotte, Lola, Lolita, Lotta, Lotte, Lotti, Lottie, Tot, Tottie. See also Carla, Carol, Caroline and Cheryl.

Charmaine

Origin/meaning: Hebrew 'garden'.
The French form of the Irish Carmel and Spanish Carmen.

Chausiku (pron. Chaooséekoo)

Origin/meaning: Swahili 'born at night'.

Chere (pron. Shehr)

Origin/meaning: French 'dear', 'darling'.
A French adjective used mainly in North America as a given name.

Variations and abbreviations: Cher, Chérie (Fr), Chery, Cherry, Sher, Sherry.

Cheryl

Origin/meaning: Old German 'man', usually given as 'womanly'.
Short form of Charlotte q.v.

Variations and abbreviations: Charil, Charyl, Cherlyn, Cherry, Sharyl, Sheryl.

Chipo

Origin/meaning: Shona 'gift'.
A Zimbabwe name.

Chiquita

Origin/meaning: Spanish 'little one'.
An endearment sometimes used as an independent name.

Chitra

Origin/meaning: Hindu 'picture'.

Chloë (pron. Klo-ee)
Origin/meaning: Greek 'a tender green shoot'.

Chris
Origin/meaning: Latin 'Christian' or 'Christ bearer'.

A short form of Christian, Christopher or Christine, sometimes used as an independent name.

Variations: Cris, Kris.

Christabel
Origin/meaning: Greek/Latin 'beautiful Christian'.

A Medieval English first name used by Samuel Taylor Coleridge as the title of one of his best-known poems, 'Christabel', 1816.

Variations and abbreviations: Chris, Christabell, Christabella, Christabelle, Christobel, Christobella, Christy.

Christiana
Origin/meaning: Latin 'Christian'.

Used as a Christian name since the early Middle Ages.

Variations and abbreviations: Cairistiona (Scot), Chris, Christian, Christiania, Christiane (Fr), Cristiana (It), Cristiona (Ir), Kristyan.

Christine/Christina
Origin/meaning: Old English 'Christian'.

The English version was Latinized as Christina. St Christine was an early Christian martyr.

Variations and abbreviations: Chris, Chrissie, Chrissy, Christa, Christen, Christer, Christiana, Christie, Christin (Ger), Christy, Christyna, Cris, Crissie, Crissy, Cristie, Cristina (It/Sp), Cristine, Cristy, Kirsteen (Scot), Kirsten (Scand), Kirstyan, Kris, Krissie, Kristina, Krystyna, Tina.

Ciara
Origin/meaning: Old Irish 'dark haired'.

The feminine equivalent of the Irish masculine Kieran.

Variation: Ciaran.

Cindy
Origin/meaning: a pet form, particularly popular in the US, of names like Lucinda and Cynthia q.v.

Variation: Sindy.

C

Claire/Clare

Origin/meaning: Latin 'bright', 'distinguished'.
The veneration of St Clare of Assisi, 1193–1253, a friend of St Francis and founder of the Order of Nuns the Poor Clares, led to the name's increasing popularity.
Variations: Chiara (It), Clair, Clara, Clarabelle, Claribel, Clarice, Clarie, Clarinda, Clarissa, Clarita (Sp), Clarrie, Klara (Ger), Klarissa.

Claudette

Origin/meaning: Latin 'lame'.
A French pet form of Claudia q.v.

Claudia

Origin/meaning: Latin 'lame'.
Used in England since the end of the 16th century, Claudia is mentioned in the second Epistle of St Paul to Timothy.
Variations: Claude (Fr), Claudette, Claudie, Claudina, Claudine, Gladys, Gwladys (Wel), Klaudia (Ger).

Clea

Origin/meaning: a name used by Lawrence Durrell in his novel sequence 'The Alexandria Quartet'. It may be a form of Clio q.v.

Clementine

Origin/meaning: Latin 'gentle', 'merciful'.
A feminine form of Clement.
Variations and abbreviations: Clementia, Clementina, Klementina.

Cleo

Origin/meaning: Greek 'fame', 'renown'.
A short form of Cleopatra which means 'renown of the father'.

Clio

Origin/meaning: Greek 'I celebrate', 'I proclaim'.
In Greek and Roman mythology Clio was the goddess of epic poetry and history.

Clodagh (pron. Clóh-duh)

Origin/meaning: Irish. It is the name of a river in Tipperary.
A 20th-century innovation, it rapidly became popular in Ireland.

Colette

Origin/meaning: Greek/Old French 'victory of the people'.
A diminutive of Nicolette. The French author, Colette, who wrote 'Gigi', boosted the name's popularity in the 20th century.
Variations: Colecta, Coletta, Collette.

Colleen

Origin/meaning: Old Irish 'girl'.

Connie

Origin/meaning: Latin 'constancy'.
A short form of Constance sometimes used as an independent name.

Constance

Origin/meaning: Latin 'constancy'.
The name of one of William I's daughters, it was introduced into England at the Conquest.
Variations and abbreviations: Con, Conni, Connie, Conny, Constancia, Constancy, Constantia, Constanze, Costanza (It), Konstanze (Ger).

Consuelo (pron. Konsooélla)

Origin/meaning: Spanish 'consolation'.
This is a short version of Our Lady of Consolation, a popular epithet of the Virgin Mary in Spain where it is Nuestra Señora
del Consúelo.
Variations and abbreviations: Connie, Consolata, Consuela. See also Mercedes.

Coral

Origin/meaning: Greek 'red-pink coral'.
A name introduced at the end of the 19th century.
Variations: Coralie (Fr), Coraline.

Cordelia

Origin/meaning: uncertain. Possibly Old Welsh 'jewel of the sea' or Latin 'warmhearted'.
The Latinized Celtic name Cordula may be the origin of the name Cordeilla, which Shakespeare adapted for the heroine of his play 'King Lear'.
Variations and abbreviations: Cordélie (Fr), Cordey, Cordie, Cordula, Cordy, Delia, Della, Kordela (Ger), Kordelia, Kordula.

Corinna

Origin/meaning: Greek, from the word 'maiden'.

An ancient Greek name sometimes used for the goddess of Spring, Persephone.

Variations: Corena, Corene, Corina, Corinne (Fr).

Cornelia

Origin/meaning: Latin, from the influential Roman family Cornelius. The name may be from 'horn' which implies kingship.

The feminine form of Cornelius q.v. It was the name of Julius Caesar's first wife.

Variations and abbreviations: Cornela, Cornelie (Fr), Cornie, Corry, Kornelia (Ger), Nelia, Nell, Nelly.

Cosima

Origin/meaning: Greek 'order', 'harmony', 'the universe'.

Italian feminine form of Cosmo q.v.

Variation: Kosima (Ger).

Courtney

Origin/meaning: either Old French 'short nose' or de Courtenay, an aristocratic family from Courtenay in France.

The family name of the West Country Earls of Devon. It was particularly successful in the US.

Variations and abbreviations: Court, Courtnay, Curt.

Cressida

Origin/meaning: Greek 'daughter of the golden one'.

The name Crysëis was wrongly used by Boccacio for the faithless daughter of Calchas. He adapted the name slightly to Chryseida and Chaucer altered it further to Criseyde.

Abbreviation: Cressy.

Crystal

Origin/meaning: Greek 'clear-ice', 'crystal'.

A modern girl's name dating from the end of the 19th century

Variations: Chrystal, Krystle.

Cynthia

Origin/meaning: Greek 'from Mount Cynthia'.

A title used for Artemis, the Greek goddess of chastity and hunting, who was born on Mount Cynthos.

Variations and abbreviations: Cimmie, Cindee, Cindie, Cindy, Cynthie. See also Phoebe.

Dagmar

Origin/meaning: Old German 'glory of the Danes'.

A Danish name. The Empress Dagmar of Russia was a sister of Queen Alexandra.

Daisy

Origin/meaning: Old English 'day's eye'. The name of a flower.

A late 19th-century name. Sometimes it was used as a pet name for Margaret, since its French equivalent, Marguerite, is the French word for a daisy.

Damayanti

Origin/meaning: Sanskrit 'subduing (men by beauty)'.

In Hindu legend, the name of a beautiful princess whose courtship with her husband, Prince Nala, was carried out by the mediation of swans.

Dana (pron. Day-nuh)

Origin/meaning: uncertain, possibly Scandinavian 'Danish'.

Danielle

Origin/meaning: Hebrew 'God has judged'.

French feminine form of Daniel q.v.

Variations and abbreviations: Danella, Danelle, Danette, Daniela (It/Sp), Darnella, Dannie, Danny.

Daphne

Origin/meaning: Greek 'laurel bush', 'bay tree'.

Daphne in Greek mythology was a nymph loved by Apollo. She called on the gods to help her elude his advances and they obliged by turning her into a laurel bush. The name came into use as a girl's name at the end of the 19th century.

Variations and abbreviations: Dafne, Daffie, Daph.

Darcy

Origin/meaning: Old French 'from Arcy', Old Irish 'dark man'.

This is a name that came to England as a last name with William the Conqueror.

Variations and abbreviations: D'Arcy, Darsey, Darsy.

Darlene

Origin/meaning: Old English 'darling'.

Modern feminine version of the much older established masculine name Daryl q.v. Found mainly in North America.

Variations and abbreviations: Darla, Darleen, Darelle, Daryl, Darylyne.

Davina

Origin/meaning: Hebrew 'darling', 'friend'.

A Scottish feminine form of David. Dating from the 17th century.

Variations and abbreviations: Davida (Eng), Davidina, Davinia, Davita, Veda, Vida, Vita.

Dawn

Origin/meaning: English 'sunrise'.

A modern 20th-century innovation. There are many names of differing origins with the same meaning including Aurora, Zara, Roxanne and Oriana.

Deborah

Origin/meaning: Hebrew 'bee'.

Deborah was a Jewish prophetess (Judges 5). The name's great popularity in the 20th century is perhaps because of the influence of film stars such as Debbie Reynolds and Deborah Kerr.

Variations and abbreviations: Deb, Debor, Debora, Debra, Debbie, Debby. See also Melissa.

Deirdre

Origin/meaning: Old Irish 'sorrowful' or 'raging'.

Deirdre was the tragic heroine of a Celtic legend, in which she committed suicide following the death of her lover and his brothers. W. B. Yeats wrote 'Deirdre' in 1907 and J. M. Synge wrote 'Deirdre of the Sorrows' in 1910, both based on the same legend.

Variations and abbreviations: Dede, Dee, Deerdre, Didi.

Delia

Origin/meaning: Greek 'from Delos'.

Delia is one of the names given to the Greek goddess Artemis, in this case because she came from the island of Delos. It may sometimes be used as a short form of Cordelia q.v.

Variations and abbreviations: Dee, Della, Didi.

Delilah

Origin/meaning: Hebrew 'delight'.

A Biblical name. Delilah betrayed Samson to the Philistines by cutting off the hair from which he derived his great strength (Judges 13–16).

Della

Origin/meaning: Old German 'noble'.

Familiar form of names such as Adèle and Delia, sometimes used as an independent name, particularly in North America.

Delmar

Origin/meaning: Spanish 'of the sea'.

Found in the US and Australia.

Variation: Delma.

Delphine

Origin/meaning: either Greek 'from Delphi' or Greek 'Delphinium' (a plant with a nectary resembling a dolphin). Delphine is the French version.

Variations and abbreviations: Delfa, Delpha, Delfina (It/Sp), Delfine (Ger), Delphina.

Denise

Origin/meaning: Greek, from the name of the god of fertility Dionysus.
French feminine version of Dennis.

Variations and abbreviations: Denice, Deniece, Denis, Denny, Denyse, Dion, Dionne.

Désirée (pron. Dáyzeeray)

Origin/meaning: Latin/French 'desired', 'longed for'.
This name arrived from France in the 20th century.

Variations: Desiderata, Desideria (Ger), Desire.

Devi

Origin/meaning: Sanskrit 'goddess'.
The feminine form of Dev that in Hindu texts is used to refer to the wife of Shiva.

Diana

Origin/meaning: Latin 'divine'. The Roman equivalent of Artemis, the Greek goddess of chastity, hunting and the moon.
The classical name came into use in Europe in the 16th and 17th centuries.

Variations and abbreviations: Deana, Deanna, Dede, Dee, Di, Diane (Fr), Dianna, Dianora (It), Didi, Dyana, Dyanna.

Dido

Origin/meaning: obscure, possibly Greek 'teacher'.
Dido was the legendary founder and Queen of Carthage.

Dilys

Origin/meaning: Welsh 'perfect' or 'pure'.
A recent Welsh name used in the last hundred years.

Dinah

Origin/meaning: Hebrew 'lawsuit' therefore 'avenged'.
In Genesis ch.34, Dinah is the daughter of Leah and Jacob. When she is dishonored by Shechem her brothers avenge her.

Variations and abbreviations: Dena, Di, Dina.

Dionne

Origin/meaning: Greek 'follower of Dionysus'.
A modern version of Denise q.v. found particularly in the US.

Variations: Dion, Dione, Dionis.

Divina

Origin/meaning: Latin 'divine' or 'super-human'.
A Latin adjective occasionally used as a first name.

Dolly

Origin/meaning: Greek 'gift of God'.
A short form of Dorothy q.v. which had been used as an independent name since the Middle Ages. It was so popular that in the 18th century it became the word which we still use today for toy babies.
Variations and abbreviations: Dol, Doll, Dollie.

Dominique

Origin/meaning: Latin 'of the Lord'.
French feminine form of Dominic q.v. equivalent of the Medieval English Dominica. It is sometimes used for a child born on Sunday, the Lord's day.

Donatella

Origin/meaning: Latin 'given'.
A pet form of Donata that is in turn a feminine form of Donato, a popular Renaissance name. Donatella is most famous for being the name of the fashion designer Donatella Versace, the sister of Gianni Versace, who took over the business in 1997.

Dora

Origin/meaning: Greek 'gift'.
A short form of Dorothy or Theodora q.v. it became popular as a name in its own right at the end of the 19th century.
Variations and abbreviations: Dodie, Doralyn, Dorelle, Dorena, Doretta, Dorja (Russ), Dorrie, Doro, Dory.

Doreen

Origin/meaning: uncertain, either Old Irish 'sullen' or an Irish diminutive of Dorothy
Introduced into England from Ireland around the turn of the century.
Variations and abbreviations: Dora, Dorene, Dorine.

Doris

Origin/meaning: Greek 'gift'.
The name of a nymph in Greek mythology and the name of a small independent country in Ancient Greece. It came into use in the 19th century. Despite its apparent classical origins it is also likely to be a variation of the once popular Dorothy q.v.
Variations and abbreviations: Dorice, Dorise, Dorita, Dorris, Dory.

Dorothy

Origin/meaning: Greek 'gift of God'.

A back-to-front version of Theodora q.v. which has the same meaning. The name was not found in England until the 16th century. At the end of the 18th century the Latinized Dorothea became fashionable. The Scottish/Irish short form Dorrit, Dickens used for his novel 'Little Dorrit', 1857.

Variations and abbreviations: Darja (Russ), Dody, Doll, Dollie, Dolly, Dora, Doreen (Ir), Dorinda, Dorofeja (Russ), Doro, Dorotea (It/Sp), Dorothea (Ger), Dorothée (Fr), Dorrit (Ir), Dortea (Dan), Dorthea (Dan), Dorthy, Dory, Dot, Dottie, Dotty.

Drew

Origin/meaning: Old German 'bearer' or Old French 'vigorous'.

This is the Medieval English form of the name Drogo, by way of the French form Dru.

Variations: Drogo, Dru.

Dulcie

Origin/meaning: Latin 'sweet'.

Since the Middle Ages there have been names derived from dulcis, the Latin word meaning sweet. They include Dulcia and Dulcibelle, a typical 18th-century variation.

Variations and abbreviations: Delcine, Dulce, Dulcea, Dulcia, Dulciana, Dulcibelle, Dulcine, Dulcinea, Dulcy.

Dusty

Origin/meaning: Old German 'brave warrior'.

Known as a boy's name until the 1960s when it was made popular as a feminine name by the singer Dusty Springfield.

Edie

Origin/meaning: Old English 'rich war'.

A form of Edith that has become fashionable as a given name in recent times.

Ebony

Origin/meaning: a name that derives from the shiny black wood.

Edina

Origin/meaning: Old English 'rich friend'.

This is a Scottish variation of Edwina, the feminine form of Edwin q.v.

Edith

Origin/meaning: Old English 'rich war'.

This is the modern form of the Anglo-Saxon name Eadgyth.

Variations and abbreviations: Eaditha (Med Eng), Eda, Ede, Edie, Edita (It), Editha, Edithe, Edwa, Edyth, Eyde, Eydie.

Edna

Origin/meaning: uncertain, Hebrew 'rejuvenation'.

A Biblical name which occurs several times in the Apocrypha.

Variations and abbreviations: Ed, Eddie, Ednah.

Edwina

Origin/meaning: Old English 'rich friend'.
A 19th-century feminine form of Edwin q.v.

Variations: Edina (Scot), Edwine.

Effie

Origin/meaning: Greek 'fair speech', implying either 'silence' or 'honor'.
A short form of Euphemia. Used in the 19th century particularly in Scotland.

Eileen (pron. Eyeleen or Evleen)

Origin/meaning: Greek 'light' or 'bright' or Old Irish 'pleasant'.
This name is often used in Ireland as the Irish equivalent of Helen q.v.

Variations and abbreviations: Aileen, Eily, Eveline.

Eirwen

Origin/meaning: Welsh 'white snow'.
A modern name with an ancient feel.

Eithne

Origin/meaning: Old Irish 'little fire', 'little fiery one'.
The modern spelling of the Old Irish name Aithne q.v.

Variation: Ethne. See also Ena.

Elaine

Origin/meaning: Greek 'light' or 'bright'.
The Medieval French form of the Greek name Helen q.v.

Variations: Elain, Elana, Elane, Elayne.

Eleanor

Origin/meaning: Greek 'bright', 'light'.
Again this is a Medieval French form of the Greek name Helen q.v. The name gained popularity because of Edward I's much loved queen, Eleanor of Castile.

Variations and abbreviations: Alienore, Eleanora, Eléanore (Fr), Elenore, Eleonore (It), Elianora, Elinor, Elinore, Ella, Ellie, Elly, Leonor (Sp), Lenore, Leonora, Leonore, Nell, Nellie, Nelly, Nora.

Elfrida

Origin/meaning: Old English 'elf-strength'.
A pre-Conquest Anglo-Saxon name.

Variations and abbreviations: Elfreda, Elfrid, Freda.

Eliana

Origin/meaning: Greek 'sun'.

This is an Italian name occasionally used in English-speaking countries.

Elise

Origin/meaning: Hebrew 'God is my satisfaction'.

A French short form of Elizabeth now used as an independent name.

Variation: Elyse.

Eliza

Origin/meaning: Hebrew 'God is my satisfaction'.

A short form of Elizabeth. Used as a pet name for Elizabeth I in the 16th century.

Variations and abbreviations: Lisa, Liza, Elisa, Elise (Fr). See also Elizabeth.

Elizabeth

Origin/meaning: Hebrew 'God is my satisfaction'.

This is the usual English spelling of the name. It comes via the Latin spelling whereas the continental spelling, using 's' instead of 'z', comes directly from the Greek.

Variations and abbreviations: Babette (Fr), Belita (Sp), Belle, Bess, Bessie, Bessy, Beth, Betsey, Betsy, Betta, Bette, Betti, Bettie, Bettina (It), Bettine (Fr), Betty, Ealasaid (Scot Gaelic), Eilis (Ir), Elisa (It), Elisabet (Scand), Elisabeth, Elisabetta (It), Elise (Fr), Elissa (It), Eliza, Elizabella, Elizabet, Elly, Elsa (Ger/Dut/Scand), Elsbeth (Scot), Else (Ger/Dut/Scand), Elsey, Elsie (Scot), Elspet (Scot), Elspeth (Scot), Elsy, Elyse, Helsa, Isabel, Isabella (Sp/It), Isabetta (It), Isobel (Scot), Lib, Libbie, Libby, Liesel (Ger), Lieschen (Ger), Lillibet, Lisa, Lisabeth, Lisavetta (Slav), Lisbeth, Lise (Ger), Liselotte (Ger), Lisette (Fr), Lissa, Liz, Liza, Lizabeth, Lizbeth, Lizzie, Lizzy, Ysabel (and see Isabel).

Ella

Origin/meaning: uncertain, probably Old German 'all'.

A popular medieval name brought to England by the Normans.

Variations: Ellaline, Ellie, Elly.

Ellen

Origin/meaning: Greek 'light' or 'bright'.

This is the form of Helen used in medieval England and pre-Conquest Scotland and Wales.

Variations and abbreviations: Ella, Ellie, Ellin, Ellyn.

Eloïse (pron. Elloweeze)

Origin/meaning: Old German 'flourishing and strong'.

Variations: Eloisa (It), Helewise (Med Eng), Héloïse (Fr).

Elsa

Origin/meaning: Old German 'noble' or Hebrew 'God is my satisfaction'.
This predominantly German name was introduced to English-speaking countries in the 19th century when Wagner used it for the heroine of his opera 'Lohengrin', 1848.

Variations: Else, Ilsa, Ilse. See also Elizabeth.

Elspeth

Origin/meaning: Hebrew 'God is my satisfaction'.
An almost exclusively Scottish variation of Elizabeth.

Variations and abbreviations: Eilasaid, Elsbeth, Elsie, Elspet, Elspie.

Eluned (pron. Éllinedd)

Origin/meaning: uncertain. Possibly a reference to the Old Welsh word meaning 'idol'.
A popular Welsh name occasionally used in England.

Variations and abbreviations: Eiluned, Elined, Linet, Luned, Lyn, Lynn, Lynnet, Lynette.

Elvira

Origin/meaning: uncertain, possibly Old German 'elf-counsel' or 'elf-ruler'.
This is a Spanish name which is found several times in literature, most notably as the woman seduced by Don Juan and as the heroine of Verdi's opera 'Ernani'.

Variation: Elvire (Fr).

Emily

Origin/meaning: Latin, from the Roman clan name Aemelius.
This is a Medieval Italian name popularized by the Italian Renaissance poet Boccaccio.

Variations and abbreviations: Amalia, Aimil (Scot), Em (Med Eng), Emalia, Emelye, Emerlee, Emilia (It/Sp), Emilie (Ger), Émilie (Fr), Emmie, Emmy.

Emma

Origin/meaning: Old German 'universal' or from the name of the Teutonic god-hero Irmin.
This name probably began as a short form of names like Ermintrude and Ermendard.

Variations and abbreviations: Em, Emm, Emmie, Emmot, Erma (Ger), Imma, Irma (Ger).

Emmanuelle

Origin/meaning: Hebrew 'God with us'.
Feminine form of Emanuel q.v.

Emmeline

Origin/meaning: Old German 'little industrious one'.

This is a diminutive of Amalburga, the original form of Amelia q.v. and introduced to England by the Normans.

Variations and abbreviations: Amelia, Em, Emblem, Emblin, Emelia, Emlin, Emlyn, Emmaline, Emmy.

Ena

Origin/meaning: Old Irish 'little fire' or 'little fiery one'.

This is an English form of the Celtic name Aine (pron. Awnye) who was Queen of the Fairies. Although generally considered Irish the name is increasingly found in Scotland.

Enid

Origin/meaning: uncertain, possibly Welsh 'tree-bark'.

This is another of the names, probably Welsh in origin, which have become more widely familiar through the tales of King Arthur and his Knights.

Erica

Origin/meaning: Old Norse 'ever-ruling'.

This is the feminine form of Eric q.v. Although popular for over 1000 years in Scandinavia it was not used in England until the 19th century.

Variations and abbreviations: Eri, Ericha, Erika (Ger/Scand), Rickie, Rikkie.

Erin

Origin/meaning: Old Irish 'peace'.

This is an alternative Celtic name for Ireland. Its use as a personal name is modern.

Variations: Erina, Erinna.

Ermintrude

Origin/meaning: Old German 'universal strength' or 'strength of Irmin'.

A pre-Conquest name, it was revived in the early 19th century.

Variations and abbreviations: Ermentrude, Ermyntrude, Irmintrude, Trudie, Trudy.

Esmé

Origin/meaning: French/Latin 'loved'.

This is a variation of Amy q.v. introduced from France to Scotland in the 16th century.

Variations: see Amy.

Esmeralda

Origin/meaning: Spanish 'emerald'.

An extremely popular Spanish name.

Variations and abbreviations: Emerald, Esmé, Esmeraldah.

Esperanza

Origin/meaning: Latin 'hope'

A name popular in Spain and now the US.

Estelle

Origin/meaning: Latin 'star'.

This is a French form of the name Stella.

Variations and abbreviations: see Stella.

Esther

Origin/meaning: uncertain. Probably Persian 'myrtle' or 'star'.

In the book of the Old Testament which carries her name, Esther is a Jewess who is chosen by King Ahasueras for her great beauty.

Variations and abbreviations: Essa, Essie, Essy, Esta, Ester (It), Ettie, Etty, Hadassah, Hester, Hesther, Hettie, Hetty.

Ethel

Origin/meaning: Old English 'noble'.

This is a simplification of Aethel. The prefix Ethel was not used on its own in pre-Conquest times but always as part of the compound names such as Ethelred or Ethelfleda.

Variations and abbreviations: Eth, Ethyl.

Eugenia

Origin/meaning: Greek 'noble', 'well-born'.

The Italian feminine form of Eugene.

Variations and abbreviations: Eugénie (Fr), Gene, Genia, Ginny.

Eva

Origin/meaning: uncertain. Possibly Hebrew 'life-giving'.

The Latinized form of Eve q.v. In English-speaking countries it was used increasingly after the publication of Harriet Beecher Stowe's book 'Uncle Tom's Cabin', 1852, which had the popular character 'little Eva'.

Evangeline

Origin/meaning: Greek 'brings good news'.

Became familiar after Henry Wadsworth Longfellow used it for his 1848 poem 'Evangeline' whose heroine is Evangeline Bellefontaine.

Eve

Origin/meaning: uncertain. Possibly Hebrew 'life-giving'.

This is the name given to the first woman by Adam.

Variations: Eva, Evie, Evita (Sp).

Eveline/Evelyn (pron. Ehv-linn in US)

Origin/meaning: Old French 'hazel-tree' or Old Celtic 'pleasant'.

The variation Evelyn, which is now more popular than the original spelling, is probably copied from the masculine Evelyn, q.v.

Variations: Avelina, Aveline, Avelyn, Eveleen, Evelina, Evelyn.

Fabia (pron. Fáybea)

Origin/meaning: Latin: of the Roman Fabius family.

This name is the root form of the diminutives Fabiana and Fabiola.

Fahmida

Origin/meaning: Arabic 'learned man'.

The Urdu feminine form of Fahim.

Variation: Fizza

Faith

Origin/meaning: Latin 'trust', 'faith'.

This, with Hope and Charity, was one of the three virtues referred to by St Paul in his first Epistle to the Corinthians.

Abbreviation: Fay.

Fanny

Origin/meaning: Late Latin 'free' or 'from France'.

A familiar form of Frances q.v. Used since the 18th century as an independent name.

Variation and abbreviation: see Frances.

Fatima (pron. Fáhteema)

Origin/meaning: Arabic 'daughter of the prophet' or 'weaned'.

Fatima was the youngest daughter of the Prophet Mohammed. There is also a similar Swahili name Fatuma (weaned) used for Fatima in parts of Africa.

Fay

Origin/meaning: either 'fairy' or an abbreviation of Faith q.v.

Like May, which may be the month or an abbreviation of Mary, Fay is a name which originated in the 19th century.

Variations: Fayanne, Faye, Fayette (Fr).

Felicia

Origin/meaning: Latin 'fortunate'.

This is a feminine form of Felix. It was popular in the Middle Ages when it was probably given to honor St Felicia, one of the many early martyrs.

Variations and abbreviations: Felice, Felicity, Felis, Félise (Fr), Phelisia.

Felicity

Origin/meaning: Latin 'happiness'.

This name was adopted by 17th-century Puritans in preference to the saint's name Felicia.

Variations and abbreviations: Fee, Felicia, Félicité (Fr), Felicidad (Sp), Felicita (It), Felicissima (It), Felizia (Ger).

Fern

Origin/meaning: Sanskrit 'feather'.

This is the name of a woodland plant renowned for its feathery fronds.

Ffion (pron. Feeon)

Origin/meaning: Welsh 'roses'.

This is the Welsh equivalent of Rose or Rosanna.

Fidda

Origin/meaning: Arabic 'silver'.

A name that is particularly popular in Jordan.

Finola

Origin/meaning: Old Irish 'white shoulders'.

A modern Irish form of Fenella.

Fiona (pron. Feeówna)

Origin/meaning: Old Irish 'fair'.

This is a pen-name invented by the Scottish novelist William Sharp, 1855–1905.

Variations: Ffiona (Wel), Fionna.

Flavia (pron. Fláyvia)

Origin/meaning: Latin: from the Flavius family.

This was a Roman name and is thought to be derived from the word flavus – yellow.

Variations: Flaviana, Flavilla.

Fleur

Origin/meaning: French 'flower'.

This is a modern equivalent of the classical name Flora q.v.

Variations: Fflyr (Wel), Flora, Florence, Flore (Med Fr), Flower.

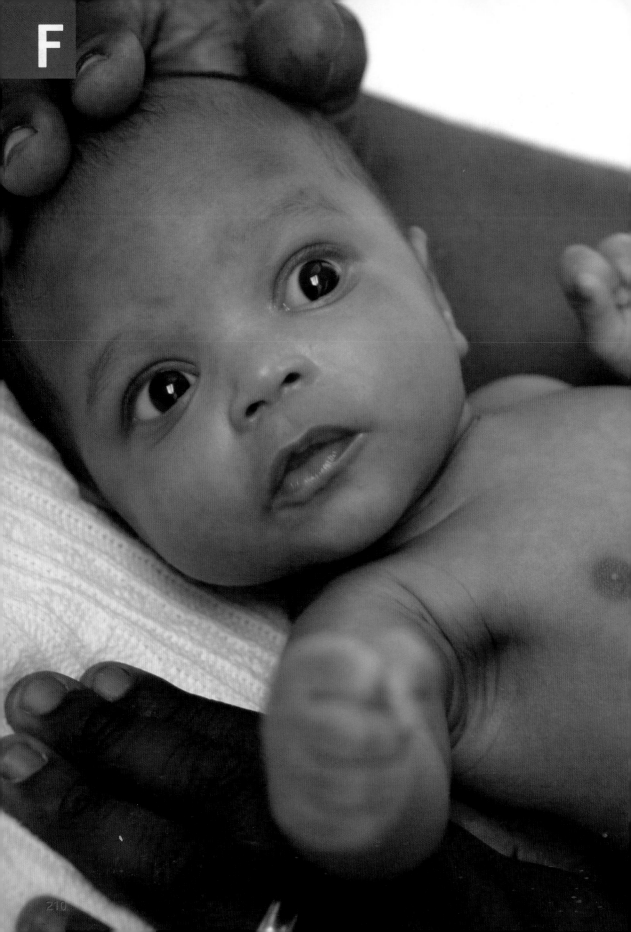

Flora

Origin/meaning: Latin. The name of the Roman goddess of flowers and spring. This name was used in the Middle Ages because of St Flora.

Variations and abbreviations: Fflyr (Wel), Fleur (Fr), Fleurette (Fr), Floella, Flor, Flore (Fr/Scot), Florella, Floretta, Floria, Floriane, Floris, Florrie. See also Fleur, Flower, Kusum.

Florence

Origin/meaning: Latin 'in bloom' or 'prosperous'.

This name, often in the Latin form of Florentia, was used in England in the Middle Ages.

Variations and abbreviations: Fiorenza (Ir), Flo, Flora, Florance, Flore, Florencia (Sp), Florentina, Florenza (It), Florentia (Ger), Florenzia (Ger), Florenzina, Floria, Florie, Florina, Florinda, Floris, Florrie, Florry, Flossie, Flossy.

Flossie

Origin/meaning: Latin 'in bloom' or 'prosperous'.

A familiar form of Florence q.v. which was sometimes used at the end of the 19th century when Florence was a vogue name.

Variations and abbreviations: see Florence.

Flower

Origin/meaning: 'a flower'.

This word, like the French Fleur, has occasionally been used as a first name.

Folukè (pron. Folóokee)

Origin/meaning: Yoruba 'placed in God's care'.

This name comes from Nigeria.

Fran

Origin/meaning: Old German 'a Frank', Medieval Latin 'from France'.

A short form of Frances q.v. sometimes used as an independent name.

Variations: see Frances.

Frances

Origin/meaning: Medieval Latin 'from France' or 'free'.

This is the feminine form of the masculine name Francis q.v. Like Francis it was introduced to England in the Tudor period.

Variations and abbreviations: Fan, Fanchette (Fr), Fanchon (Fr), Fancy (US), Fannie, Fanny, Fran, Francelia, Francesca (It), Francesse, Francine, Francisca (Sp/Port), Francoise (Fr), Francyne, Frangag (Wel), Frank, Frankie, Frannie, Franny, Franziska (Ger), Frasquita (Sp), Zissi.

Francesca (pron. Franchéska)

Origin/meaning: Medieval Latin 'from France'.

This is the Italian form of Frances q.v. It is the earliest form of the name although a name of similar origin, Franka, predates it.

Variations and abbreviations: see Frances.

Françoise (pron. Frónswahze)

Origin/meaning: Medieval Latin 'from France'.

This is the French form of Frances q.v. Like the Italian Francesca it dates from the 13th century and probably became established as a Christian name because of the fame of St Francis of Assisi who lived then. See Frances.

Freda

Origin/meaning: Old German 'peaceful friend'.

A short form of Frederica q.v., Alfreda or Winifred q.v. An alternative spelling of Frieda.

Frederica

Origin/meaning: Old German 'peace-rule'.

The feminine form of Frederick q.v. It dates from the 18th century when many masculine names were feminized on the Latin pattern by adding 'a'. Other examples are Augusta and Georgina.

Variations and abbreviations: Federica (It), Fred, Fredi, Freddie, Freddy, Fredericka, Frédérique (Fr), Friederike (Ger), Fritza, Fritzi, Rica, Ricki, Rickie, Ricky, Rikky, Rixi.

Freya

Origin/meaning: Old Norse. The goddess of love and of the night.

Freya was the equivalent in Norse mythology of the Roman goddess Venus.

Variations and abbreviations: Freia, Freija, Freja, Frigga.

Friday

Origin/meaning: Old Norse 'Freya's day' (Freya was the Norse goddess of love), or old English 'peace-strong' a corruption of Frideswide.

Frideswide (pron. Frids'wid)

Origin/meaning: Old English 'peace-strong'.

One of the few pre-Conquest names which survived the Norman Conquest. St Frideswide, d.735, was daughter of a Mercian king.

Variations and abbreviations: Frediswid, Frévisse (Fr), Friday, Frideswid, Frithswith (Old Eng), Fryswyde.

Gabrielle

Origin/meaning: Hebrew 'strong man of God'.
The Italian Gabriella and French/German Gabrielle are fairly recent feminine variations in English-speaking countries.

Variations and abbreviations: Gabey, Gabi, Gabie, Gabriela, Gabriel (Ger), Gabrielle (Fr), Gaby, Gabby, Gavrila (Russ).

Galina

Origin/meaning: Greek 'peace' or 'tranquility'.
A Russian name, which was very fashionable there in the 1960s. Also used in German-speaking countries.

Variations and abbreviations: Gala, Galya.

Gauri

Origin/meaning: Sanskrit 'white'.
In Hindu mythology a name of Shiva's wife, who after being teased by her husband for her dark complexion, meditated until it had turned fair.

Variation: Gowri

Gay

Origin/meaning: French 'merry', 'cheerful'.
This name, taken directly from the adjective, has come into use over the last 100 years.

Variations: Gae, Gaye.

Gaynor

Origin/meaning: Old Welsh 'fair and yielding' or 'white wave'.
This is a form of the Welsh name Guinevere q.v. the name of the wife of King Arthur.

Variations: Gaenor (Wel), Ganor, Gaynore, Guanor (Scot).

Geeta

Origin/meaning: Hindustani 'Holy Book'.
This is the Hindu equivalent of the Bible, being a collection of the sayings of Krishna.

Variation: Gita.

Gemma (pron. Jemma)

Origin/meaning: Latin 'jewel'.
A popular Italian name, its use in English-speaking countries dates only from this century

G

Genevieve (pron. Jéneveev)
Origin/meaning: uncertain. It includes the Gaulish French word for 'tribe' but the rest is unknown. An old French name, often considered a form or close relative of Guinevere q.v.
Variations and abbreviations: Geneviève (Fr), Genovefa (Ger), Genoveffa (It), Genoveva, Ginette, Vevo.

Georgette/Georgia
Origin/meaning: Greek 'farmer'.
Feminine forms of George q.v.

Georgiana
Origin/meaning: Greek 'farmer'.
A feminine form of George q.v. By the mid-19th century the slightly simpler form Georgina had superseded it.
Abbreviation: Georgie.

Geraldine
Origin/meaning: Old German 'spear-rule'.
This name originated as an adjective meaning 'of the Fitzgerald family'. Fitzgerald was the family name of the Earls of Kildare.
Variations and abbreviations: Geralda, Geralde (Ger), Geraldina, Geraldine (Fr), Gerolda, Gerrie, Gerry, Giralda (It), Jerrie, Jerry.

Gerda
Origin/meaning: Norse mythology. Gerda was the wife of Frey.
Gerda was used by the Danish writer Hans Christian Andersen for his story 'The Snow Queen'.

Germaine
Origin/meaning: Latin 'a German'.
This is the feminine form of German(us) through the French form Germain.
Variation: Germana (It).

Gertrude
Origin/meaning: Old German 'spear-strength'.
This was the name of one of the Valkyries, twelve maidens who accompanied the greatest warriors killed in battle to Valhalla to feast with Odin the chief of the gods.
Variations and abbreviations: Gartrude, Gattie, Gatty, Geldrude (It), Gerda, Gertie, Gertraud (Ger), Gertrud (Ger/Scand), Gertruda, Gertrudis (Ger), Gerty, Trudie, Trudy.

Gilda

Origin/meaning: Old English 'golden'.
A medieval name which probably began as a nickname.

Variations: Golda, Goldie, Goldy.

Gillian

Origin/meaning: from Julius, a Roman family name, possibly meaning 'dowry'.
This name developed in the Middle Ages as a feminine form of Julian.

Variations and abbreviations: Gill, Gillet, Gillie, Gilly, Giula (It), Giuletta (It), Giuliana (It), Jillian, Juli, Julia, Juliana, Juliann, Julie (Fr), Julienne, Juliane, Juliet, Julietta, Juliette (Fr), Julita, Julitta.

Gina (pron. Jéena)

Origin/meaning: Latin 'queen'.
This is a short form of Regina, a medieval name.

Ginger

Origin/meaning: a pet form of Virginia q.v. or a nickname for people with red hair.

Ginny

Origin/meaning: either Latin from Roman family Verginius ('Spring') or Latin 'maidenly'.
A short form of Virginia q.v. now commonly used as an independent name.

Gisela

Origin/meaning: Old German 'pledge'.
It has been an independent name for over a thousand years.

Variations and abbreviations: Ghislaine, Gila, Gisa, Gisèle (Fr), Giselle, Gisella (It).

Gladys

Origin/meaning: Latin 'lame' from Claudius, the name of two eminent Roman families. This is one of many Welsh surviving forms of Roman names.

Variations and abbreviations: Glad, Gladusa (Cornish), Gladuse (Cornish), Gwladus (Wel), Gwladys (Wel).

Gloria

Origin/meaning: Latin 'glory'.

Not used as a name until the late 19th century when it seems to have been introduced in the US.

Glynis

Origin/meaning: Welsh Celtic 'valley', 'glen'.

The feminine form of Glyn q.v.

Variations: Glenda, Glenna, Glennis, Glenys, Glynnis, Glynwen.

Godiva

Origin/meaning: Old English 'God's gift'.

Godiva was the wife of Leofric, Earl of Chester, and a generous benefactress of religious institutions.

Grace

Origin/meaning: Latin 'grace'.

Although used in the Middle Ages this name really established itself in England in the 17th century. Puritans on both sides of the Atlantic used it in the sense of God's favor or bounty.

Variations: Engracia (Sp), Gracia (Med Eng), Gracie, Gratia, Gratiana, Grayce, Grazia (It).

Gráinne

Origin/meaning: 'love'.

One of the most popular of the native Irish names brought back into use by the Celtic

Variations: Grace, Graidhne (Ir), Grainé, Grania.

Greta

Origin/meaning: Persian?/Greek/Latin 'pearl' or French/English 'daisy'.

A German and Scandinavian short form of Margaret q.v.

Variations: Greda, Greet (Dut), Grete, Gretchen (Ger), Gretel. See also Margaret.

Gudrun

Origin/meaning: Old English 'secret writing'.

Used by D. H. Lawrence in his novel 'Women in Love', 1920. In Scandinavian legend Gudrun was a model of patience.

Guinevere

Origin/meaning: Old Welsh 'fair and yielding' or 'white wave'. The wife of King Arthur.

Variations and abbreviations: Gaenor (Wel), Ganor, Gaynor (Med Eng), Gaynore, Genevieve, Ginevre (It), Guener, Guenever, Guenevere, Guenieve, Guenna, Gwenhwyvar (Old Wel), Gwenore (Med Eng), Jenifer (Cor), Jennifer, Vanora (Scot), Wander (Scot).

Gwawl

Origin/meaning: Welsh 'light'.

One of the native names coming back into use in Wales.

Gwen

Origin/meaning: Welsh 'white', 'fair'.

An independent name, the equivalent of the masculine Gwyn, q.v.

Variations: Gwenda, Gwenno.

Gwendolyn

Origin/meaning: Welsh 'white (fair) moon/circle/brow'.

Like several other Welsh names, Gwendolyn spread beyond Wales in the 19th century.

Variations and abbreviations: Guendolen, Guendoloena, Guenna, Gwen, Gwenda, Gwendolen (Wel), Gwendolin, Gwennie, Gwynne, Winnie, Wynne.

Gwyneth

Origin/meaning: Welsh 'white/fair maiden'.

This may be the same name as Gyneth, the daughter of King Arthur. Another meaning sometimes given is the area of North Wales known as Gwynedd.

Variations and abbreviations: Gwyn, Gwynaeth, Gwynedd, Gynedd.

Hannah

Origin/meaning: Hebrew 'grace', 'graceful'.

The name of the mother of the prophet Samuel.

Variations and abbreviations: Hana, Hanna, Hanni, Hannie, Hanny. See also Ann, Anna, Nancy.

Harriet

Origin/meaning: Old German 'home-ruler'.

An English feminine form of Henry from its Medieval English form Harry.

Variations and abbreviations: Harri, Harrie, Harrietta, Harriette, Harrio, Harriot, Hat, Hattie, Hatty.

Hasina

Origin/meaning: Swahili 'good'.

An East African name.

Variation: Hasanati.

Hayfa

Origin/meaning: Arabic 'slender'.

Hayley

Origin/meaning: Old English 'high clearing'.

A last name used as a first name.

Hazel

Origin/meaning: Old German 'hazel-tree'.

One of the many names taken from flowers and trees at the end of the 19th century.

Heather

Origin/meaning: Middle English 'heather'.

It was first used, with many other flower names, at the end of the 19th century.

Hebe (pron. Héebee)

Origin/meaning: Greek 'youth'.

In Greek mythology Hebe was the daughter of Zeus and Hera.

Hedda

Origin/meaning: Old German 'struggle'.

A short form of Hedwig q.v. long used in Germany and Scandinavia as an independent name.

Variations and abbreviations: see Hedwig.

Hedwig (pron. Hédveeg)

Origin/meaning: Old German 'battle struggle'.

This is the modern German form of a name which has existed for about 1500 years.

Variations and abbreviations: Avice (Eng), Avis, Edvige (Fr), Edwige (It), Haduwig, Hadwig, Heda, Hedda, Heddy, Hedy, Hedvig (Swed), Hetta, Hetti.

Helen

Origin/meaning: Greek 'light' or 'bright'.

This was the name of an early saint, the Empress Helen(a), 255–330.

Variations and abbreviations: Aileen (It), Eileen (Ir), Elaine (Old Fr), Elana, Elane, Elayne, Eleanor, Eleanora, Eleen, Elena (Sp/It), Eleni (Gr), Elenore, Eleonore, Elianora, Elinor, Elinore, Ella, Ellen, Ellene, Ellie, Elly, Ellyn, Elyn, Helena, Helene, Hélène (Fr), Ilene, Lana, Lena, Lenka (Russ), Lenore, Leonora, Nell, Nellie, Nelly.

Helena (pron. Helenuh)

Origin/meaning: Greek 'light' or 'bright'.

The Latinized form of the Greek name Helen q.v. Shakespeare used it in 'A Midsummer Night's Dream' and in 'All's Well That Ends Well'.

Variations and abbreviations: see Helen.

Helga

Origin/meaning: Old Norse 'holy'.

This name was introduced into England by Scandinavian invaders in the 9th century.

Variation: Olga (Russ).

Heloise (pron. Elloweeze)

Origin/meaning: Old German 'flourishing and strong'.

The Norman French version of an Old German name. The usual English form is Eloïse q.v.

Variations and abbreviations: see Eloïse.

Hema

Origin/meaning: Sanskrit 'gold'.

A name found throughout India. The masculine equivalent is Hemchandra.

Henrietta

Origin/meaning: Old German 'home-ruler'.

This is the Latinized form of Henriette, the French feminine form of Henry (Henri).

Variations and abbreviations: Enrichetta (It), Enriquetta (Sp/Port), Etta, Ettie, Etty, Hat, Hattie, Hatty, Heinrike (Ger), Hendrika (Dut), Henka, Hendrickje, Henna, Henrie, Henrieta, Henriette (Fr), Henryetta, Hetti, Hettie, Hetty.

Hermia

Origin/meaning: Greek mythology. Hermes was the messenger of the gods.
This is a feminine form of Hermes. Shakespeare used it for one of the characters in his play 'A Midsummer Night's Dream', 1594.

Hermione (pron. Herm´yohnee)

Origin/meaning: Greek mythology. Hermes was the messenger of the gods.
This, like Hermia q.v. is a feminine form of Hermes.

Hero

Origin/meaning: Greek 'chosen one'.
In Greek mythology Hera was the sister/wife of Zeus, the supreme god.

Hester

Origin/meaning: uncertain. Probably Persian 'myrtle' or 'star'.
A form of Esther q.v. which was popular in the 17th century.

Variations and abbreviations: Hetty, Hestor.

Hilary

Origin/meaning: Medieval Latin 'cheerful'.
The masculine and feminine forms of this medieval name are the same. The feast day of St Hilary (Hilaire) of Poitiers, 315–367, is January 14th.

Variations: Hilaire (Fr), Hilar (Ger), Hilario (Sp/Port), Hilarius (Dut/Ger/Scand), Ilario (It).

Hilda

Origin/meaning: Old German/Old English 'battle'.
Hild was the chief of the twelve Valkyrie in Norse mythology who rode through battles choosing who was to be slain and taken in glory to Valhalla.

Variations: Hild, Hilde, Hildy.

Holly

Origin/meaning: Old English 'holly tree'.
This is one of the flower names which came into fashion at the end of the 19th century.

Honey

Origin/meaning: Old English 'nectar'.
During the Middle Ages honey was used instead of sugar to sweeten food and drink and the word became a form of endearment.

Hope

Origin/meaning: Old English 'hope'.
This is one of the three virtues listed by St Paul in his first Epistle to the Corinthians.

Horatia (pron. Horáyshea)

Origin/meaning: Latin, from Horatius, the name of a patrician Roman clan.
The feminine form of Horace/Horatio.

Hyacinth

Origin/meaning: Greek 'hyacinth flower' or 'a red precious stone'.
In Greek mythology, Hyacinth was a beautiful boy loved by the sun god Apollo and Zephyr the West Wind.

Variations and abbreviations: see Jacintha.

Hypatia (pron. Hipáyshea)

Origin/meaning: Greek. Uncertain.
In 1853, Charles Kingsley, author of 'The Water Babies', and 'Hereward the Wake', wrote a novel based on the life of Hypatia (375–415) of Alexandria.

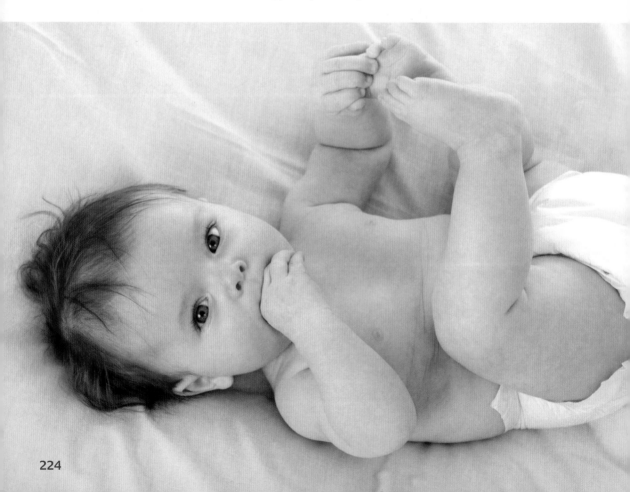

Ianthe (pron. Eeánnthee)

Origin/meaning: Greek 'violet flower'.

A name from Greek mythology; Ianthe was one of the sea nymphs.

Variation: Iantha. See also Violet and Hyacinth.

Ida

Origin/meaning: Old German 'industrious'.

Possibly derived from an Old German name Idaberga, the name was introduced into England by the Normans.

Ife (pron. Eefée)

Origin/meaning: Yoruba 'love'.

A popular Nigerian name.

See also Amy, Lerato.

Ignatia (pron. Ignáyshea)

Origin/meaning: uncertain. Possibly Latin 'fiery'.

A feminine form of Ignatius q.v. Usually used by Catholics.

Ila

Origin/meaning: Sanskrit 'world'.

Imogen

Origin/meaning: uncertain. Sometimes given as Old Irish 'girl' or 'daughter' or Greek 'beloved child'.

The regular use of this name in England dates from the present century, although a similar name, Imagina, was used in Europe in the Middle Ages.

Variations and abbreviations: Imagina, Imogene, Imogine, Immy, Innagon, Innogen.

India

Origin/meaning: Sanskrit 'river' or 'river Indus'.

The name of the country has sometimes been used by people who were born there.

Indira

Origin/meaning: Sanskrit 'moon'.

This is based on the same word as the name Indu q.v.

Indu (pron. Indhú)

Origin/meaning: Sanskrit 'moon'.

Indu was a famous female scholar who lived many thousands of years ago.

See also Chandra, Indira, Selina.

Inez

Origin/meaning: Greek 'pure', 'chaste'.

The Anglicized version of Ines, which is the Spanish equivalent of Agnes, q.v.

Variations: Ines, Inessa, Ynes, Ynez.

Inge

Origin/meaning: Old Norse/Old German Ingvi or Ing.

This name is extremely popular in Scandinavia and German-speaking countries.

Variations: Ing, Inga. See also the masculine name Ingmar.

Ingrid

Origin/meaning: Old Norse/Old German 'Ingvi's ride' or 'beloved of Ingvi'.

Another name containing the name of the hero-god Ingvi or Ing.

Abbreviations: Inga, Inge, Inger.

Iona (pron. Eye-ówna)

Origin/meaning: either Greek 'violet coloured stone' or the Scottish Hebridean island.

Irene (pron. Eiréenee or Éireen)

Origin/meaning: Greek 'peace'.

Eirene is the Greek goddess of peace. Although its use in English-speaking countries is comparatively recent, the name is a very old one.

Variations and abbreviations: Eirena, Eirene, Irena, Irina (Slav), Ira, Rena, Rene, Rina.

Iris

Origin/meaning: Greek 'rainbow'.

In Greek mythology Iris was a goddess who acted as the messenger of the gods.

Irma

Origin/meaning: Old German 'universal'.

This name originated as a pet form of longer names such as Irmtraud and became a first name in English-speaking countries at the end of the 19th century.

Isabel

Origin/meaning: Hebrew 'God is my satisfaction'.

This is an early medieval development of Elizabeth q.v. which began in Spain and Provence. It became Ilsabeth and then Islabeau.

Variations and abbreviations: Bell, Bella, Belle, Ib, Ibbie, Ibby, Ilsa (Ger), Ilse (Ger), Isa (Scot), Isabeau (Fr), Isabella (It), Isabelle, Isabetta, Ishbel (Scot), Isobel (Scot), Issie, Issy, Izabel, Ysabel.

Isadora

Origin/meaning: uncertain. Possibly Greek 'gift of Isis' (an Egyptian goddess).

The feminine form of an ancient Greek masculine name, Isidore. the name was made famous in the US by the American dancer/choreographer Isadora Duncan, 1878–1927.

Variation: Isidora.

Iseult

Origin/meaning: either Old Welsh 'fair one' or Old German 'ice-rule'.

This is the Celtic form of Isolda q.v.

Ismenia

Origin/meaning: Greek 'learned'.

A medieval name possibly connected with Ismene (pron. Isménee) the daughter of Oedipus and Jocasta.

Variations and abbreviations: Ismay, Ismena, Ismene, Ysmena.

Isolda

Origin/meaning: either Old Welsh 'fair one' or Old German 'ice-rule'.

Isolda is the Latinized form of the German name.

Variations and abbreviations: Essylt, Isaut, Iseut, Iseult, Isold, Isolde (Ger), Isolt, Isota, Yseult, Ysold, Ysolda, Ysolde, Ysolt, Ysonde.

Ivy

Origin/meaning: Old English 'ivy plant'.

One of the flower and plant names which were popular at the end of the 19th century.

Jacintha (pron. Jassinta)

Origin/meaning: Greek 'hyacinth flower', 'hyacinth jewel' (red topaz, zircon or garnet). This is an English version of Hyacinth.

Variations and abbreviations: Cynthia, Cynthie, Giancinta (It), Hyacinth, Hyacintha, Hyacinthe, Hyacinthia, Hyacinthie (Ger), Jacinta (Sp), Jacinthe, Jacynth.

Jacqueline

Origin/meaning: uncertain. Possibly Hebrew 'supplanter'.

This is a feminine form of James from the French Jacques.

Variations and abbreviations: Jacki, Jackie, Jacky, Jaclyn, Jacquelyn, Jacqui.

Jacquetta

Origin/meaning: uncertain. Possibly Hebrew 'supplanter'.

A French feminine form of James from the French masculine form Jacques.

Variations: Jacquenetta, Jacquenette, Jacquette, Jaquetta.

Jade

Origin/meaning: Old French/Spanish 'jade', a semi-precious stone.

Used as a name since the late 19th century when gem names became fashionable.

Variation: Ijada (Sp).

Jameela

Origin/meaning: Arabic 'beautiful'.

A popular Muslim name.

Variation: Jamila. See also Belle.

Jane

Origin/meaning: Hebrew 'Jehovah has favored'.

This feminine form of John came into fashion in England in the 16th century.

Variations: Jana, Janey, Janie, Jayne. See also Joan.

Janet

Origin/meaning: 'Little Jane' a diminutive of Jane. Hebrew 'Jehovah has favored'.

This has long been an independent name rather than a mere pet form of Jane.

Variations and abbreviations: Jennet (Med Eng), Jonet, Netta, Nettie. See also Joan.

Janice

Origin/meaning: Hebrew 'Jehovah has favored'.

A US form of Joan, probably from Jan, the short form of another variation, Jane.

Variation: Janis. See also Joan.

Jasmine

Origin/meaning: Arabic/Persian 'jasmine flower'.
This is the English version of the Arabic Yasmin.

Variations and abbreviations: Gelsomina (It), Jasmin (Ger), Jasmina, Jessamine (Fr), Jessamy, Jessamyn, Jess, Jessie, Jessy, Yasmin (Arab).

Jayanti

Origin/meaning: Sanskrit 'victorious'.
The feminine form of Jayant, and found in Hindu texts as an epithet of Durga, Shiva's wife, and as the name of Indra's daughter.

Jayashree

Origin/meaning: Sanskrit 'victory'.
A popular Indian name.

Jean

Origin/meaning: Hebrew 'Jehovah has favored'.
This is a Scottish form of the English name Joan.

Variations: Jeanie, Jeanne (Fr), Jeannette.

Jemima

Origin/meaning: Hebrew 'dove'.
This is a 17th-century Biblical name. Jemima was one of Job's three daughters.

Variations and abbreviations: Jamima, Jem, Jemie, Jemmie, Jemmy, Mimie.

Jennie/Jenny

Origin/meaning: since the 1920s this has been the most common as a short form of the newly fashionable name Jennifer.
Prior to that it was considered a familiar form of Jane or Jean.

Jennifer

Origin/meaning: Old Welsh 'fair and yielding' or 'white wave'.
This is the Cornish form of the Old Welsh name Gwenhywvar (Guinevere).

Variations and abbreviations: Jen, Jenifer, Jenni, Jenny. See also Guinevere.

Jessica

Origin/meaning: Hebrew 'God beholds'.
Used by Shakespeare as the name of Shylock's daughter in 'The Merchant of Venice'.
It is probably a version of the Biblical Iscah.

Variations and abbreviations: Gessica (It), Jesca, Jess, Jessalin, Jessie, Jessy.

Jessie

Origin/meaning: Hebrew 'Jehovah has favored'.
A Scottish short form of Janet, itself a feminine form of John.

Variations and abbreviations: Jess, Jessy.

Jill

Origin/meaning: from Julius, a Roman family name, possibly meaning 'dowry'.
This short form of Gillian/Jillian/Juliana has been used since the Middle Ages. It is currently popular as an independent name.

Joan

Origin/meaning: Hebrew 'Jehovah has favored'.
The most usual Medieval English feminine form of John q.v. It was often spelt Johan.

Variations and abbreviations: Gianna (It), Giannina (It), Giovanna (It), Hanna (Ger), Jan, Jana (US), Janella, Janelle, Janet, Janetta, Janette, Janey, Jania, Janice, Janie, Janine, Janis, Janith, Janka, Janna (Ger), Jannelle, Jany, Janyte, Jayne, Jean (Scot), Jeanette (Fr), Jeanie, Jeanne (Fr), Jeannette (Fr), Jeannine (Fr), Jennet, Jenni, Jennie, Jenny, Jenyth, Jess, Jessie, Jessy, Jinny, Jo-Ann, Joan, Joana, Joanna, Joanne (Fr), Johanna (Ger), Joni, Jonie, Juana (Sp/Port), Juanita (Sp/Port), Netta, Nettie, Shena (Scot), Sheena (Scot), Sian (Wel), Siné (Scot), Sinead (Ir).

Joanna

Origin/meaning: Hebrew 'Jehovah has favored'.
This is the Latinized version of the medieval feminine form of John, Joan.

Variations and abbreviations: Jo, Joana, Jo-Ann, Joanne (Fr), Johanna (Ger).

Jocasta

Origin/meaning: Greek 'shining moon'.
In Greek legend Jocasta is the mother of Oedipus who unwittingly kills his father and marries his mother.

Jocelyn

Origin/meaning: Old German 'man of the Goths'.
This pre-Conquest name was introduced into England by the Normans and until the 20th century was used exclusively as a male name.

Variations and abbreviations: Joceline, Josceline, Joscelyn, Joss, Josselyn, Joycelin.

Jodi/Jody

Origin/meaning: Hebrew 'Jewish woman', 'from Judah'.
A modern diminutive of Judith q.v., currently a vogue name in North America, where it originated.

Variations: Jodie. See also Judith.

Joelle

Origin/meaning: Hebrew 'Jehovah is god'.

A US feminine form of Joel q.v. created by adding a typical French feminine ending.

Variations: Joella, Joellen.

Jonquil

Origin/meaning: the name of a flower similar to the narcissus.

This is an unusual flower name which became popular at the end of the 19th century.

Jordan

Origin/meaning: Hebrew 'flowing down'.

Jordan has been used as a masculine and feminine name since the Crusaders brought back the name of this river from the Holy Land in the Middle Ages.

Josephine

Origin/meaning: Hebrew 'May Jehovah increase'.

This is a French feminine diminutive form of Joseph q.v.

Variations and abbreviations: Fifi, Fina, Giuseppa (It), Giuseppina (It), Jo, Jo-Jo, Jolene (US), Josée (Fr), Josefa (Ger), Josefina (Sp/Port), Josefine, Josepha, Joséphine (Fr), Josette, Josie, Josy, Pepita (Sp), Peppina (It).

Josie

Origin/meaning: Hebrew 'May Jehovah increase'.

A short form of Josephine used mainly in the US.

Variations: Josy. See also Josephine.

Joy

Origin/meaning: Latin 'rejoicing', French 'joy'.

A medieval Christian name.

Joyce

Origin/meaning: French Celtic 'champion'.

The English form of Judoc(us), or Josse, the name of a 7th-century Breton saint.

Variations: Joice, Joisse (Med Fr), Josse (Med Eng), Joycelin.

Judith

Origin/meaning: Hebrew 'Jewish woman', 'from Judah'.

Judith was the heroine of the Apocryphal Book of Judith.

Variations and abbreviations: Giuditta (It), Jodi, Jodie, Jody, Judi, Judie, Judintha, Juditha (Ger), Judy, Judye, Jutta.

Julia

Origin/meaning: from Julius, a Roman family name, possibly meaning 'dowry'.
This is the direct equivalent of the masculine Julius.

Variations and abbreviations: Giulia (It), Jule, Jules, Julie (Fr).

Juliana

Origin/meaning: from Julius, a Roman family name possibly meaning 'dowry'.
The Latin feminine version of Julian q.v.

Variations and abbreviations: Giuliana (It), Juliane, Julianne, Julienne, Julie.

Julie

Origin/meaning: from the Roman family name Julius, possibly meaning 'dowry'.
The French form of Julia q.v., which became very popular in English-speaking countries in the 20th century.

Variations and abbreviations: see Julia.

Juliet

Origin/meaning: 'little Julia'. From the Roman family name Julius.
Shakespeare based his play 'Romeo and Juliet' on a poem by Arthur Brooke called 'The Tragical History of Romeus and Juliet', 1562.

Variations and abbreviations: Jule, Juliette (Fr). See also Gillian.

Jumoke (pron. J'mókhi)

Origin/meaning: Yoruba 'everyone loves the child'.
A Nigerian name that can be used for both boys and girls.

June

Origin/meaning: the sixth month of the year.
The month may have taken its name from Juno, the Chief of the goddesses and the patron of all female concerns from birth to death. The name June has come into use in the 20th century with one or two examples in the 19th century.

Juno

Origin/meaning: Old Irish, uncertain, possibly 'lamb'.
A variation of Oonagh q.v. best known for Sean O'Casey's play 'Juno and the Paycock', 1924.

Justine

Origin/meaning: Latin 'just'.
The French feminine version of Justin q.v.

Variations: Giustina (It), Justina (Sp).

Kailas (pron. Kyelahs)

Origin/meaning: Sanskrit. The name of a holy mountain in the Himalayas.

Hindus believe that the God Shiva and Parvati q.v. his wife live on Mount Kailas.

Kamala

Origin/meaning: Sanskrit 'pale red'.

The feminine form of Kamal and found often in Hindu classical texts, including as a name of the goddess Lakshami, wife of Vishnu.

Kamaria (pron. Kamaréea)

Origin/meaning: Swahili 'moon-like'.

A popular name in East Africa.

Karen

Origin/meaning: uncertain. Possibly Greek 'pure'.

A Scandinavian form of Katharine q.v. It was introduced into the US by Scandinavian immigrants and has subsequently spread to other English-speaking countries.

Variations: Caren, Carin, Karim. See also Katharine.

Kashmira

Origin/meaning: Kashmin 'from Kashmir'.

A name given because Kashmir is considered a holy area.

Kate

Origin/meaning: uncertain. Possibly Greek 'pure'.

This is a short form of Katharine q.v. Shakespeare's Katherina Minola, the 'Shrew' of his play 'The Taming of the Shrew', 1594, is referred to as Kate.

Variations: Katie, Katy. See also Katharine.

Katharine/Katherine

Origin/meaning: uncertain. Possibly Greek 'pure'.

Tradition has it that Katherine of Alexandria was one of the virgin martyrs who died in Alexandria early in the 4th century after protesting about the worship of idols.

Variations and abbreviations: Caitlin (Ir), Caitrin, Caren, Carin, Caryn, Cass, Cassie, Cassy, Catalina (Sp), Catarina, Cate, Catelin (Med Eng), Caterina (It), Catharina, Catharine, Cathee, Catherina, Catherine (Fr), Cathie, Cathleen (Ir), Cathlene, Cathrine, Cathryn, Cathy, Catia (It), Catie, Catlin (Med Eng), Catriona (Scot), Caty, Ekaterina (Ger/Russ), Karen (Scand), Karin, Kass, Kassia, Kassie, Kata, Katalin, Kate, Katerina, Katerine, Katey, Katha, Katharina (Ger), Kathi, Kathie, Kathleen (Ir), Kathryn, Kathy, Katia (Ger), Katie, Katina, Katinka (Russ), Katja (Russ), Katrina (Gk), Katrinka, Katya, Kay, Kaye, Kit, Kittie, Kitty, Treena, Trina.

Kathleen

Origin/meaning: uncertain. Possibly Greek 'pure'.

The Irish diminutive form of Katharine q.v.

Variations and abbreviations: Cath, Cathee, Cathleen, Cathie, Catty, Kay, Kath, Kathie, Kathy. See also Katharine.

Kay

Origin/meaning: uncertain. Possibly Greek 'pure'.

A short form of Katharine q.v.

Keira

Origin/meaning: Old Irish 'dark haired'.

A variation of Ciara that has become known because of the British actress Keira Knightley.

Kelly

Origin/meaning: Gaelic 'descendant of War'.

Celtic surname most commonly found in Ireland, now popular as a girl's first name.

Variation: Kellie.

Kerrie

Origin/meaning: 'from Kerry', an Irish place-name, meaning the place of dark-haired people.

Variations: Keriann, Kerianne, Kerry, Kerryn. See also Kieran.

Kezia

Origin/meaning: Hebrew 'cassia' (a type of cinnamon).

Kezia was one of the three beautiful daughters of Job. The name was used by the Puritans.

Variation: Keziah.

Khadija

Origin/meaning: Arabic 'born prematurely'.

Khadija was the wife of Mohammed.

Variation: Kedeja.

Kibibi

Origin/meaning: Swahili 'little lady'.

An East African name.

See also Martha.

Kim

Origin/meaning: Old English 'cyne' – 'royal'. From the surname Kimball 'royal hill'.
This name became popular for boys after the publication in 1901 of Rudyard Kipling's book
'Kim'. It has now become equally popular for girls.

Kimberley

Origin/meaning: Old English 'from the royal meadow'.
This is an English last name which is popular as a girl's name in the US and Australia.

Variations and abbreviations: Kim, Kimmie.

Kirsten

Origin/meaning: Latin 'Christian'.
The Scandinavian form of the English names Christine, Christina and Christiana.

Variations and abbreviations: Kerstin, Kerstina, Kirsteen (Scot), Kirsty, Kris, Krissy, Kirstin,
Kristin, Kristina, Kristine. See also Christiana, Christine.

Kirsty

Origin/meaning: Latin 'Christian'.
This is a Scottish pet form of Christine/Christiana.

Variations: Kirstie. See also Kirsten and Christine.

Kitty

Origin/meaning: uncertain. Possibly Greek 'pure'.
A pet form of Katharine q.v.

Kumari

Origin/meaning: Sanskrit 'maiden, daughter'.
A feminine form of Kumar that is found throughout Hindu texts.

Kusum (pron. Kuhsoom)

Origin/meaning: Sanskrit 'flower'.
Popular throughout India.

Variation: Kusum kumari.

Kyle

Origin/meaning: Gaelic 'narrow strait or sound'.
This is a place-name from Scotland which has become a last name. In the latter half of the
20th century it was used as a feminine first name, particularly in the US. The familiar form
Kylie is a native word in Western Australia for a boomerang.

Variations: Kylie, Kyly.

Laetitia (pron. Letisha)

Origin/meaning: Latin 'joy', 'delight'.

Laetitia was occasionally found during Middle Ages but didn't establish until the 18th century.

Variations and abbreviations: Lätitia (Ger), Lece (Fr), Lecia, Leda, Letice, Leticia, Letitia, Letizia (It), Lettice (Eng), Letty.

Lakshmi (pron. L'kshmee)

Origin/meaning: Hindu. The name of the goddess of wealth and prosperity, the wife of Vishnu.

Lalita

Origin/meaning: Sanskrit 'playful'.

A name found in Hindu texts, in particular as the name of the female cowherd who became a playmate of the adolescent Krishna.

Variation: Lalit.

Lana

Origin/meaning: a short form of either Helen (Greek 'light' or 'bright') or Alanna (Celtic 'beautiful').

Lara

Origin/meaning: uncertain. Possibly Greek 'cheerful'.

A Russian short form of Larissa q.v. Byron used it for his poem 'Lara', 1814.

Variations and abbreviations: See Larissa.

Larissa

Origin/meaning: uncertain. Possibly Greek 'cheerful' or Pre-Hellenic 'castle'.

Larissa, with the short form Lara, has been one of the most popular names in the Soviet Union since the 1960s.

Variations and abbreviations: Lara, Larisa.

Lata (pron. L'ta)

Origin/meaning: Sanskrit 'climbing plant', 'bower'.

Laura

Origin/meaning: Latin 'bay tree' or 'from Laurentium' (city of laurels).

A feminine form of Laurence q.v. which evolved as a short form of the original Laurencia.

Variations and abbreviations: Laure (Fr), Laureen, Laurel, Lauren, Laurence (Fr), Laurencia, Laurenzia, Lauretta (It), Laurette, Laurie, Laurine, Lora (It), Loreen, Loren, Lorene, Lorenza (It), Loretta, Lorette (Fr), Lori, Lorrie.

Laurel

Origin/meaning: Latin 'laurel' or 'bay tree'.
Used in the 19th century when flower names were in vogue.
Variations and abbreviations: See Laura.

Lauren

Origin/meaning: Latin 'bay tree' or 'from Laurentium' (city of laurels).
Like Laura this is a short form of Laurencia, the feminine form of Laurence q.v.
Variations and abbreviations: See Laura.

Lavinia

Origin/meaning: uncertain. Possibly 'from Lavinium' (a town near Rome). Sometimes given as 'purified'.
Lavinia is a name from Roman literature. In Virgil's poem the 'Aeneid' Aeneas, a Trojan hero, escapes after the fall of Troy and after many years of wandering reaches Italy.
Abbreviation: Leni.

Layla

Origin/meaning: Arabic 'intoxicating'.
In Arab literature, the story by 7th-century poet Qays Ibn al-Mulawwah about his love for his cousin Layla is as well known as Romeo and Juliet and their names are similarly associated with love and devotion.

Leah

Origin/meaning: Hebrew 'heifer'. Sometimes given as 'weary'.
Leah was the first wife of Jacob, one of the patriarchs of the Old Testament.

Lee

Origin/meaning: Old English 'meadow'.
An English last name adopted in the 19th century as a first name.
Variations: Lea, Leigh.

Leela

Origin/meaning: Sanskrit 'play'.
Found in Hindu texts, it is associated with amorous sport or feigning love.

Leila (pron. Layla)

Origin/meaning: Persian 'night' or 'dark-haired as night'.
A popular Muslim name. It is found in the Persian legend of Leila and Majnoun.
Variations: Layla, Leilah, Lela, Lelah, Lila.

Lena

Origin/meaning: Greek 'light' or 'bright' or Hebrew 'Woman of Magdala'.

A short form of Helena, now an independent name.

Variation: Leni.

Léonie

Origin/meaning: Greek 'lion'.

A French feminine form of the popular French name Leon q.v.

Variations and abbreviations: Leo, Leona, Leonia (It), Leonzia (It).

Leonora

Origin/meaning: Greek 'bright', 'light'.

An Italian form of Eleanor/a q.v. similar to the German name Lenore.

Variations and abbreviations: Leonore (Ger), Leonor, Lora.

Lerato

Origin/meaning: Tswana 'love'.

A name from Botswana in South Africa.

See also Amy, Ife.

Lesley

Origin/meaning: Scots Gaelic 'garden by the pool'.

This spelling of the Scottish last name is generally the one used for girls.

Variations and abbreviations: Les, Lesli, Leslie, Lesly, Lezley, Lezlie.

Lettice

Origin/meaning: Latin 'joy', 'delight'.

The English form of Laetitia q.v. It was extremely popular throughout the Middle Ages.

Variations and abbreviations: see Laetitia.

Libby

Origin/meaning: Hebrew 'God is my satisfaction'.

A short form of Elizabeth q.v. sometimes given as an independent name.

Variations and abbreviations: Lib, Libbie. See also Elizabeth.

Liesl

Origin/meaning: Hebrew 'God is my satisfaction'.

A variation of Elizabeth that was the name of the eldest child in the 1965 Oscar-winning musical 'The Sound of Music'.

Lilith

Origin/meaning: Hebrew 'belonging to the night' or Assyrian 'goddess of storms'.
In non-Biblical Hebrew mythology, Lilith was a wife of Adam before he gave his rib to create Eve.

Lillian

Origin/meaning: Hebrew 'God is my satisfaction'.
This is one of dozens of variations of the name Elizabeth.

Variations and abbreviations: Lili, Lilian, Liliane, Lilias (Scot), Lilla, Lilli (Ger), Lillias (Scot), Lillie, Lilyan.

Lily

Origin/meaning: Greek 'lily' or pet form of Elizabeth (Hebrew 'God is my satisfaction').
In use since the late 19th century fashion for flower names.

Variations and abbreviations: Lil, Lilli, Lillie, Lilly. See also Susannah and Elizabeth.

Linda

Origin/meaning: Old German 'serpent'.
Linda is a short form of the many pre-Conquest names which contained the word. The best known nowadays are Belinda and Rosalind. Serpent may seem a strange meaning but in fact it was very flattering. In German mythology the serpent was regarded as a magical creature. Linda is also the Spanish word for pretty.

Variations: Lindi, Lindy, Lynda.

Lindsay

Origin/meaning: Old English. Uncertain, possibly 'Lincoln's island'.
A Scottish aristocratic last name adopted as a male and female first name.

Variations and abbreviations: Lin, Lindsey (Eng), Linsay, Linsey, Lyn, Lynsey.

Lisa/Liza

Origin/meaning: Hebrew 'God is my satisfaction'.
Short forms of Elizabeth.

Variations: Elisa, Elise, Eliza, Elizabeth, Lissa.

Lois (pron. Lóys or Lówis)

Origin/meaning: Greek, meaning uncertain.
A Biblical name taken by 17th-century Puritans. Lois Lane is the girlfriend of the comic-strip character Superman.

Lola

Origin/meaning: a Spanish diminutive of Dolores (Spanish 'sorrows') or Carlota (the Spanish form of Charlotte 'man').

Variation: Lolita.

Lorna

Origin/meaning: this name was invented by the novelist R. D. Blackmore for his classic novel 'Lorna Doone', 1869. The name was apparently adapted from the title of the Marquess of Lorne.

See also Fiona, Miranda, Ophelia, Pamela, Perdita, Vanessa and Wendy.

Lorraine

Origin/meaning: French 'from Lorraine' (an area of France).

This has only come into use since the middle of the 20th century.

Variations and abbreviations: Larain, Lorain, Loraine, Lorri, Lorrayne.

Lottie

Origin/meaning: Old German 'man', by association 'womanly'.

A common familiar form (like Tottie) of Charlotte, a feminine form of Charles q.v.

Variations: Lotte, Lotty. See also Charlotte.

Louisa/Louise

Origin/meaning: Old German 'glorious battle'.

These are the Latin and French feminine forms of the French name Louis q.v.

Variations and abbreviations: Lodovica (It), Loise, Lou, Louie, Louise (Fr), Louisette, Lu, Ludowika (Ger), Luigia (It), Luisa (It/Sp), Luise (Ger), Lulu.

Lourdes

Origin/meaning: from the place where St Bernadette of Lourdes, 1844–1879, the miller's daughter claimed to see visions of the Virgin Mary and where healing miracles take place.

Loveday

Origin/meaning: Medieval English 'born on loveday'.

A loveday was an annual day set aside for settling disputes. In the 17th century it also came to mean a day when the young people of a town or village could look for a partner.

Lubna

Origin/meaning: Arabic 'storax tree'.

Taken from the tree with sweet sap that is used to make incense and perfume. Lubna is the heroine of a famous Arab love story.

Lucasta (pron. Lookásta)

Origin/meaning: Latin 'light'.

A poetic form of Lucia/Lucy q.v. used in the 17th century.

See also Lucy and Althea.

Lucia

Origin/meaning: Latin 'light'.

The original Latin feminine form of Lucius q.v. from which the English Lucy and French Lucille are derived.

Variations and abbreviations: see Lucy.

Lucinda

Origin/meaning: Latin 'light'.

This is a 17th-century form of Lucy.

Variations: Lucinde. See also Lucy.

Lucretia

Origin/meaning: Latin, belonging to the Roman family Lucretius.

This is a classical name revived in Italy during the Renaissance period.

Variations: Lucrèce (Fr), Lucrecia (Sp), Lucresse, Lucrezia (It).

Lucy

Origin/meaning: Latin 'light'. Lucy is the English form of Lucia, a Roman name.

Variations and abbreviations: Luc, Lucasta (17th century), Luce (It), Lucetta, Lucette, Luci, Lucia (Ger/It/Lat), Luciana (It), Lucienne (Fr), Lucilia, Lucilla (It), Lucille (Fr), Lucina (It), Lucinda (17th century), Lucinde, Lucine, Lucky (US), Luz, Luzi, Luzia (Ger).

Lulu

Origin/meaning: Old German 'glorious battle', Arabic 'pearl'.

A pet form of Louisa/Louise q.v. or a Muslim name quite unconnected with the European name.

Lydia

Origin/meaning: Greek 'from Lydia' (an ancient kingdom of Asia Minor renowned for its wealthy King, Croesus). This pre-Christian name occurs in the Acts of the Apostles.

Lynn/Lynne

Origin/meaning: Old English 'pool' or a short form of the Welsh Eluned q.v. Possibly 'idol'. The short form, now used independently, of Eluned or its French variation Lynette, which came into general use in the 19th century.

Variations: Lyn , Lynette.

Lynnet

Origin/meaning: uncertain. Possibly connected with the Old Welsh word meaning 'idol'. This is a variation of the well-established Welsh name Eluned q.v. from the short form, Lyn.

Variations and abbreviations: Eiluned, Elined, Eluned, Linet, Linette, Linnet, Luned, Lyn, Lynelle, Lynette, Lynne, Lynnet, Lynnette.

Lysia

Origin/meaning: uncertain.

This is the traditional name given to the twin of St Thomas the Apostle.

Madeleine

Origin/meaning: Hebrew 'woman from Magdala'.

This name comes from a corruption of Magdalene. The old pronunciation was 'maudlin' which, because Mary Magdalene was patron saint of penitents, came to mean tearful.

Variations and abbreviations: Mad, Maddelena (It), Maddie, Maddy, Madeline (Eng), Madelon (Fr), Madeline (US, Madlen, Madlon, Mado, Magda, Magdalena (Ger/Lat/Scand), Magdalene (Eng), Magdelone (Dan), Malena, Malina, Lena, Lene.

Madhur

Origin/meaning: Sanskrit 'sweet'.

A word usually used to describe sounds and tastes that has recently become a given name.

Madhuri (pron. Madtoorée)

Origin/meaning: Sanskrit 'sweet'.

This name comes from madhu, the Sanskrit word for honey or spring.

Madonna

Origin/meaning: Latin 'my lady'.

An honorific title for the Virgin Mary that started being used as a given name in America amongst those of Italian descent.

Maeve

Origin/meaning: Old Irish, meaning uncertain.

Maedbh was Queen of Connaught in the 3rd century who fought a great battle over a brown bull, the subject of an epic poem.

Maia (pron. M´yuh)

Origin/meaning: Latin 'exalted'.

The name of a Roman goddess, the mother of Mercury. She may be based on a more ancient Indian deity, associated with visions.

Variations: Maija (Fin), Maja (Ger/Scand).

Maida

Origin/meaning: Old English 'maiden, virgin'.

Variation: Mayda

Mandisa (pron. Mandéeza)

Origin/meaning: Xhosa 'sweet'.

A name from the South of Africa.

Mara
Origin/meaning: Hebrew 'bitter'.
A form of the Hebrew name usually translated as Mary or Miriam.
Variations: Marah

Marcella
Origin/meaning: Latin 'little Marcus' from the name of Mars the Roman god of war. Marcella, the feminine form, has been used occasionally in English-speaking countries.
Variations: Marcella (Sp), Marcelia, Marceline, Marcelle (Fr), Marcellina (It), Marcelline.

Marcia (pron. Márssia or Marsha)
Origin/meaning: 'of Mars' (the Roman god of war) i.e. 'warlike'.
This name comes from the Roman family name Marcius.
Variations and abbreviations: Marcelia, Marcie (Fr), Marcy, Marquita, Marsha (US).

Margaret
Origin/meaning: Persian?/Greek/Latin 'pearl' or Medieval French/English 'daisy'.
Variations and abbreviations: Daisy, Greta, Gretel, Gritty, Madge, Mag, Maggie, Maggs, Maggy, Maisie, Mamie, Margareta (Swed/Ger), Margarete (Ger/Dan), Margaretha (Dut/Ger), Margarette, Margarita (Sp), Margaux, Marge, Marged (Wel), Margery, Marget, Marghanita, Margherita (It), Margie, Margit (Swed), Margita (Swed), Margo, Margot, Margred (Wel), Margrethe (Dan), Margriet, Marguerita, Marguerite (Fr), Margy, Marina, Marjie, Marjorie, Marjory, May, Meg, Megan (Wel), Meggie, Meggy, Meghan, Megs, Meta, Mog, Peg, Pegeen, Peggi, Peggie, Peggoty, Rita.

Margery
Origin/meaning: Persian?/Greek/Latin 'pearl' or French/English 'daisy'.
An alternative English spelling of Marjorie q.v. which is a form of Margaret q.v.
Variations and abbreviations: see Margaret.

Marguerite
Origin/meaning: Persian?/Greek/Latin 'pearl' or French/English 'daisy'.
This is the French form of Margaret q.v.
Variations and abbreviations: see Margaret.

Maria
Origin/meaning: uncertain. Possibly Hebrew 'bitter' or 'wished for child'.
The Latin form of Mary used to translate the original Hebrew Mrym. All other forms of the name stem from it.
Variations and abbreviations: see Mary.

Mariah
Origin/meaning: Hebrew 'bitter' or 'wished for child'.
A variation on Mary that has greatly increased in popularity, most likely because of the singer Mariah Carey.

Mariana/Marianne
Origin/meaning: uncertain. Possibly Hebrew 'bitter' or 'longed for child'.
The Spanish and Italian diminutives of Mary (Maria), meaning 'little Mary'.
Variations and abbreviations: see Marion.

Marie
Origin/meaning: uncertain. Possibly Hebrew 'bitter' or 'longed for child'.
The French form of Mary.
Variations and abbreviations: see Mary.

Marietta
Origin/meaning: Hebrew 'bitter' or 'longed for child' plus Antoinetta (from the Roman Antonius family).
A contraction of Marie-Antoinette.

Marilyn
Origin/meaning: Hebrew 'bitter' plus Old English 'pool'.
A US combination of two popular names, Maria and Lyn. Its great popularity in the 1950s is undoubtedly due to the film star Marilyn Monroe (Norma Jean Baker), 1926–1962.

Marina
Origin/meaning: uncertain. Usually given as Latin 'of the sea'.
May also be a form of Mary q.v. Occasionally used in England in the Middle Ages.
Variation: Marinetta.

Marion
Origin/meaning: uncertain. Possibly Hebrew 'bitter' or 'wished for child'.
Marion means 'little Mary'. It has been used as an independent name since the Middle Ages.
Variations: Marian, Mariana (It/Sp), Marianna (It), Marianne (Fr), Maureen (Ir). See also Mary.

Marjorie
Origin/meaning: Persian?/Greek/Latin 'pearl' or French/English 'daisy'.
A Scottish pet form of Margaret, used as an independent name since the 12th century.
Variations: Margery, Marjory. See also Margaret.

Marlene (pron. Marrlayna)
Origin/meaning: Hebrew 'bitter' plus 'of Magdala'.
A combination of Maria and Lene (a common German short form of Magdalena).

Marsha
Origin/meaning: Latin 'of Mars' (the Roman god of war), i.e. 'warlike'.
An American form of Marcia q.v. which reflects the American pronunciation.

Martha
Origin/meaning: Aramaic 'lady'.
Martha was the sister of Mary Magdalen and Lazarus. She was upbraided by Christ for allowing her chores to distract her from sitting and listening to him.
Variations: Marja (Russ), Marta (It), Marte, Marthe (Fr), Mari, Martie, Martita, Marty.

Martina
Origin/meaning: Latin 'of Mars' (the Roman god of War) i.e. 'warlike'.
Variations and abbreviations: Marta, Martie, Martine (Fr), Marty, Martyna, Tina.

Mary
Origin/meaning: uncertain. Possibly Hebrew 'bitter' or 'wished for child'.
The name in Hebrew was spelt only with consonants – MRYM.
Variations and abbreviations: Maia, Maidie (Wel), Mair, Maire (Fr), Mairi (Scot), Maja (Ger), Mame, Mamie (US), Manette (Fr), Manon (Fr), Mara, Maria (It/Sp), Mariam, Mariamne, Marian, Mariana, Marianna, Marianne, Marice, Marie (Fr), Mariel, Marietta, Mariette (Fr), Marilyn, Marion, Mariquilla, Mariquita (Sp), Maris, Marisa, Mariska, Marita (Sp), Maritsa, Marja (Slav), Marla, Marya, Maryann, Maryanne, Marysa, Maryse, Marscha (Russ), Masha (Russ), Maura, Maure (Ir), Maureen (Ir), Maurita, May, Meriel, Meryl, Mimi, Minette, Minnie, Minny, Miriam, Mitzi, Moira (Scot), Moire (Scot), Mollie, Molly, Moyra (Scot).

Matilda
Origin/meaning: Old German 'battle strength'.
This is the Latin form of an Old German name, introduced into England by the Normans.
§**Variations and abbreviations:** Mahault (Med Fr), Maitilde (Ir), Majalda (It/Port), Matelda (It), Mathilda, Mathilde (Fr/Ger), Matilde (Sp), Mattie, Matty, Maud, Maude, Maudie, Mawt (Med Eng), Mechtilde, Tilda, Tillie, Tilly.

Maud
Origin/meaning: Old German 'battle strength'.
A medieval form of Matilda. Tennyson's poem 'Maud', 1855, may have contributed to its popularity in the 19th century.
Variations and abbreviations: Maude, Maudie, Mawt. See also Matilda.

Maureen

Origin/meaning: uncertain. Possibly Hebrew 'bitter' or 'wished for child'.
This is the Irish diminutive of Mary (Maire) and means 'little Mary'.

Mavis

Origin/meaning: French 'song thrush'.
A modern name which first appeared in the 19th century.

Mawusi (pron. Mawusée)

Origin/meaning: Ewe 'in the hands of God'.
A name from Ghana.

Maxine

Origin/meaning: Latin 'little great one'.
A French feminine diminutive of Max, the short form of Maximilian q.v. It dates from the 19th century.

May

Origin/meaning: Sanskrit 'growth', 'burgeoning'. The name of the fifth month of the year. In the 20th century this name has usually been given as the name of the month. May was considered a special month in the year, associated with festivity.
Variations: Mae, Mai (Fr/Ger/Scand), Maye.

Meave

Origin/meaning: Old Irish 'joy'.
A name from Irish legend, Meave was considered the equivalent of the English Mab, the fairy who manipulated men's dreams.

Meena

Origin/meaning: Sanskrit, either from meen (fish) or meena (enamel work which shines like fishes' scales).

Meenakshi (pron. Meenakshée)

Origin/meaning: Sanskrit 'eyes like a fish'.
This is the equivalent of the English expression 'doe's eyes' and is a flattering description.

Meera (pron. Meeráh)

Origin/meaning: from the Rajasthan area, meaning obscure.
Meera was one of the most famous Hindu saints. She was a devotee of Krishna and wrote many poems about him. Gandhi gave this name to Jane, his adopted English daughter.

Megan

Origin/meaning: Persian?/Greek/Latin 'pearl' or French/English 'daisy'.
This is a comparatively recent Welsh pet form of Margaret q.v.

Melanie

Origin/meaning: Greek 'black', 'dark-haired'.
St Melania the younger, 383–439, was a rich woman who converted her husband
to Christianity.

Variations and abbreviations: Mel, Mela, Malania (It), Mélanie (Fr), Melinda, Melloney,
Melly, Melony.

Melinda

Origin/meaning: uncertain. Sometimes given as 'loved' or 'dark-haired'.
This 20th-century name seems to be a combination of several names which are favorites in
the US such as Melanie and Linda.

Variations and abbreviations: Linda, Lynda, Malinda, Melinde, Mindy (US)

Melissa

Origin/meaning: Greek 'bee' or 'Melissa officianalis' the Latin name for the herb lemon balm.
Used in pre-Christian Greece and by 16th and 17th-century poets to evoke that era.

Variations and abbreviations: Lisa, Lissa, Malissa, Mel, Melisa, Melitta, Milly, Missie, Missy.

Melody

Origin/meaning: Greek 'a song being sung'.

Mercedes

Origin/meaning: Spanish 'mercies'.
This is part of a standard Spanish description of the Virgin Mary, Maria de Mercedes –
Mary of Mercies. The main word became a name in its own right.
See also Consuelo, Mercy.

Mercy

Origin/meaning: Medieval Latin 'pity'.
This name was one of the abstract virtue names popular with the 17th-century Puritans.

Variation: Merry.

Meredith

Origin/meaning: Welsh 'great?/lord'.
This was a Welsh masculine first name, with the accent on the second syllable.

Variations and abbreviations: Bedo (Wel), Maredudd (Wel), Meredudd (Wel), Merry.

Meriel

Origin/meaning: Old Irish 'bright sea'.
An old form of Muriel q.v.

Merle

Origin/meaning: French 'blackbird'.
This is a French last name which may indicate an ancestor who was fond of whistling.

Meryl

Origin/meaning: Hebrew 'bitter' and Latin 'famous in war'.
A familiar form of the common double name Mary Louise, brought to prominence by the US actress Meryl Streep.

Mhonum

Origin/meaning: Tiv 'mercy'.
This is a Nigerian name.

Mia

Origin/meaning: uncertain. Possibly Hebrew 'bitter' or 'wished for child'.
A European short form of Mary (Maria) made familiar by the US actress Mia Farrow.

Variations and abbreviations: see Mary.

Michelle (pron. M'shell)

Origin/meaning: Hebrew 'Who is like the Lord?'.
A French feminine form of Michael q.v. It became common in the 1960s after the success of the Beatles song 'Michelle'.
Variations and abbreviations: Michaela (It), Michela (It), Michèe (Fr), Micheline (Fr), Mick, Mickie, Micky.

Mildred

Origin/meaning: Old English 'mild strength'.
This was the name of a Saxon saint who died about 700. The daughter of King Merewald of Mercia she was an abbess renowned for her gentleness.
Variations and abbreviations: Meldred (Med Eng), Mil, Mildrid, Millie, Milly.

Millicent

Origin/meaning: Old German 'work-strong'.
This is the usual modern form of a name which goes back to the time of the Emperor Charlemagne, 742–814.
Variations and abbreviations: Lissa, Mel, Melicent, Mélisande (Fr), Melisenda (Sp), Melisendra, Mellicent, Mellisent, Mellie, Melly, Milicent, Milli, Millie, Millisent, Milly.

Mimi

Origin/meaning: uncertain. Possibly Hebrew 'bitter' or 'wished for child'.
A European familiar form of Mary and Miriam.

Minnie

Origin/meaning: Hebrew 'bitter' or Old German 'helmet of resolution'.

A Scottish familiar form of Mary q.v. now an independent name, or short form of Wilhelmina.

Variations and abbreviations: Min, Mina, Minna, Minne, Minni, Minka (Slav). See also Mary and Wilhelmina.

Mirabel

Origin/meaning: Latin 'wonderful'.

A name found occasionally since the Middle Ages.

Variations and abbreviations: Mira, Mirabella, Mirabelle (Fr).

Miranda

Origin/meaning: Latin 'admirable'.

This name was probably invented by Shakespeare who used it for the heroine of his play 'The Tempest', 1611.

Variations and abbreviations: Mira, Myra. See also Fiona, Lorna, Pamela, Perdita, Stella, Vanessa, Wendy.

Miriam

Origin/meaning: uncertain. Possibly Hebrew 'bitter' or 'wished for child'.

This is a translation of the name which appears in Hebrew as MRYM and is translated as Mary.

Variations and abbreviations: Mariamne, Mimi, Mirjam (Ger), Miryam (Fr), Mitzi (US), Myrjam (Ger).

Miucca

Origin/meaning: unknown, but familiar in fashion circles for being the name of the iconic Italian fashion designer Miucca Prada.

Modron

Origin/meaning: a goddess of Welsh Celtic legend, mentioned in the collection of Welsh folk tales, 'The Mabinogion'.

Mohini

Origin/meaning: Sanskrit 'bewitching woman'.

In some Hindu legends, the name taken by Vishnu when he took on the guise of a beautiful woman in order to interrupt the meditation of Shiva.

Moira (pron Moy-ra)

Origin/meaning: uncertain. Possibly Hebrew 'bitter' or 'wished for child'.

This is a Scots version of Mary q.v. now used as an independent name.

Variation: Moyre. See also Mary.

Molly

Origin/meaning: uncertain. Possibly Hebrew 'bitter' or 'wished for child'.
A familiar form of Mary, often used as an independent name.
Variation: Mollie.

Mona

Origin/meaning: Old Irish 'little noble one'.
At the beginning of the 19th century it became more widespread as people became interested in native Irish language and culture.

Mona

Origin/meaning: Arabic 'hope'.
A Muslim name quite unconnected with the Irish name above.

Monica

Origin/meaning: uncertain. Sometimes given as Latin 'monk' or 'adviser'.
St Monica, 331–387, was the mother of St Augustine. In his writings he explains how she contributed to his conversion to Christianity.
Variations and abbreviations: Mona, Monika (Ger), Monique (Fr).

Morna

Origin/meaning: Gaelic 'affection'.
In James Macpherson's translation of the 3rd-century Ossianic poems published in the 18th century, Morna is the name of Fingal's mother.

Morowa

Origin/meaning: Akan 'queen'.
A Ghanian name. Other African names meaning 'queen' are Thema (also used in Ghana) and Torkwase (used in Nigeria).

Morwenna

Origin/meaning: Old Welsh 'wave', 'of the sea'.
St Morwenna was a 6th-century saint, the patron of Morwenstow in Cornwall, and the name was used in Cornwall as well as Wales.
Variations and abbreviations: Morwen, Morwinna, Mwynen.

Mukta (pron. Mookta)

Origin/meaning: Sanskrit 'pearl'.
A name found throughout India. It honors Muktabai, a saintly Hindu woman.

Muriel

Origin/meaning: Old Irish 'bright sea'.
This is the Norman version of a Celtic name.

Variations: Meriel, Miriel, Murial, Muriella, Murielle.

Muteteli (pron. Mutetáyli)

Origin/meaning: Rwanda 'dainty'.
A name used in the Central African Republic of Rwanda.

Myfanwy (pron. Mivvánwee)

Origin/meaning: Welsh 'my rare one'.

Variations and abbreviations: Fanny, Myfi, Myvanwy.

Myra

Origin/meaning: a coined literary name used in the 17th and 18th centuries. Myra was the name of a city in Asia Minor. It was used by, among others, Sir Fulke Greville (Lord Brooke), 1554–1628, who may have originated it, and George Crabbe, 1754–1832.

Variations: Mira, Myrrah.

Myrtle

Origin/meaning: Greek. The name of a sweet-smelling flowering shrub.
There are several legends and superstitions surrounding the myrtle tree. These include the belief that eating myrtle leaves conferred the power to detect witches. The myrtle was also associated with Venus the Greek goddess of love.

Variations and abbreviations: Mertle, Mirtle, Myrrha, Myrta, Myrtah, Myrtice, Myrtilla.

Nadia (pron. Nahdeea)

Origin/meaning: Russian 'hope'.

This is the typical familiar form of the Russian name Nadezhda.

Variations and abbreviations: Nada, Nadina (It), Nadine (Fr), Nadja. See also Hope.

Nadika

Origin/meaning: Sanskrit 'river'.

A 'nadika' is also a measurement of time equaling 360 'pranas' (breaths) or 24 minutes.

Najma (pron. Naíma)

Origin/meaning: Arabic 'benevolent'.

A popular Muslim name.

Variation: Naeemah.

Nalini

Origin/meaning: Sanskrit 'lovely'.

Nancy

Origin/meaning: Hebrew 'graceful'.

A derivative of Hannah and Ann q.v.

Nanette

Origin/meaning: Hebrew 'graceful'.

A diminutive of Nan, a familiar form of Ann q.v. now found as an independent name. It enjoyed a short vogue in the wake of the musical 'No, No, Nanette'.

Naomi (pron. Nayóhmee)

Origin/meaning: Hebrew 'joy', 'delight'.

This name is the equivalent of the medieval name Pleasance. At about the time that Pleasance was becoming obsolete Naomi came into use.

Nasreen

Origin/meaning: Parsi 'wild rose'.

Natalia

Origin/meaning: Latin 'birth', i.e. Christmas day.

This is a name derived from the phrase 'natale domini' (birth of the Lord). It used to be given to girls born at the Christmas season and is an exact equivalent of Noël/Noëlle q.v.

Variations and abbreviations: Natalie (Fr), Natalina (It), Natalja, Natalya, Nathalia, Nathalie, Natasha (Russ), Natty, Nettie.

Natalie

Origin/meaning: Latin 'birth', i.e. Christmas day.

The French and German form of Natalia q.v. currently popular in English-speaking countries.

Variations and abbreviations: see Natalia.

Natasha

Origin/meaning: Latin 'birth', i.e. Christmas day.

The Russian diminutive of Natalia. It has been used since the 19th century in Britain when Russian novels were popular.

Abbreviation: Tasha.

Nellie

Origin/meaning: Greek 'bright' or 'light'.

A familiar form of Eleanor or Helen, both of which have the same meaning, and occasionally of Cornelia q.v.

Variations and abbreviations: Nell, Nelly.

Nerissa

Origin/meaning: Greek 'sea nymph'.

Nerissa was one of the Nereids who were the daughters of the sea god Nereus.

Nerys (pron. Néh-rees)
Origin/meaning: Welsh 'lord'.

Nessa
Origin/meaning: Greek 'pure', 'chaste'.

An English familiar form of Agnes q.v. similar to the Welsh version, Nesta.

Variation: Nessie.

Netta
Origin/meaning: this is a familiar form of names ending in -et (such as Janet and Annette).

Variations: Nettie, Netty, Nita (Sp).

Nicola
Origin/meaning: Greek 'victory of the people'.

This is the Latinized feminine form of Nicholas q.v. It has recently become extremely popular in Britain.

Variations: Colette, Nichola, Nicole (Fr), Nicoletta (It), Nicolette (Fr), Nikol (Ger/Dut), Nikoline (Ger).

Nicole
Origin/meaning: Greek 'victory of the people'.

The French feminine form of Nicholas. It is used in many other countries and is particularly popular in Australia.

Variations and abbreviations: see Nicola.

Nigella
Origin/meaning: Old Irish 'champion'.

A rare feminine form of Nigel q.v. It is the Latin feminine form of the Latin Nigellus. By a happy coincidence, it is also the Latin name for the flower Love-in-the-Mist.

Nina
Origin/meaning: Hebrew 'graceful', or Spanish 'small girl'.

A Russian diminutive form of Ann, this name came into use in England along with other Russian names like Natasha and Nadine.

Nita
Origin/meaning: a Spanish diminutive of names like Juanita and Anita.

Now used as an independent name. The English equivalent is Netta q.v.

Noëlle

Origin/meaning: French 'Christmas'.

This is a modern French feminine form of Noël created on the pattern of a French adjective.

Variation: Noëlla. See also Natalia.

Nona

Origin/meaning: Latin 'ninth'.

A name given to a ninth child or girl when people had large families. It is occasionally used today without any consideration of its meaning but for its pleasant easy sound.

Nora

Origin/meaning: Latin 'honor' or 'beauty'.

An Irish short form of Honora which has been popular since the Middle Ages.

Variations: Norah, Noreen.

Norma

Origin/meaning: Latin 'rule'.

This Latin word seems first to have been 'borrowed' as a name by Bellini for his opera 'Norma', 1831.

Nuala

Origin/meaning: Old Irish 'white shoulders'.

An Irish short form of Fenella through the form of Finnuala.

Nur Jehan

Origin/meaning: Sanskrit 'light of the world'.

This was the name of the wife of Jehangir q.v., 1569–1627, the third Mogul Emperor of India.

Variation: Nur Jahan.

Octavia

Origin/meaning: Latin 'eighth'.

A name given to an eighth girl or eighth child. Octavia, d.11 bc, was the sister of the Emperor Augustus and second wife of Mark Antony, who deserted her for Cleopatra.

Odette

Origin/meaning: Old German 'of the fatherland', 'rich'.

The German and French diminutive form of the Old German name Oda.

Variations and abbreviations: Oda, Odetta (It), Odile, Ottilie.

Olga

Origin/meaning: Old Norse 'holy'.

The root of this name is the Norse word helga – holy – and it is found in Russia because the founder of the Russian monarchy
was a Viking.

Olive

Origin/meaning: Latin 'olive tree', 'olive branch'.

The olive, so vital to the southern European way of life, became a symbol of peace because in war the enemy would destroy the precious olive trees.

Variations and abbreviations: Liva, Livia, Livie, Livy, Nola, Nollie, Olivia, Olivette, Ollie, Olva.

Olivia

Origin/meaning: Latin 'olive tree'.

The Italian version of Olive q.v.

Variations and abbreviations: see Olive.

Olwen

Origin/meaning: Old Welsh 'white footprint'.

In 'The Mabinogion', the collection of Welsh Celtic folk tales, Olwen was the daughter of a giant. Her beauty was so great that white trefoils appeared on the ground where she trod.

Variation: Olwyn.

Olympia

Origin/meaning: Greek 'from Olympia'.

Olympia was a religious centre in Ancient Greece and the site of the Olympic Games. The name is sometimes given as 'from Olympus', the mountain home of the gods and therefore 'celestial'.

Variations: Olimpe (Fr), Olimpia (It), Olympe (Fr), Olympias.

Ondine (pron. Ondeen)

Origin/meaning: Latin 'water sprite'.

The French form of Undine q.v.

Oni

Origin/meaning: Benin 'desired'.

A Nigerian name.

Oonagh (pron. Oohnah)

Origin/meaning: Old Irish, uncertain, possibly 'lamb'.

This name is also found in Scotland, another Celtic area.

Variations and abbreviations: Juno, Ona, Oona, Una.

Opal

Origin/meaning: Sanskrit 'precious stone'.

This is one of the jewel names which have been used since the 19th century.

Ophelia

Origin/meaning: uncertain. Possibly Greek 'help' or 'serpent'.

This name seems to have been a literary name coined in the 16th century when classical Greek influence was strong. Best known in Ophelia in Shakespeare's 'Hamlet', c.1600.

Oriana

Origin/meaning: Latin 'risen', 'dawn'.

A name coined in the 16th century as a flattering title for Queen Elizabeth I and the new era which she symbolized.

Oriel

Origin/meaning: uncertain, possibly Old German 'fire-strife' or Latin 'golden'.

This name was found in the Middle Ages and it probably has origins in a pre-Conquest name.

Orsola

Origin/meaning: Latin 'little she bear'.

An Italian variation of Ursula q.v.

Ottilie

Origin/meaning: Old German 'of the fatherland' or 'rich'.

One of the main variations, with Odile and Odette, of the Old German name Oda.

Variations and abbreviations: Otti, Ottilia (It), Ottoline.

Padma

Origin/meaning: Sanskrit 'lotus'.
A name found throughout Hindu texts for both men and women, although in modern times its use as a feminine name is more common.

Pamela (pron. Pámela or Paméela)

Origin/meaning: this name has no real meaning, although it is sometimes given as 'all-honey' because of a similarity to these Greek words.

Variations and abbreviations: Pam, Pamella, Pammie, Pammy. See also Lorna, Miranda, Perdita, Ophelia, Vanessa, Wendy.

Parvati

Origin/meaning: Hindu 'mountain dweller'.
Parvati is a Hindu goddess, wife of Lord Shiva.

Parvin (pron. Parrvín)

Origin/meaning: Persian or Arabic. Meaning uncertain.
This Muslim name is found in both Pakistan and India.

Pascale

Origin/meaning: Hebrew/Latin 'of the Passover' or 'of Easter'.
A primarily French name, one of the most popular names in post-war France.

Variations: Pascaline (Fr), Pasqua (It).

Patience

Origin/meaning: Latin/Old French 'calm endurance'.
One of the abstract virtues used as names by 17th century Puritans in England and New England. In England it was sometimes used for men as well as women.

Abbreviation: Pat.

Patricia

Origin/meaning: Latin 'patrician', i.e. aristocratic.
The feminine form of Patrick q.v.

Variations and abbreviations: Paddie, Pat, Patrice (Fr), Patrizia (It), Patsy, Patti, Pattie, Patty, Tricia, Trish, Trisha.

Paula

Origin/meaning: Latin 'small'.
A German feminine version of Paul q.v. It has been used occasionally in England since the Middle Ages, probably to honor the Roman St Paula, 347–404.

Pauline

Origin/meaning: Latin 'small'.

A French feminine form of Paul q.v. and Paulinus often given to honor St Paulina.

Variations and abbreviations: Paola (It), Paolina (It), Paule (Fr), Paulene, Pauletta, Paulette (Fr), Paulina (Sp), Paulyn, Polly.

Peggy

Origin/meaning: Persian?/Greek/Latin 'pearl' or French/English 'daisy'.

One of the English short forms of Margaret, probably the result of childish attempts to say Meggy.

Variations and abbreviations: Peg, Pegeen (Ir), Peggotty.

Penelope (pron. Pen-éll-opee)

Origin/meaning: uncertain. Possibly connected with the Greek word for a bobbin.

This is a name from Homer's poem 'The Odyssey'. Penelope was the wife of Odysseus.

In Ireland it has sometimes been used to 'translate' the native Fionnghuala.

Variations and abbreviations: Pen, Penny, Poppy.

Perdita

Origin/meaning: Latin 'lost'.

This is a name made up by Shakespeare for his play 'A Winter's Tale'.

Perpetua

Origin/meaning: Latin 'continuous' or 'universal'.

The meaning of this name is similar to Constance. St Perpetua was martyred with St Felicity at Carthage in 203.

Peta

Origin/meaning: Greek 'stone'.

An occasional feminine form of Peter q.v.

Petra

Origin/meaning: Greek 'stone'.

This is the feminine form of Petrus, the Latin form given to the name Peter in medieval documents.

Variations and abbreviations: Peta, Piera, Petrina, Pierina. See also Petronella.

Petronella

Origin/meaning: Latin, from Petronius, a Roman family name.

In the Middle Ages this name was mistakenly believed to be the name of St Peter's daughter, a mythical St Petronilla who was honored as a saint.

Variations and abbreviations: Petronel, Petronia (It), Petronilla (It).

Petula

Origin/meaning: Latin 'pert' or 'seeker'.

A name made familiar by the English singer and actress Petula Clark.

Abbreviation: Pet.

Philippa

Origin/meaning: Greek 'lover of horses'.

The Latin feminine form of Philip q.v.

Variations and abbreviations: Filippa (It), Filippina (It), Phil, Philipine, Pippa, Pippy.

Philomena

Origin/meaning: Greek 'love of song'.

St Philomena was the name of two early Roman martyrs. The renewed veneration of St Philomena in the 19th century brought about a revival of her name particularly in Italy.

Variations and abbreviations: Filippa (It), Filippina (It), Phil, Philomela (Ger), Philomene (Fr).

Phoebe (pron. Feebee)

Origin/meaning: Greek 'shining one'.

In Greek mythology Phoebe was another name for Artemis (Roman – Diana) the goddess of the moon. Her counterpart, Apollo, god of the sun, was also known as Phoebus.

Variations: Febe (It), Phebe. See also Cynthia.

Phyllida

Origin/meaning: Greek 'leafy'.

A literary form of Phyllis q.v. much used in the 17th century.

Variations: Filada, Filide (It), Fillida, Philida, Phillada, Phillida.

Phyllis

Origin/meaning: Greek 'leafy'.

Phyllis was a Greek maiden who thought she had been forsaken by her lover and hanged herself. The gods pitied her and turned her into an almond tree. The name was used by Greek and Roman poets to signify an unspoiled country girl.

Variations and abbreviations: Fillis, Phillis, Phyl. See also Phyllida.

Pia (pron. Péeya)

Origin/meaning: Latin 'devout'.

This is an Italian and Spanish name occasionally used in English-speaking countries.

Pippa

Origin/meaning: Greek 'lover of horses'.

An Italian short form of Philippa q.v. now used in Britain as an independent name.

Placida (pron. Plassida)

Origin/meaning: Latin 'calm'.

An adjective occasionally used as a girl's name.

Plaxy

Origin/meaning: Greek 'busy'.

An old Cornish name said to be a form of the Greek name Praxedes.

Polly

Origin/meaning: uncertain. Possibly Hebrew 'bitter' or 'wished for child'.

A familiar form of Mary, through Molly. Currently enjoying a minor vogue as an independent name.

Variations and abbreviations: see Mary.

Pollyanna

Origin/meaning: Hebrew 'bitter' plus Hebrew 'graceful'.

A double name equivalent of Mary-Anne (Polly is a familiar form of Mary).

Poppy

Origin/meaning: either a flower name or the Greek short form of Penelope.

Poppy has enjoyed a minor vogue in Britain in recent years.

Portia (pron. Pórsha)

Origin/meaning: either Latin 'sharing' or from Porcius, a Roman family name which may take its meaning from the word pig.

Variation: Porzia (It).

Primrose

Origin/meaning: Latin 'earliest rose'.

Flower names were a new fashion at the end of the 19th century.

Priscilla

Origin/meaning: Priscus was a Roman family name, probably meaning 'strict' or 'correct'. This is a pre-Christian name adopted as a Christian name by 17th-century Puritans because it is found in the Bible.

Variations and abbreviations: Prisca (Ger/It), Priscille (Fr), Priska (Ger), Prissy, Cilla.

Priti (pron. Préetee)

Origin/meaning: Sanskrit 'love'.
Found throughout India. See Amanda, Amy.

Prudence

Origin/meaning: Latin 'caution', 'discretion'.
A virtue name most common in the 17th century when it was popular amongst the Puritans. It is occasionally used in modern times.

Variation: Prue, Pru.

Prunella

Origin/meaning: Latin/French 'plum colored'.
This is a rare name.

Variation: Prunelle (Fr).

Queenie

Origin/meaning: English 'little Queen'.

A late 19th-/early 20th-century girls' pet name, sometimes, at the height of its popularity, given as an independent name.

Variations and abbreviations: Queen, Queena, Queeny, Quenie. See also Victoria.

Querida

Origin/meaning: Spanish 'beloved'.

Quinta

Origin/meaning: Latin 'fifth', 'fifth born'.

The female equivalent of Quentin q.v. usually used either for a fifth daughter or a fifth child.

Variations: Quintilla (It), Quintina (It).

Rabia (pron. Rabéea)

Origin/meaning: Arabic 'spring'.

This is a popular Muslim name.

Variations: Rabiah, Rabiyyah.

Rachel

Origin/meaning: Hebrew 'ewe'.

Always a popular Jewish name this became a Christian name as well in the 17th century. At that time Rachael was the usual spelling and that old-fashioned spelling is again popular today.

Variations and abbreviations: Rae, Rachael, Rachele (It), Rachelle (Fr), Rahel (Ger), Rakel (Swed), Raquel (Sp), Raquela, Ray, Rey, Shelley, Shelly.

Radha

Origin/meaning: Sanskrit 'success'.

Found throughout Hindu texts but most famous for being the name of the favorite consort of Krishna. It is often used as a prefix to form other names.

Rajni (pron. Rjni)

Origin/meaning: Sanskrit 'night'.

Found throughout India.

Rajani

Origin/meaning: Sanskrit 'the night'.

In Hindu texts, a name of Durga, the wife of Shiva.

Ramona

Origin/meaning: Old German 'strength protection', 'counsel protection', i.e. 'strong', or 'wise protector'.

The Spanish feminine form of Raymond q.v. The best known feminine form, perhaps because of the song of the same name.

Variations: Raimonda (It), Raimunde (Ger), Raymonde (Fr), Reimunde (Ger).

Raphaela

Origin/meaning: Hebrew 'God has healed'.

A feminine form of Raphael q.v. used in Europe and occasionally found in English-speaking countries.

Variation: Raffaella (It).

Raquel

Origin/meaning: Hebrew 'ewe'.
Spanish form of Rachel q.v. given wider popularity because of Raquel Welch, the US
film actress.

Rebecca

Origin/meaning: uncertain. Probably originates in a language of people neighboring Israel.
Sometimes given as 'faithful wife' or 'strongly bound'. It was an immensely popular name in
the 17th century period of Biblical names, especially in Puritan New England.

Variations and abbreviations: Becca, Beckie, Becky, Bekki, Reba, Rebeca (Sp), Rebeka,
Rebekah, Rebekka (Ger), Rivkah (Heb).

Rehema

Origin/meaning: Swahili 'compassion'.
An East African name.

René

Origin/meaning: Greek 'peace'.
Short form of Irene q.v. sometimes given as an independent name.

Variation: Renie.

Rhoda

Origin/meaning: either Greek 'from Rhodes' (the isle of roses) or 'rose bush'.
This is one of the pre-Christian Greek names found in the Bible (Acts, ch.12) which was
adopted as a Christian name by
17th-century Protestants. A quite separate Arabic name, Roda, means 'to be satisfied'.

Variations and abbreviations: Rhode, Rhody.

Rhona

Origin/meaning: uncertain. Possibly Old Welsh Rhonwen 'slender, fair' or Old German
Ronalda 'power-might'.

Rhonda

Origin/meaning: uncertain. Possibly connected with the Rhondda area of Wales.

Rhonwen

Origin/meaning: Old Welsh 'slender, fair'.
A name sometimes considered to be the origin of the supposedly Saxon name Rowena.

Ria

Origin/meaning: either a short form of Maria meaning 'bitter' or a variation of the name of the goddess Rhea.

Rita

Origin/meaning: Persian?/Greek/Latin 'pearl' or Medieval French/English 'daisy'. The short form of Margarita, the Spanish form of the name Margaret q.v.

Roberta

Origin/meaning: Old German 'fame bright'.

A feminine form of Robert q.v. found mainly in Scotland and also in Italy.

Variations and abbreviations: Bobbie, Roberte (Fr).

Robina

Origin/meaning: Old German 'fame bright'.

A feminine form of Robin q.v. found mainly in Scotland. In the US Robin is used for girls, although in Britain it is regarded as exclusively masculine.

Variations: Robbie, Robby, Robena, Robin, Robinia, Robyn.

Rokeya

Origin/meaning: Arabic 'she rises on high'.

This is a Muslim name.

Variation: Rukiya.

Roma

Origin/meaning: Italian, the city of Rome.

Occasionally used as a girl's name. A modern fashion.

Rona

Origin/meaning: uncertain. Possibly Old Welsh Rhonwen 'slender, fair' or Old German Ronalda 'power-might'.

The popularity of this name in Scotland suggests it is considered a feminine form of the Scottish masculine name Ronald and is a quite separate name from Rhona.

Rosalie

Origin/meaning: uncertain. Either Latin 'roses and lilies' or possibly Latin 'rosalia' a festival of flowers.

The original form Rosalia is still current in Italy but the name came to English-speaking countries via France and in the French form Rosalie.

Variations and abbreviations: Ros, Rosaleen (Ir), Rosalia (It), Rose, Rozalie, Roz.

Rosalind

Origin/meaning: Old German 'horse serpent'. Usually given as Spanish 'beautiful rose'. The original Old German name was taken to Spain by the Goths. Despite the meaning the Old German is a flattering name since a serpent was considered a sacred creature (see Belinda). However in Spain it was naturally re-interpreted as the Spanish words 'rosa' – 'rose', and 'linda' – 'beautiful'.

Variations and abbreviations: Ros, Rosalinda (Sp), Rosaline, Rosalyne, Rosalynd, Roseline, Rosie, Roslindis, Rozalind.

Rosaline

Origin/meaning: Old German 'horse serpent'. Usually given as Spanish 'beautiful rose'. A form of Rosalind q.v.

Variations and abbreviations: see Rosalind.

Rosamund

Origin/meaning: Old German 'horse protection', Latin 'pure rose'.
Like Rosalind q.v. this Old German name was re-interpreted in the Middle Ages, in this case using the Latin 'rosa' – 'rose', and 'munda' – 'pure'.

Variations and abbreviations: Ros, Rosamund, Rosamunda (Sp), Rosamunde (Ger), Rosemonde (Fr), Rosmunda (It), Roz, Rozamond, Rozamund.

Rosanna

Origin/meaning: a combination of the names Rose and Anna.
This name has been found in various spellings since the Middle Ages.

Variations and abbreviations: Roanna, Ronnie, Rosanne, Roseanna, Roseann, Rozanna, Rozanne, Zanna, Zanny.

Rose

Origin/meaning: Old German 'horse', Latin 'rose'.
This name was probably derived originally from the Old German Hros, meaning horse. The horse, like the serpent, was considered a god by the Saxons, as the white horses cut into chalk hillsides testify.

Variations and abbreviations: Ffion (Wel), Rhoda, Ross, Rosie, Rosy, Roze.

Rosemary

Origin/meaning: either a combination of two names Rose and Mary (Hebrew 'bitter')
or a plant name.
The herb rosemary takes its name from the Latin words 'ros' – 'dew', and 'marinus' –
'of the sea'.

Variations and abbreviations: Mary Rose, Romy, Rosemarie (Fr), Rose Marie, Rosie, Rosy.

Rosita

Origin/meaning: Latin 'little rose'.

A Spanish diminutive of Rose q.v. Popular among Catholics as the pet name of St Rose of Lima, 1586–1617.

Roushan

Origin/meaning: Arabic 'dawn'.

A Muslim variation of Roxane q.v.

Variation: Roshanna.

Rowena

Origin/meaning: uncertain. Possibly Old English 'fame friend' or Old Welsh 'slender, fair'.

Variations and abbreviations: Rhonwen, Rona, Ronwen, Rhona.

Roxane (pron. Rocksahn)

Origin/meaning: Persian 'dawn'.

It was the name of the wife of Alexander the Great and has been used from time to time in literature.

Variations and abbreviations: Rossana (It), Roushan (Arabic), Roxana, Roxanna, Roxanne, Roxy. See also Aurora, Dawn, Zarah.

Ruby

Origin/meaning: English 'red gemstone'.

A name taken directly from the name of a precious stone that became, along with other gemstone names, popular in 19th century England. While out of fashion for most of the 20th century, the start of the new century has seen the revival of such names.

Ruth

Origin/meaning: obscure. Sometimes given as Hebrew 'vision of beauty', also Medieval English 'compassion'.

Since Ruth was a Moabite it is unlikely this is a Hebrew name. A book of the Old Testament is given over to her story.

Variations: Ruthann, Ruthe, Ruthie.

Sabiah

Origin/meaning: Arabic 'morning'.
This is a popular Muslim name.
Variations: Sabah (East African), Sabera.

Sabina (pron. Sabeena)

Origin/meaning: Latin 'Sabine woman'. The Sabines were an ancient tribe whose lands bordered on Rome.
This Roman name survived because it was the name of several saints. In Britain Sabin became both a masculine and feminine variation in the Middle Ages. Sabina became the feminine form.
Variations: Sabin, Sabine (Ger/Fr), Sabyn, Savina (It), Savine (Fr).

Sabrina

Origin/meaning: the Latin name for the River Severn.
Milton in his play 'Comus' retells the Old British legend that Queen Guendolen, spurned by her husband Locrine, raised an army, defeated him and forced his mistress and his daughter Sabre to fly.
Variation: Sabrin.

Sacha (pron Sah-shuh)

Origin/meaning: Ancient Greek 'defender of men'.

A short form of Alexander, or Alexandra q.v. frequently found recently as an independent first name for both boys and girls.

Variations and abbreviations: Sascha, Sasha.

Sadie

Origin/meaning: Hebrew 'princess'.

A familiar form of Sarah q.v.

Variations: Sadye, Saidee.

Sally

Origin/meaning: Hebrew 'princess'.

A form of Sarah q.v. which involves a typical change of letter from r to l. It has been given as a totally independent name.

Variations and abbreviations: Sal, Sallee, Sallie.

Salma

Origin/meaning: Arabic 'safe'.

A popular Muslim name that has become popular world-wide, and has recently become familiar thanks to the Hollywood actress Salma Hayek.

Variation: Solama.

Salome

Origin/meaning: Aramaic 'peace'.

This is a Greek form of the Hebrew word Shalom. It is the name given by tradition to the daughter of Herodias who danced before Herod in return for the head of John the Baptist.

Variations: Saláma (Arabic), Salomé (Fr), Salomi, Salomy. See also Solomon.

Samantha

Origin/meaning: uncertain, possibly Aramaic 'listener' or feminine of Samuel.

Samantha appears to be a mainly 20th-century name 'manufactured' by films and television.

Variations and abbreviations: Sam, Samanta (It), Samanthy, Sammie, Sammy. See also Darren, Tracey, Kelly.

Sandhya (pron. Sandayéah)

Origin/meaning: Sanskrit 'evening'.

Sandy

Origin/meaning: Greek 'defender of men'.

A familiar form of Alexandra q.v.

Variations: Sandi, Sandie.

Sandra

Origin/meaning: Greek 'defender of men'.

The Italian short form of Alexandra (Alessandra) q.v.

Variations and abbreviations: Sandi, Sandie, Sondra, Zandra.

Sapphira (pron. Safféera)

Origin/meaning: Greek 'sapphire'.

This is a Biblical name which has been used occasionally since the Middle Ages.

Variations: Sapphire, Sephira.

Sarah

Origin/meaning: Hebrew 'princess'.

The Biblical Sarai was given to Abraham's wife by God. Although known in the Middle Ages, it only became widespread during the 17th century period of Biblical names.

Variations and abbreviations: Sadie, Sal, Sally, Sara, Saraid (Ir), Sari (Hung), Sarina, Sarita, Sarra, Sharai, Shari (Hung), Sorcha (Ir), Zara, Zarah, Zaria. See also Sharon, Soraya.

Saraid

Origin/meaning: Old Irish 'excellent' or Hebrew 'princess'.

Like Sorcha q.v. this native Irish name is also used as an equivalent of Sarah and therefore claims two meanings.

Sarswati (pron. Sarraswatti)

Origin/meaning: Hindu, the goddess of education, wife of Brahma.

A long-established name found throughout India. Sarswati is credited with the invention of Sanskrit. She is always portrayed as extremely beautiful.

Sati

Origin/meaning: Sanskrit 'virtuous wife'.

This was the name of the first incarnation of Parvati, wife of Shiva.

Scarlett

Origin/meaning: Middle English 'rich red'.

This word is assumed to have come from a Persian word for a rich cloth, usually deep red in color, called Saqirlat. Made famous by the heroine of Margaret Mitchell's book 'Gone With the Wind', 1936.

Variation: Scarlet.

Selina

Origin/meaning: probably Latin 'heavenly'. Sometimes given as Greek 'moon'.

This comes from the French version, Céline. It first appeared as an English name at the end of the 17th century when French influence was very strong.

Variations and abbreviations: Celene, Celia, Celina, Céline, Selena, Selene, Selia, Seline. See also Celeste, Celia, Chandra.

Selma

Origin/meaning: Old German 'helmet of God'.

A short form of the rare Old English name Anselma.

Variation: Zelma.

Selma

Origin/meaning: Arabic 'secure'.

A popular Muslim name quite unrelated to the European name.

Senga

Origin/meaning: Greek 'pure', 'chaste'.

A Scottish name, thought to be simply a reversed spelling of Agnes.

Septima

Origin/meaning: Latin 'seventh'.
A name given to a seventh daughter or seventh child.

Seraphina

Origin/meaning: Hebrew 'burning', 'ardent'.
The name of one of the early saints.
Variations: Serafina (It), Seraphite (Sp).

Serena (pron. Seréena)

Origin/meaning: Latin 'calm', 'serene'.
A name found occasionally since the Middle Ages.

Shakira

Origin/meaning: Arabic 'be grateful'.
A Muslim name.
Variations: Shakila, Shakura (East African).

Shanti

Origin/meaning: Sanskrit 'tranquil'.
Originally a word used to denote the peaceful mental state achieved through meditation, in later Hindu texts Shanti appears as the name of the daughter of the deity Daksha.

Sharon

Origin/meaning: Hebrew place-name. Possibly also Hebrew 'princess'.
The phrase 'rose of Sharon' appears in the Song of Solomon. Rose-of-Sharon became abbreviated to simple Sharon.
Variations and abbreviations: Sharai, Shari, Sharron, Sharry, Sharyn.

Sheela

Origin/meaning: Sanskrit 'good character'.
Originally one of the six perfections to be striven for in Buddhism. It was not used as a female name until the late medieval period.
Variation: Sheila.

Sheila

Origin/meaning: Latin 'blind'. From the aristocratic Roman Caecilius family.
The Anglicized form of Shelagh/Sighile, which is itself the Irish form of Cecilia q.v.
Variations: Sheela, Sheelagh Sheelah, Sheilah, Shelagh Shelly.

Shelley

Origin/meaning: Old English 'clearing on a bank'.
A last name sometimes used as a feminine first name. Also a familiar form of names such as Michelle, Sheila, Shirley, Rachel, Rochelle.
Variation: Shelly.

Shena

Origin/meaning: Hebrew 'Jehovah has favored'.
Scots form of Joan or Jane, a phonetic spelling of the Scots Gaelic Sìne.
Variations: Sheena, Sìne.

Sherry

Origin/meaning: a familiar form of names like Chérie, Sharon, Charlotte, etc.
Sometimes given as an independent name.

Shirley

Origin/meaning: Old English 'bright clearing'.
An English place-name which became a last name. As a first name, it seems to be a direct result of Charlotte Brontë's novel 'Shirley', 1849.
Variations and abbreviations: Sher, Shir, Shirl, Shirlee, Shirleen, Shirlene, Shirline.

Shobha

Origin/meaning: Hindu 'decoration', 'beauty'.
A name found throughout India.

Siân (pron. Shahn)

Origin/meaning: Hebrew 'Jehovah has favored'.
This is the native Welsh form of Jane q.v.
Variations: Siani, Sìne (Scot), Sinéad (Ir), Sioned, Siwan (Wel).

Sibyl

Origin/meaning: Greek. The name given to the women who put the prophecies of the oracles into words.
The name was introduced into England by the Norman Conquest. In the 19th century Disraeli's novel 'Sybil', 1845, revived interest in the name, although mistakenly spelt with the vowels reversed.
Variations and abbreviations: Cybil, Cybill, Sib, Sibelle, Sibbie, Sibby, Sibel, Sibilla (It), Sibylla, Sibylle (Fr/Ger), Sybil, Sybilla, Sybille.

Sidney

Origin/meaning: Latin/Greek 'follower of Dionysios'.

This aristocratic last name is a contraction of St Denis, a French place name. As a first name it had the additional boost to its popularity of being the last name of the much admired Elizabethan poet Sir Philip Sidney, 1554–1586.

Variations and abbreviations: Sid, Syd, Sydney.

Sidony (pron. Sidónee)

Origin/meaning: Greek/Latin 'fine cloth'.

The medieval word sendal, or sendon (from a Greek word) was used to describe a fine cloth and by implication in some cases, a winding sheet. Girls born on or about the date of the Feast of the Holy Sendon (winding sheet) were sometimes called Sidony.

Variations and abbreviations: Sid, Sidney, Sidonia (It), Sidonie (Fr/Ger), Sindonia, Zdenka (Slav).

Sienna

Origin/meaning: Latin 'from Siena'.

The name is taken from the Italian city and has become familiar as a first name because of Sienna Miller, the English actress.

Simone (pron. Séemon)

Origin/meaning: uncertain. Usually given as Hebrew 'hearkening'.

This is the French feminine form of Simon q.v.

Variations: Simona (It), Simonetta, Simonette, Simonne (Fr).

Sinead (pron. Shináyd)

Origin/meaning: Hebrew 'Jehovah has favored'.

This is the feminine form of Sean, the Irish form of John. It approximates to the English Jane.

Variations: Siàn (Wel), Sìne (Scot), Sinéidín (dim.). See also Joan.

Siobhán (pron. Shiváwn)

Origin/meaning: Hebrew 'Jehovah has favored'.

The Irish form of Joan q.v.

Sita

Origin/meaning: Hindu. Mythological. An incarnation of Lakohmi, the wife of Vishnu. Sita was the wife of Rama, himself one of the incarnations of the god Vishnu. The adventures of Rama and Sita are told in many poems and stories including the famous epic poem 'The Ramayana'.

Sonia

Origin/meaning: Greek 'wisdom'.

This is a Slavic familiar form of Sophie q.v. It is particularly popular in Russia and is frequently found in Scandinavia.

Variations and abbreviations: Sonja, Sonnie, Sonya.

Sophia

Origin/meaning: Greek 'wisdom'.

The Italian form of Sophie q.v.

Variations and abbreviations: see Sophie.

Sophie

Origin/meaning: Greek 'wisdom'.

This is the English and French form of the name Sophia. The name came to England with the Hanoverians at the beginning of the 18th century. Sophie was the name of George I's daughter, and became fashionable very rapidly.

Variations: Sofia (Ger/It/Russ), Sofie, Sonia (Slav), Sonja, Sonya, Sophia (It), Sophy.

Soraya

Origin/meaning: Sanskrit/Persian 'good princess'.

An Arab name made more generally familiar by Queen Soraya, former wife of the late Shah of Persia.

Sorcha (pron. Sorshah)

Origin/meaning: Old Irish 'bright' or Hebrew 'princess'.

This native Irish name has come to be used as the Irish equivalent of Sarah and therefore has two meanings.

Stacey

Origin/meaning: Greek 'resurrection'.

A short form of Anastasia q.v. which has become more popular than the original.

Variations and abbreviations: Stace, Stacy.

Stella

Origin/meaning: Latin 'star'.

This name was used from time to time in the Middle Ages to honor the Blessed Virgin Mary, one of whose titles is Stella Maris 'Star of the Sea'. Jonathan Swift, 1667–1745, gave the name Stella to a friend, Esther Johnson. It is a direct translation of Esther which is the Persian word for star.

Variations: Estella (It/Sp), Estelle (Old Fr), Estrella (Sp).

Stephanie

Origin/meaning: Greek 'wreathed', 'crowned'.

This is the feminine form of Stephen q.v. It was originally a French name, spelt Stéphanie.

Variations and abbreviations: Etiennette (Fr), Stef, Stefania (It), Stefanie (Ger), Steffie, Steph, Stephana, Stephani, Stephie, Stevana, Stevena.

Sudha (pron. Soo-thoh)

Origin/meaning: Hindu 'moon', 'nectar'.

See Chandra.

Sunita

Origin/meaning: Hindu 'well-behaved'

Found mainly in Central and Western India.

Sukey

Origin/meaning: Hebrew 'graceful white lily'.

Old-fashioned familiar form of Susan q.v. popular in the 18th century.

Variation: Suki.

Susan

Origin/meaning: Hebrew 'graceful white lily'.

A short form of Susannah q.v. used in the 18th century and which by the 19th century had overtaken the original in popularity.

Variations and abbreviations: see Susannah.

Susannah

Origin/meaning: Hebrew 'graceful white lily'.

This name, originally Shushannah, has the same meaning as Shushan, the royal city of Assyria.

Variations and abbreviations: Siusan (Scot), Sosanna (Ir), Sue, Sukey, Suki, Susana (Sp), Susanna (It), Susanne (Fr/Ger), Susette, Susi, Susie, Susy, Suzanna, Suzanne (Fr), Suzette (Fr), Suzi, Suzy, Zsa Zsa (Hung), Zusi.

Suzanne/Suzette/Suzan

Origin/meaning: Hebrew 'graceful white lily'.

French forms of Susannah q.v.

Sylvia

Origin/meaning: Latin 'of the woodland'.

This is the feminine alternative of Silvester (Silvius) q.v.

Variations and abbreviations: Silva, Silvana (It), Silverie (It), Silvestra (It), Silvia, Silviana (It), Silvie, Sylviane (Fr), Sylvie (Fr), Sylvetta, Zilvia.

Tabitha

Origin/meaning: Aramaic 'antelope', 'gazelle'.

This is the translation of the Greek name Dorcas and both versions are given in the Acts of the Apostles.

Tacita (pron. Tássita)

Origin/meaning: Latin 'silent'.

Feminine of the Old Roman name Tacitus, still viable today, especially in Italy.

Tamara

Origin/meaning: Hebrew 'palm tree'.

A popular name in Eastern Europe but rare in English-speaking countries.

Variations and abbreviations: Tamar, Tammie, Tammy.

Tammy

Origin/meaning: Aramaic 'little twin'.

This is a pet form of the feminine versions of Thomas, Tamsin and Thomasina.

Variations and abbreviations: Tam, Tammi, Tammie.

Tamsin

Origin/meaning: Aramaic 'twin'.

A feminine version of Thomas q.v. popular in Tudor times.

Variations and abbreviations: Tam, Tamasin, Tamasine, Tammy, Tamzin, Thomasin, Thomasina.

Tanya

Origin/meaning: uncertain. Possibly 'little queen'.

A Russian short form of Tatiana q.v. now used as an independent name.

Variations: Tanhya, Tania, Tonya.

Tatiana

Origin/meaning: uncertain, sometimes given as 'little father', 'little queen'.

One of the five most popular girls' names in Russia.

Variations and abbreviations: Tanhya, Tania, Tanya, Tonya.

Teri

Origin/meaning: Greek 'late summer'.

A short form of Theresa that has become a popular girl's first name.

Tess

Origin/meaning: uncertain, possibly Greek 'from Tharasia' or 'reaper'.
An English short form of Theresa q.v. now used as an independent name.

Variations: Tessa, Tessie, Tessy.

Thelma

Origin/meaning: literary, invented by Marie Corelli for her novel 'Thelma: a Norwegian Princess', 1887.

Theodora

Origin/meaning: Greek 'gift of God'.
The feminine form of Theodore q.v.

Variations and abbreviations: Dora, Fedora (Russ), Fjodora (Russ), Teodora (It), Thea, Theo.

Theresa

Origin/meaning: obscure, possibly Greek 'from Tharasia' or 'reaper'.
This name first took root in Spain. Its sudden introduction to the rest of Catholic Europe was due to the popularity of St Teresa of Avila, 1515–1582, the Spanish nun and mystic.

Variations and abbreviations: Teresa (Sp/It), Terese, Theresita (Sp), Teressa, Terri, Terrie, Terry, Tess, Tessa, Tessie, Tessy, Thérèse (Fr), Theresia (Ger), Tracey, Tracy.

Thora

Origin/meaning: Old Norse 'strength', 'thunder'.
This is a Scandinavian feminine name from Thor, the Norse god of war and thunder.

Variations: Thorina, Thyra, Tora (Swed), Tyra.

Tiffany

Origin/meaning: Greek 'manifestation of God'.
Medieval English form of Theophania.

Tiger Lily

Origin/meaning: taken from the flower and familiar as a first name since being used as a name by British celebrity, the late Paula Yates, for her daughter with INXS star, Michael Hutchence, now also deceased.

Tilly

Origin/meaning: Old German 'battle strength'.
A pet form of Matilda.

Variations: Tillie.

Tina

Origin/meaning: a short form of names ending in -tine or -tina, e.g. Clementine, Christine.

Toni

Origin/meaning: Latin. From Antonius, one of the great Roman families.
This is a popular short form of Antonia q.v.

Variations: Tonia, Tonie.

Tracey

Origin/meaning: uncertain, possibly Greek 'from Tharasia' or 'reaper'.
This is an English familiar form of Theresa.

Variations: Tracie, Tracy.

Tricia

Origin/meaning: Latin 'patrician'.
A popular short form of Patricia, often used as an independent name.

Variations: Trish, Trisha.

Trudy

Origin/meaning: Old German 'strength' or 'spear strength'.
This is a short form of Gertrude which in the second half of the 20th century has been more popular than the original.

Variations: Druda, Traude (Ger), Traute (Ger), Trude (Den), Trudel, Trudi, Trudie.

Ulla

Origin/meaning: Latin 'little she bear' or Old German/Old English 'wolf ruler'.
A short form of either Ursula or Ulrike used as an independent name. It is most popular in Scandinavia. The Scandinavian influence brought the name to Scotland.

Ulrike

Origin/meaning: Old German/Old English 'wolf ruler'.
The feminine of Ulrich.

Variations and abbreviations: Ulla, Ulrica (It), Ulricha, Ulrika (Scand).

Uma

Origin/meaning: Hindu. A goddess, one of the incarnations of Parvati, wife of the great god Shiva.

Una (pron. Yéwna)

Origin/meaning: Latin 'one'.

A name first used by Spenser in his poem 'The Faeri Queen'. Sometimes, pronounced Oona, it is also used as a variant spelling of the Irish Gaelic name Oonagh.

Undine

Origin/meaning: Latin 'water sprite'.

A name invented by the 16th-century Swiss alchemist and astrologer Paracelsus from the Latin word unda, meaning wave. He used it to describe a water sprite.

Variation: Ondine (Fr).

Ursula

Origin/meaning: Latin 'little she-bear'.

St Ursula (probably 3rd or 4th century) was one of the martyrs of the Roman Empire. She and her companions were martyred for their Christianity by the Huns at Cologne. The discovery of a vast cache of bones at Cologne in the 12th century was used to support the story.

Variations and abbreviations: Orsa, Orsola (It), Ulla, Ursa, Ursala, Ursel, Ursina (It), Ursola (Sp), Ursule (Fr), Ursulina, Uschi (Ger). See also Orson.

Usha (pron. Oosha)

Origin/meaning: Sanskrit 'dawn'.

Found throughout Hindu texts including as the daughter of heaven, renowned for her beauty.

Valentina

Origin/meaning: Latin 'strong', 'healthy'.

The feminine version of Valentine q.v. although occasionally called by the original version.

Variations and abbreviations: Val, Valentine.

Valerie

Origin/meaning: Latin 'strong', 'influential'. From the patrician Roman family of Valerius. The English feminine form of this name was brought over from France in the 19th century.

Variations and abbreviations: Val, Valeria (It), Valeriane, Valérie (Fr), Valery, Valerye, Valeska (Slav).

Vanessa

Origin/meaning: a pet name invented by the 18th-century writer Jonathan Swift for his friend Esther Vanhomrigh.

He amalgamated the first syllable of her last name with -essa, a short form of Esther.

Variations and abbreviations: Nessa, Vanna.

Varsha

Origin/meaning: Sanskrit 'rain'.

A name found throughout India.

Veena

Origin/meaning: Sanskrit 'sitar'.

A name found throughout India. In Indian mythology this instrument is used by Narad (pron. Nard) the messenger of the gods.

Velma

Origin/meaning: Old German 'helmet of resolution'.

A short form, popular in the US, of Wilhelmina q.v. from the German pronunciation.

Venetia

Origin/meaning: used since the Middle Ages and taken from Venice, the romantic city of northern Italy.

Vera

Origin/meaning: Latin 'true', Russian 'faith'.

Probably in England a 19th-century short form of Veronica q.v. now used as an independent name. It may however be a direct use of the Russian name which is pronounced Vyera.

Variations: Véra (It), Vere, Veria, Verla.

Verena

Origin/meaning: Old German 'defender', 'protector'.
A martyr whose feast falls on September 1st. The name's introduction to England was probably through Mrs Yonge's popular novel 'The Heir of Redclyffe'. Sometimes used as a short form of Veronica.

Variations and abbreviations: Rena, Véran (Fr), Verina, Verine, Verna.

Verity

Origin/meaning: Middle English word 'truth'.
Used since the 17th century when Puritans chose virtues and Biblical names as an alternative to Catholic saints' names.

Variation: Verily.

Veronica

Origin/meaning: Latin 'true icon/image'.
The name traditionally given to the woman who wiped the face of Christ with a cloth while he was walking to Calvary. The image of Christ's face was said to be left on the cloth she used. Not surprisingly perhaps she is patron saint of photographers.

Variations and abbreviations: Nicky, Ronnie, Vera, Verena, Veronika (Ger), Véronique (Fr), Vroni.

Vesta

Origin/meaning: the name of the Latin goddess of the hearth.
Occasionally found as a first name.

Vicky

Origin/meaning: Latin 'victory'.
Short form of Victoria q.v. now found as an independent name.

Variations: Vicki, Vickie, Vikki, Vikky.

Victoria

Origin/meaning: Latin 'victory'.
Rare in England before the reign of Queen Victoria, 1837–1901. Victoria was the Queen's second name and had been one of the names of her German mother, the Duchess of Kent.

Variations and abbreviations: Queenie, Vic, Vicki, Vickie, Vicky, Victoire (Fr), Victorine, Viktoria (Ger), Viktorine, Vita, Vitoria (Sp), Vittoria (It), Vittorina (It).

Vida

Origin/meaning: Hebrew 'beloved'.
A short form of feminine versions of David q.v., e.g. Davida.

Villette

Origin/meaning: Old German 'helmet of resolution'.

Regional French version of William q.v.

See also Wilhelmina.

Viola

Origin/meaning: Latin 'violet flower'.

This Latin word for a violet was used occasionally during the Middle Ages as a feminine first name. It was chosen by Shakespeare for his heroine in 'Twelfth Night'.

Variations and abbreviations: Vi, Violante, Viole, Vye. See also Yolande, Violet.

Violet

Origin/meaning: Latin 'the violet flower'.

The English word violet is first found as a name in Scotland in the 16th century, but it was not until the 19th century that the name became fashionable in England.

Variations and abbreviations: Vi, Violante (Fr), Violetta (It), Violette (Fr), Vye. See also Ianthe, Yolande, Viola.

Virginia

Origin/meaning: either Latin from the Patrician Roman family Verginius (spring) or Latin 'maidenly', 'virginal'.

The American plantation (later State) of Virginia, was named by Sir Walter Raleigh to honor Elizabeth I, England's Virgin Queen in 1584.

Variations and abbreviations: Ginger, Ginni, Ginnie, Ginny, Jinny, Jinney, Verginia, Virgie, Virginie (Fr).

Vita

Origin/meaning: Latin 'life', 'full of life'.

This Latin word was not used as a name until comparatively recently.

Vivian

Origin/meaning: Latin 'full of life'.

In the 19th century Tennyson used Vivien, for one of his poems of the Arthurian legends, 'Vivien and Merlin' and the poem helped to popularize the name.

Variations and abbreviations: Bibiana, Viv, Vivien, Viviana (It), Viviane (Ger), Vivianne, Vivie, Vivienne (Fr), Vivyan. See also Vita.

Voletta

Origin/meaning: Old French 'a veil'.

Variations and abbreviations: Volet, Vollet (both pron. Vollay).

Wallis

Origin/meaning: Old Scots 'from Wales', 'foreign'.
A last name used as a girl's first name – a common practice in the Southern United States.

Wanda

Origin/meaning: uncertain. Possibly Old German 'stem' or 'branch'.
Very popular in Germany at the end of the 19th century, it was introduced into England by the novelist Ouida, who gave the name to the heroine of her book 'Wanda', 1883.
Variations: Vanda (It), Wenda.

Wendy

Origin/meaning: invented by J. M. Barrie for his book 'Peter Pan', 1904.
Apparently he had the idea because Margaret Henley, the small daughter of a friend, nicknamed him 'friendy-wendy'.
Variations: Wendi, Wendie, Wendye. See also Fiona, Lorna, Miranda, Ophelia, Pamela, Perdita, Vanessa.

Wilhelmina

Origin/meaning: Old German 'will helmet' i.e. 'helmet of resolution'.
A feminine form of William q.v. brought to England from the Netherlands and Germany during the 18th century.
Variations and abbreviations: Billie, Billy, Guglielma (It), Guillema, Guillemette (Fr), Guillelmina (Sp), Guillelmine (Fr), Gullelma, Min, Mina, Minna, Minni, Minnie, Minny, Valma, Velma, Vilhelmina (Slav), Villette (Fr), Vilma, Wilella, Wilhelmine, Willa, Willamina, Williamina, Wilma, Wilmette, Wylma.

Willa

Origin/meaning: Old German 'helmet of resolution'.
Short form, popular in the US, of Wilhelmina.

Winifred

Origin/meaning: Old German 'peaceful friend', Old Welsh 'blessed reconciliation'.
Although this name is traditionally given the first meaning it is equally likely that it is the English version of the Old Welsh name Gwenfrewi (through the Latin Wenefreda).
Variations and abbreviations: Freda, Fredi, Freddie, Venefrida (It), Wenefrede, Wenefride, Winefred, Win, Winnie, Winnifred, Winny, Wyn.

Winona

Origin/meaning: Sioux Indian 'first born daughter'.
Variation: Wenona.

Xanthe (pron. Zanthee)

Origin/meaning: Greek 'yellow'.

Variation: Xantha.

Xenia (pron. Zennia)

Origin/meaning: Greek 'hospitable', 'guest'.

Variations and abbreviations: Xena, Zena, Zenia.

Yasmin

Origin/meaning: Arabic/Persian 'jasmine flower'.
The Arab original of the better known English form Jasmine q.v.

Variation: Yamina. See also Jasmine.

Ynez

Origin/meaning: Greek 'pure', 'chase'.
A spelling of Inez, the Spanish form of Agnes q.v.

Yolande

Origin/meaning: Latin 'violet flower'.
A French name which developed from Violaine, or Violante, Medieval French forms of Viola, the Latin word for violet.

Variations and abbreviations: Iola, Iolande (It), Iolanthe (Ger), Jolanda (It), Jolanthe (Ger), Yolanda (Sp), Yolanthe. See also Violet, Ianthe.

Yvette

Origin/meaning: Old German 'yew'.
Like Yvonne, a feminine version of Yves, the French form of Ivo.

Variations: Evette, Ivette.

Yvonne

Origin/meaning: Old German 'yew'.
A French feminine version of Yves, Yvon, the French forms of Ivo.

Zaha
Origin/meaning: origin unknown but familiar in architecture circles for being the name of the award-winning architect Zaha Hadid.

Zainab
Origin/meaning: Arabic 'beautiful'.
A Muslim name, Zainab was the eldest daughter of Mohammed.
Variation: Zainabu (E African).

Zakiya
Origin/meaning: Arab 'intelligent'.
This is a popular Muslim name.

Zandra
Origin/meaning: Greek 'defender of men'.
An abbreviation of Alexandra q.v.

Zarah
Origin/meaning: possibly Arabic 'flower', or Hebrew 'sunrise', 'dawn'. Possibly also a variant of Sarah 'princess'.
Variations: Zara, Zariah, Zerah, Zora. See also Dawn, Roxane.

Zarina
Origin/meaning: African 'golden'.

Zelda
Origin/meaning: uncertain. May be a contraction of Griselda, 'gray battle maid'.
A 20th-century name.

Zelma
Origin/meaning: Old German 'helmet of God'.
A form of Anselma/Selma q.v.

Zena
Origin/meaning: Greek 'hospitable'.
An Anglicized version of Xenia q.v.

Zillah

Origin/meaning: uncertain. May be Hebrew 'shade'.
A Biblical name (Genesis ch.4), one of the [ ] wives of Lamech (the ot[ ]
Sometimes said to be a popular name among gypsies, it is otherwi[ ]
used the name for the maid in her novel 'Frost in May'. It is also
Brontë's 'Wuthering Heights'.

Zinnia

Origin/meaning: a tropical plant.
One of the flower names occasionally used.

Zita

Origin/meaning: Etruscan 'young girl'. Sometimes given as Greek Zeta, the sixth letter of the Greek alphabet. It may sometimes be a short form of names, e.g. Rosita, which end in Sita or Zita.

Zoë

Origin/meaning: Greek 'life'.
Initially used because of its meaning to translate the Biblical Hebrew word for Eve, the mother of mankind, into Greek, Zoë became a name in its own right.
Variations: Zoa, Zoé (Fr).

Zoila

Origin/meaning: Spanish 'be cheerful'.
A rare but stylish name that was once popular in Spain and parts of Latin America. The male form is Zoilo.

Zsa Zsa (pron. Jhah-Jhah)

Origin/meaning: Hebrew 'lily' or 'princess'.
Hungarian form of Susan or Sarah made familiar by American/Hungarian actress Zsa Zsa (Sari) Gabor.

Zuleika (pron. Zoolíka)

Origin/meaning: Arabic 'fair', 'beautiful'.
A favorite Persian name. Max Beerbohm's satirical novel 'Zuleika Dobson', 1911, gave it some popularity in England.
Variation: Suleika (Ger).